Revolutionary Subject

Benjamin Kohlmann is Professor of English at the University of Regensburg (Germany), working on the relationship between literature and politics. He is the author of *Committed Styles: Modernism, Politics, and Left-Wing Literature* and *British Literature and the Life of Institutions: Speculative States*. He co-founded and co-edits the book series Literature & Politics at Oxford University Press.

Revolutionary Subjects

A Radical History of the Bildungsroman

Benjamin Kohlmann

VERSO
London • New York

For Katharina and Clara

First published by Verso 2026

The manufacturer's authorized representative in the EU for product safety (GPSR) is LOGOS EUROPE, 9 rue Nicolas Poussin, 17000, La Rochelle, France
Contact@logoseurope.eu

1 3 5 7 9 10 8 6 4 2

Verso
UK: 6 Meard Street, London W1F 0EG
US: 207 East 32nd Street, New York, NY 10016
versobooks.com

Verso is the imprint of New Left Books

ISBN-13: 978-1-8042-9727-8
ISBN-13: 978-1-8042-9729-2 (US EBK)
ISBN-13: 978-1-8042-9728-5 (UK EBK)

British Library Cataloguing in Publication Data
A catalogue record for this book is available from the British Library

Library of Congress Cataloging-in-Publication Data

Names: Kohlmann, Benjamin, 1981- author
Title: Revolutionary subjects: a radical history of the bildungsroman / Benjamin Kohlmann.
Description: London; New York: Verso, 2026. | Includes bibliographical references and index.
Identifiers: LCCN 2026010594 (print) | LCCN 2026010595 (ebook) | ISBN 9781804297278 paperback | ISBN 9781804297292 ebook
Subjects: LCSH: Bildungsromans--History and criticism | Socialism in literature | Radicalism in literature | Politics and literature | LCGFT: Literary criticism
Classification: LCC PN3448.B54 K64 2026 (print) | LCC PN3448.B54 (ebook)
LC record available at https://lccn.loc.gov/2026010594
LC ebook record available at https://lccn.loc.gov/2026010595

Typeset in Minion Pro by Hewer Text UK Ltd, Edinburgh
Printed and bound by CPI Group (UK) Ltd, Croydon CR0 4YY

Youth does not bear its solution within it: it must collapse and be rent apart.

Jean-Paul Sartre, 'Preface' (1960)
to Paul Nizan's *La Conspiration*

And so he worked on. And he did not feel the mountain and the darkness and the loneliness. Tonight the barriers were down, the walls had fallen, he was at one with himself and with the world around, he was who he was.

Werner Bräunig, *Rummelplatz* (1959–66)

Contents

Acknowledgements

The gestation of this book has shared a number of features with the protagonists whose lives are narrated in the radical bildungsroman: for a long time, I struggled to begin; sometimes, I thought I lacked the energy to carry on; and, at other moments, I was worried that I might lose sight of the end. But working on this book has also been a reminder that writing (like other kinds of work) is a collective enterprise that is made possible through the generosity and support of others.

The project took shape as a book following an expression of interest by Sebastian Budgen and a serendipitous intervention by the late Fredric Jameson. I thank them both for believing in this project at an early stage.

I am grateful to my students and colleagues at the University of Regensburg for their intellectual companionship. Clare Hall, Cambridge, provided an ideal place for the exploration of new ideas and directions – it was a happy sabbatical spent there as a visiting fellow that made it possible for me to complete the manuscript.

It's impossible to list all the individuals who supported this project either through conversations or by commenting on drafts of chapters. As is often the case, fortuitous comments made by friends and colleagues transformed the book and substantially improved it. Heartfelt thanks go to Janice Ho and Matt Taunton, two of my favourite people: my conversations with them have enriched this project (and its author) in countless ways. I also owe special debts of gratitude to Ian Afflerbach, Ingo Berensmeyer, Dan Blanton, Peter Boxall, Patrick Bray, Michaela Bronstein, Georgia Christinidis, Katerina Clark, Santanu Das, Ben Harker, Owen Holland, Steve Lee, Bettina Lerner, Scott McCracken, Jo McDonagh, Liz

Miller, Franco Moretti, Nasser Mufti, Tue Andersen Nexø, Sonali Perera, Ivana Perica, Helen Small, Matthew Stratton, David Trotter, Anna Vaninskaya and Dirk Wiemann.

Several of the chapters in this book first took shape as guest lectures. I am enormously grateful to audiences who provided food for thought as my arguments took shape. I owe special thanks to colleagues and friends at UC Berkeley, Cambridge University, the CUNY Graduate Center, Doshisha University (Kyoto), Edinburgh University, Exeter University, the University of Gour Banga, Leibniz University Hannover, the University of Konstanz, the London Modernism Seminar, Manchester University, LMU Munich, Oxford University, University College London, the University of East Anglia, and the Leibniz-Zentrum für Literatur- und Kulturforschung Berlin.

Thanks are also due to Kalina Janeva and Nick Walther for their excellent editorial work on the manuscript. It was once more a delight to work with indexer extraordinaire Paula Clarke Bain.

Finally, it is a pleasure to acknowledge the generous support of the German Research Foundation (DFG), which helped to fund the research for this project.

Portions of this book were published in an early exploratory article almost exactly ten years ago: 'Toward a History and Theory of the Socialist Bildungsroman', *Novel: A Forum on Fiction*, 48.2 (2015), 167–89. Parts of Chapter 3 were published in *Modern Language Quarterly* 86.4 (2025), 353–78. My translation of Karl August Varnhagen von Ense's 'Im Sinne der Wanderer' was published with an introduction in *PMLA* 138.1 (2023), 102–9. I am grateful for the permission to reprint this material here. The epigraph from Werner Bräunig's *Rummelplatz* is reprinted in Samuel P. Willcocks's (excellent) English translation, with kind permission of Seagull Books.

Unless indicated otherwise, all translations are my own.

This book is for Katharina and Clara. Work never felt like work, thanks to them.

Introduction

World Literature and the Work of Revolution

Towards the end of *The Tower* (*Der Turm*, 2008), Uwe Tellkamp's monumental fictional reckoning with the final years of the German Democratic Republic (GDR), the novel's twenty-something protagonist, Christian, finds himself scraping frozen soil off a bucket wheel that belongs to a gigantic surface-mining excavator. An ill-judged comment during his mandatory military service has put Christian on the wrong side of the regime, and his hopes for a career as a doctor are dashed. Christian is singled out by the authorities for ideological 're-education' – he is sent to work in an open-pit mine in the Lausitz region near the East German–Polish border, and his military service is extended by two years. The Socialist Unity Party of Germany (SED), the country's authoritarian ruling party, is trying to break Christian's spirit and bring him back into alignment with state ideology:

> His job was to clean the bucket wheel . . . The bucket wheel stopped at the highest point and Christian, as nimble as an orang-utan once he had become accustomed to the work, would clamber up the struts, gratings and railed walkways to the front of the boom at the end of which, about fifteen metres from the body of the excavator, his work began: knocking off the clumps of soil stuck to the wheel. Christian hacked away like a murderer, on his back he could sense the eyes of the driver, who, from the lower cab, was examining the darkness above the calm glow of his cigarette . . . When it was freezing the soil, in the minute it took him to get from the recreation room to the bucket wheel, became as hard as a tree trunk, and then Christian could only hack and split and cut the

> dark brown mass off in shavings and splinters, working as hard as he could, driven on by the fear of being caught by the wheel as it suddenly started to turn.[1]

Christian's back-breaking work – set against the dramatic backdrop of outsized machinery and the wind-swept, gaping cavity of the mine – leaves him at the mercy of natural (and political) forces beyond his control. But the scene also puts a brutal end to a biographical narrative that might, under other conditions, have offered an account of Christian's continued growth and flourishing – a story that might have unfolded according to the generic parameters of the bildungsroman. Tellkamp's novel calls up elements of the bildungsroman genre, but it crucially replaces the protagonist's self-actualization – the growth of a rich and rounded personality that finds its place in a sustaining social order – with the image of a coercive re-education (*Umerziehung*) that corrals the errant individual back into the communal fold.[2] In a perverse twist on the genre, Christian's existential crisis mirrors the terminal crisis of the state that seeks to humiliate him. Tellkamp invites his readers to draw these kinds of connections. The title of his novel alludes to the Tower Society of Goethe's *Wilhelm Meisters Lehrjahre* (*Wilhelm Meister's Apprenticeship*, 1796), the foundational text in the bourgeois bildungsroman tradition: the absolute (albeit benign) educational influence that Goethe's fictional secret society exerts over Wilhelm's life is mirrored in the sinister hold that the GDR's secret police exercises over Christian's fortunes.

Tellkamp uses the structure of the bildungsroman to convey an acute sense of historical crisis – the implosion of the GDR in 1990 and the rapid unravelling of the Soviet experiment in the years that followed. For one, the scene in the open-pit mine offers a grim inversion of the bildungsroman's conventional developmental trajectory by replacing the vision of the protagonist's fully realized self with the authoritarian state's attempt to obliterate that very self ('Nemo', or 'Nobody', is the nickname

1 Uwe Tellkamp, *The Tower: Tales from a Lost Country* (London: Penguin, 2014), pp. 913–15.

2 On the ubiquity of *Umerziehung* in GDR political discourses about individual growth, see Verena Zimmermann, *'Den neuen Menschen schaffen': Die Umerziehung von schwererziehbaren und straffälligen Jugendlichen in der DDR (1945–1990)* (Köln: Böhlau, 2004). Hunter Bivens offers an important account of the literary dimensions of 're-education' in *The East German Novel of Socialist Construction: Laboring Affect* (Rochester, NY: Camden House, 2026).

Christian acquires among the other pit workers).[3] But the scene also inverts the conception of work that underpins more traditional bildungsromane. Work, in Tellkamp's novel, is no longer the medium of enriching experiences of self-formation and social belonging but an instrument callously wielded by a totalitarian state against its own population. As the literary scholar Franco Moretti has argued, in the nineteenth-century European bildungsroman, work had typically served to integrate self and world: the bildungsroman's master narrative – a youthful individual breaks away from the community, experiences a process of bildung, and finally returns fully formed to the bosom of the community – depends on the individual's ability to see their work both as vocationally connected to their inner self *and* as contributing to the common good.[4] Starting with Goethe's *Lehrjahre*, many nineteenth-century European bildungsromane conclude with the vision of a self completely at home in the world: 'The soul in such a novel', Georg Lukács influentially argued in his early work *The Theory of the Novel* (1914–15), 'carries within itself, as a sign of its tenuous, but not yet severed link with the transcendental order, a longing for an earthly home which may correspond to its ideal.'[5]

This conventional account of the bildungsroman's politico-cultural work has a long and venerable history. It is closely bound up with the intellectual genealogy that locates the genre's origins in the early nineteenth century, notably in the work of the German philosopher G. W. F. Hegel. According to Hegel's influential gloss on bildung in his lectures on aesthetics, individuals who undergo a process of formation learn to see existing social structures not as alien impositions on the self but as an extension of their own being. This recognition, Hegel contends, entails 'the acknowledgment of the seemingly external laws . . . as something I myself have brought into being and to which I am therefore bound by an identification much more intense than rational choice or freedom.'[6] It is in this sense that Goethe's *Wilhelm Meisters Lehrjahre*, Gottfried Keller's *Der grüne Heinrich* (*Green Henry*, 1855/79) and other canonical nineteenth-century bildungsromane conclude with the happy alignment of subjective desires and objective reality.

3 Tellkamp, *The Tower*, p. 667.

4 Franco Moretti, *The Way of the World: The Bildungsroman in European Culture* (London: Verso, 2000).

5 Georg Lukács, *The Theory of the Novel: A Historico-Philosophical Essay on the Forms of Great Epic Literature* (Cambridge, MA: MIT Press, 1999), p. 132.

6 I borrow this paraphrase of Hegel's position from Fredric Jameson's *Hegel Variations: On the* Phenomenology of Spirit (London: Verso, 2010), p. 105.

Literary scholars know this story all too well. They have pointed to the links that exist between the nineteenth-century bildungsroman's vision of community (Lukács's 'earthly home') and the historical emergence of the nation-state.[7] According to these accounts, the reintegration of individual and (national) community at the end of the nineteenth-century bildungsroman serves to hem in the formlessness of youth associated with the cataclysmic socio-political changes wrought by the French Revolution and industrial modernity. Emerging in reaction to these events, so the story goes, the bildungsroman aimed to contain the disruptive social energies that threatened further revolution in the wake of 1789 and 1848. When it is described in this way, the bildungsroman looks like the artistic equivalent of the nationalist policies that were enshrined at the 1815 Congress of Vienna and that sought to undo the geopolitical changes of the period 1789–1815. These reactionary policies find an echo in the bildungsroman's conventional celebration of the everyday and the pleasures of domesticity: the bildungsroman naturalizes social reality by offering readers the aestheticized image of an organic community in which the individual can find fulfilment. The nineteenth-century bildungsroman, claims Moretti, narrates how revolution 'could have been avoided'.[8]

This is all well as far as it goes. Crucially, however, this account of the bildungsroman's political work has eclipsed a rich alternative genealogy of the genre, which my book sets out to reconstruct and reclaim. This counter-tradition evolved alongside the bildungsroman's more familiar hegemonic forms from the early nineteenth century onwards, and it is firmly allied to left political causes. It asks what happens when the habits and routines inculcated by capitalist society – the bildung that we inhabit like a second skin – wear thin. The radical bildungsroman does not show how revolution 'could have been avoided' but, instead, requires us to imagine the conditions under which a more egalitarian and fully internationalist dispensation might finally emerge. Works in the genre run from early socialist readings of Goethe's *Meister* novels (especially

7 See Pheng Cheah, *Spectral Nationality: Passages of Freedom from Kant to Postcolonial Literatures of Liberation* (New York: Columbia University Press, 2003), esp. pp. 239–47; Jed Esty, *Unseasonable Youth: Modernism, Colonialism, and the Fiction of Development* (New York: Oxford University Press, 2013). Tobias Boes's literary history of the bildungsroman stresses the genre's national boundedness but also considers the more expansive ('cosmopolitan') affiliations envisioned by the genre: *Formative Fictions: Nationalism, Cosmopolitanism, and the Bildungsroman* (Ithaca, NY: Cornell University Press, 2012).

8 Moretti, *Way of the World*, p. 64.

the neglected *Wilhelm Meisters Wanderjahre* [*Wilhelm Meister's Journeyman Years*, 1821/1829]) to Nikolay Chernyshevsky's *What Is to Be Done?* (1863), Martin Andersen Nexø's *Pelle the Conqueror* (1906–19) and Maxim Gorky's *Mother* (1906); but they also include later texts such as Doris Lessing's *The Golden Notebook* (1962) and Maryse Condé's *Hérémakhonon* (1976), as well as novels by Peter Weiss, Ngũgĩ wa Thiong'o, Paul Nizan, Ding Ling and Nanni Balestrini, and films such as Jean-Luc Godard's 1967 *La Chinoise* (with its revolutionary protagonist Guillaume Meister) and Li Wenhua's re-education film *Breaking with Old Ideas* (1975) from the Chinese Cultural Revolution. Taken together, these works address a marked absence in the Marxist tradition – what the British philosopher Gillian Rose called Marxism's lack of a developed 'concept of formation and re-formation (*Bildung*)'. Responding to this perceived lack, the novels and films I explore here set out to develop models of 'revolutionary subjectivity' that supplement and enrich canonical Marxist 'accounts of structural change'.[9]

My book makes the bildungsroman visible as a global genre by tracing its radical commitments across the nineteenth and twentieth centuries and into the twenty-first. The writers and filmmakers whose remarkable works form the core of this study comprise a geographically and diachronically expansive set of artists. My selection of case studies from different national contexts is intended to highlight the generic flexibility of the left bildungsroman, as well as its portability across diverse national artistic traditions and its adaptability to a wide spectrum of ideological and historical concerns. The socialist project, as it emerges from these works, is not reducible to some fictitious party-line orthodoxy. Instead, the lines of influence that connect these writers and artists resemble what the American cultural historian Michael Denning has called the 'Novelists' International' – a loose and non-formalized network of left-wing artists whose works were energized by communist politics but whose 'history is by no means congruent with that of the official "socialist realisms" of the communist regimes'.[10] The radical novel of formation, as I describe it here, is characterized by an experimental retooling of key conventions and motifs of the bildungsroman. As such, it is best understood not as a transhistorically fixed and stable literary genre but as a set of formally innovative texts that repurpose

9 Gillian Rose, *Hegel contra Sociology* (London: Verso, 2009), p. 233.

10 Michael Denning, 'The Novelists' International', in *Culture in the Age of Three Worlds* (London: Verso, 2004), pp. 51–72 (52).

individual bildung motifs and constellate them into new narrative patterns in order to centre (classed, gendered, racialized) subject positions that are not ordinarily foregrounded in the bourgeois bildungsroman. Similar to the global traditions of working-class writing analysed by the literary scholar Sonali Perera, we need to understand this formal fragmentation and retooling as the genre's 'condition of possibility rather than as a failing' – as an enabling factor in the genre's global spread rather than as a symptom of its inability to measure up to some fictitiously pure bourgeois literary model.[11] The radical bildungsroman's formal malleability – which frequently strains against the artistic rigidity implied by the term *genre* – is key to its longevity as well as to its continued political force. This formal richness, I argue, serves a broadly universalist political project. The radical novel of formation presents us with intricately delineated characters who are embedded in detailed historical settings, but this does not mean that the experience of politics articulated in these texts is therefore merely particularist. On the contrary, it is precisely through their complex attention to particular sites and modalities of the political struggle that these novels achieve their embodied universalism.

The radical bildungsroman forms a vital strand of socialist world literature whose history extends across some two hundred years from the early 1800s to the present. Texts in the genre are linked by a discernible set of shared concerns and political convictions. They take it as axiomatic that any radical politics deserving of its name must start out from the needs and aspirations of human beings who learn to inhabit shared political ground by formulating collective political demands. Instead of positing as normative a single model of revolutionary subjectivity (for example, the collective subject of the revolutionary proletariat), the radical bildungsroman explores a wide range of identities. My discussion in this book will move from orthodoxly communist writers to socialist authors who eschew traditional Marxian categories, and to feminist and postcolonial novels that further expand such conceptual frameworks. These texts share an overarching understanding of the political struggle as a drawn-out, halting and uneven process rather than as a singular moment of political conversion or revolutionary rupture. We can recover this understanding of the political struggle through close engagement with the literary form of these texts; and, as I

11 Sonali Perera, *No Country: Working-Class Writing in the Age of Globalization* (New York: Columbia University Press, 2014), p. 7.

argue later in this chapter, we can productively conceptualize it in analogy to the locally circumscribed and future-oriented teleologies of *work*. The radical bildungsroman articulates an egalitarian vision of (self-) formation as strenuously collaborative (in the root sense of *collaboration* as a type of work that is performed collectively). In so doing, the genre affords us an understanding of political praxis that emphasizes the hard-won quality of revolutionary change.

Most of the novels I discuss in this book were written before 1989. Unlike Tellkamp's disillusioned protagonist, the bildungshelden in these texts remain committed to the utopian promise of the socialist project: they treat experiences of alienation – the divorce of subject and object, world and meaning, self and community – not as an insurmountable crisis but as the starting point for a range of new emancipatory political projects. A central contradiction explored in the radical bildungsroman is that between socialist internationalism and the bildungsroman's traditional privileging of a national frame of reference: the genre maintains an uneasy relationship with the telos of national closure precisely because the retreat into the borders of the nation would seem to acknowledge the failure of socialist internationalism. To think about the left bildungsroman, therefore, is to think about the impossibility of narrative closure – about the elusiveness of socialism's 'earthly home' and the fundamental open-endedness of the political struggle. To put it another way: whereas, as the literary scholar Jed Esty writes, in the traditional bildungsroman '[t]he nation-state stabilizes the bourgeois revolution into a narratable form', this recourse to the nation-state threatened to make the international dimension of the socialist revolution unnarratable.[12]

In what follows, I set out the larger stakes of my argument. The first half of the Introduction will trace the left bildungsroman's historical origins in the 1830s and 1840s by showing that socialist critics drew on the Goethean category *Weltliteratur* to articulate the bildungsroman's emancipatory and internationalist horizons. What emerges from these nineteenth-century debates, and from my book as a whole, is a history of socialist writing that does not narrowly identify *Weltliteratur* with the globalizing forces of capital, as Marxist literary historians have often tended to do. Instead, in the words of Ngũgĩ wa Thiong'o, this radical counter-tradition mobilizes the 'universalist tendency' that lies 'at the heart of the constitution of Goethe's world literature' and that forms 'the

12 Esty, *Unseasonable Youth*, p. 47.

nonimperial heart of the modern and postmodern'.[13] The second half of the Introduction will offer examples from a number of global contexts to suggest that the left bildungsroman articulates these radical universalist aspirations by framing the political struggle in terms of the patterns and temporalities of *work*. I develop this conceptual model of bildung-as-work by turning to one of the key texts of Marxist humanism, Lukács's *Ontology of Social Being* (written over the course of the 1960s, late in Lukács's career), which argues for the salience of *work* as an explanatory socio-cultural heuristic. The left bildungsroman's understanding of radical praxis as a form of work is important, I argue, because it makes it possible to reimagine political action outside the debilitating binarisms of revolutionary euphoria versus historical pessimism, (total) victory versus (total) defeat. The genre teaches us to view experiences of defeat and deferral as necessary aspects of the socialist struggle, and, in doing so, it can help us imagine anew the modalities of political survival and radical change.

Radical Bildung and *Weltliteratur*: Goethean Legacies

The scene from Tellkamp's *The Tower* with which I began prises open a gulf between self and society as Christian is subjected to forced labour by an authoritarian state that falsely claims to defend the ideals of the October Revolution. In Tellkamp's novel, the separation of (social) world and self is so absolute that it appears irreversible – in this sense, *The Tower* can be said to mark a late endpoint to the rich history of the radical bildungsroman that I tell in this book. If we want to reclaim the political vitality of the left bildungsroman, we must learn to bracket the unrelenting sense of historical disappointment that characterizes later accounts of the socialist project by writers such as Tellkamp. The present section begins this work of reconstruction by charting the early genesis of the left bildungsroman – a history that can be traced back to a set of revisionary socialist readings of Goethe's *Meister* novels from the 1820s and 1830s. Much scholarship on the bildungsroman (including Lukács's influential discussion in *Theory of the Novel*) has turned to the *Lehrjahre* to argue that the genre is inextricably wedded to the social

13 Ngũgĩ wa Thiong'o, 'Globalectical Imagination: The World in the Postcolonial', in Ngũgĩ wa Thiong'o, *Globalectics: Theory and the Politics of Knowing* (New York: Columbia University Press, 2012), pp. 44–62 (55).

status quo. This single-minded focus on the *Lehrjahre*, I suggest here, has severely restricted our understanding of the genre's ability to integrate radical political ideas. By contrast, the most significant socialist accounts of the bildungsroman to emerge from the 1830s and 1840s typically home in on the later *Wanderjahre*, a text that tests the boundaries of the novel form itself, and one which contemporary critics sometimes find too disjointed to merit the label of bildungsroman at all. Goethe's socialist readers of the 1830s and 1840s believed that the *Wanderjahre* offered an account of bildung that was radically different from the one envisioned in the *Lehrjahre*.

What was it about Goethe's bildungsromane that made these novels so compelling to socialist readers? The *Lehrjahre* relates the story of Wilhelm Meister, a young man torn between adopting the life of a merchant (thereby following the wishes of his father, who expects Wilhelm to enter the family business) and pursuing his passion for the theatre. Although much of the novel's narrative energy is generated by Wilhelm's youthful (intellectual, artistic, creative) adventures, he finally gives up on his aspiration to establish a new national theatre. Embracing his father's middle-class values, Wilhelm eventually chooses to pursue upward mobility by becoming engaged to the aristocratic Natalie rather than his sweetheart Mariane. As many critics (from Lukács's *Theory of the Novel* onwards) have pointed out, Wilhelm's path to maturity in the *Lehrjahre* entails a renunciation of youthful desire and the realization of his new commitment to an economically productive life. Unbeknownst to Wilhelm, however, his bildung has been furthered all along by the machinations of the *Turmgesellschaft*, a secret society whose members mysteriously appear at key moments in Wilhelm's life and orchestrate much of his apprenticeship (for example, it is Jarno, a member of the society, who first sparks Wilhelm's interest in the theatre by introducing him to Shakespeare). Through the theatre, Wilhelm also encounters a series of minor figures and wandering actors, all of whom contribute to the ongoing process of his emotional and intellectual bildung. Most famous among these is Mignon, the androgynous and itinerant child that Wilhelm adopts. As Goethe's narrator notes, Mignon's uncertain parentage and erratic behaviour are signs of her 'irregular bildung'.[14] Importantly, however, this 'irregular bildung' is presented not as an

14 Johann Wolfgang von Goethe, *Wilhelm Meisters Lehrjahre*, in *Werke*, vol. 7, ed. Erich Trunz (Hamburg: dtv, 1998), p. 96.

imperfection but as a symptom of Mignon's yearning for an unattainable homeland: her wanderings across Europe have left her without a stable identity, a fact that is reflected in her 'strange' (*sonderbar*) transnational pidgin ('broken German, mixed with French and Italian').[15]

Whereas the *Lehrjahre* focuses on Wilhelm's fortunes, the *Wanderjahre* turns more explicitly to questions of social organization. It is true that the book features a plotline involving Goethe's eponymous bildungsheld Wilhelm, but this plot is 'woven into a complex and not in any way obviously unified tapestry'.[16] The *Wanderjahre* opens with Wilhelm's decision to undertake a journey that will lead him (and his son Felix) away from the domestic life he shares with Natalie ('not more than three days shall I remain under one roof,' Wilhelm declares: 'I shall leave no lodging without distancing myself at least one mile from it'[17]). The loose narrative structure of the *Wanderjahre* echoes Wilhelm's self-imposed wanderings: the book is broken up into what Marc Redfield calls a disorientating 'mélange of novellas, letters, speeches, journal entries, technical writing, poetry, and aphorisms'.[18] The *Wanderjahre*'s residual plot traces the outline of Wilhelm's life as he is repeatedly brought into contact with utopian schemes for the restructuring of society. While Felix undergoes a process of bildung in the so-called 'Pedagogical Province' (a utopic community designed to prepare its students for a life of practical and socially minded activity), the main utopian charge of the book's social vision is associated with the enigmatic figure of the *Oheim* – the 'uncle' (Oheim) of Wilhelm's friend Lenardo – and with the Bund ('League'), which the Oheim helps to support and finance. The uncle and the Bund are central to the *Wanderjahre*'s utopian-socialist vision: while the Oheim voices some of the text's most radically socialist ideas (these include the 'transformation of private into public property' and the 'transcendence of property as such'[19]), the Bund endeavours (unsuccessfully) to initiate a settlement scheme in North America that will translate these abstract aspirations

15 Ibid., p. 110.

16 Marc Redfield, *Phantom Formations: Aesthetic Ideology and the Bildungsroman* (Ithaca, NY: Cornell University Press, 1996), p. 99.

17 Johann Wolfgang von Goethe, *Wilhelm Meisters Wanderjahre, oder die Entsagenden*, in *Werke*, vol. 8, ed. Erich Trunz (Hamburg: dtv, 1998), p. 12.

18 Redfield, *Phantom Formations*, p. 100.

19 I borrow both phrases – *Besitz werde Gemeingut* and *Aufheb[ung] des Besitzes* – from Karl Grün, one of the socialist critics who found much to admire in the *Wanderjahre* during the revolutionary 1840s. See Grün's *Ueber Göthe vom menschlichen Standpunkte* (Darmstadt: Leske, 1846), pp. 281, 283.

into practice by creating democratically organized communes in the New World.

To the extent that the Bund publicly advertises its commitment to democratic cooperation, it offers a stark contrast to the *Lehrjahre*'s secretive, quasi-Masonic *Turm* (Tower) Society. The Bund's utopian socialism spoke to revolutionary thinkers and writers of the 1830s and 1840s precisely because the attempt to set up utopian communes in North America could be read as a coded engagement with the popular-democratic experiments that culminated in the revolutions of 1848: 'The protagonists of Goethe's novel decide to emigrate to America,' noted the German radical Karl Grün in one the most important socialist readings of the *Meister* novels to emerge from the revolutionary ferment of the 1840s: '[The protagonists'] ideals cannot be brought to fruition in Europe' because present social conditions stand in the way of their realization.[20] Radicals like Grün equated the formal openness of the *Wanderjahre* – the novel's erring plotlines, its inconclusive stops and starts – with the hopes and frustrations experienced by the period's socialist revolutionaries: whereas the classical bildungsroman 'ends with its own negation, a state in which development is arrested and mundane reality suddenly yields up a hidden immanent meaning', for Grün the *Wanderjahre* encapsulates a radically different understanding of bildung as an ongoing work-like struggle in which the transformation of the self is bound up with the revolutionary desire to transform existing social structures.[21] The *Wanderjahre*'s formal openness, Grün argues, does not encode the indefinite deferral of revolutionary change; instead, it indicates the vagaries and incertitude that are a necessary feature of the socialist struggle for a better world. Grün's observations about the *Wanderjahre* resonate with the larger body of radical bildungsromane I explore in this book. For example, Peter Weiss's early novel *Vanishing Point* (*Fluchtpunkt*, 1962) closes by showing that its exiled protagonist must learn to inhabit the 'world of a fugitive': like other political exiles, he must embrace 'my lostness, my uprootedness' in the hope of making this 'not-belonging' the source of a future internationalism.[22]

The years leading up to 1848 saw the emergence of a rich crop of socialist readings of Goethe's *Wilhelm Meister* novels. These interpretations reacted against the stiflingly conformist atmosphere that followed

20 Ibid., pp. 308–9.

21 Ibid., p. 279.

22 Peter Weiss, Leavetaking *and* Vanishing Point (London: Calder and Boyars, 1966), pp. 130, 55.

the Congress of Vienna, and they captured the hopes that inspired the pan-European revolutionary wave of 1848 in which proletarian and bourgeois elements joined forces against the ossified monarchical structures of Europe's *anciens régimes*. These readings sought to rescue Goethe's novels of formation – in particular *Wilhelm Meisters Wanderjahre* – from adulatory accounts that turned Goethe into the stalwart of Weimar classicism and that saw in him the embodiment of a Biedermeyer-esque political quietism. This appropriation of Goethe was partly strategic because it enabled socialists to extend their cultural influence by claiming the period's preeminent *bürgerlich* writer as one of their own. But the interest in the *Lehrjahre* and *Wanderjahre* also suggests that revolutionaries were looking for literary forms that might render intelligible the hopes and frustrations of the political struggle. It comes as a real surprise to learn that the bourgeois bildungsroman and the radical bildungsroman evolved in parallel for several decades. However, we also need to recognize that the socialist interest in the genre first found expression in the medium of literary criticism – in the works of figures such as Karl August Varnhagen von Ense, George Sand, Ludolf Wienbarg, Karl Grün, Alexânder Jung and Ferdinand Gregorovius.[23] It was not until the second half of the nineteenth century, when the surging communist movement drew support through the mobilization of cultural and artistic forms that left bildungsromane began to be written in sizable numbers.

Paying attention to the socialist reception of the *Wanderjahre* helps to defamiliarize conventional accounts of the bildungsroman genre that take their cue from the *Lehrjahre*, but it also expands our understanding of the formal and thematic parameters of the genre's left variant. 'The *social* idea that is expressed in *Wilhelm Meister*, especially in the *Wanderjahre*, needed our own present to render it fully apparent,' writes Gregorovius at the start of his book *Goethe's* Wilhelm Meister – *Its Socialist Elements Developed* (1849).[24] Gregorovius's comment captures the gist of many other contemporaneous radical accounts of the *Wanderjahre* by suggesting that attention to the *Wanderjahre*'s 'socialist

23 George Sand noted in a letter to Bettina von Arnim that had Goethe lived in France, his *Wanderjahre* would have helped French writers make strides towards a fully committed socialist literary tradition ('il serait, en fait d'idées socialistes, notre maître'). See Sand, 'Lettre à Bettina von Arnim, 18 mars 1845', in *Correspondance*, vol. 6, ed. Georges Lubin (Paris: Garnier, 1969), pp. 824–7 (826).

24 Ferdinand Gregorovius, *Göthe's* Wilhelm Meister *in seinen socialistischen Elementen entwickelt* (Königsberg: Bornträger, 1849), p. iv.

elements' also makes possible a revisionary reading of the *Lehrjahre*.[25] Properly understood, Gregorovius argues, the two *Meister* novels complement each other: while the *Lehrjahre* focuses on the rich psychological formation of an individual (*die innerliche humane Vollendung des Einzel-Menschen*), the *Wanderjahre* is concerned to show the growth of complex social structures (*System der Gesellschaft*) in which humans will be able to flourish collectively.[26] Many pre-1848 socialist readers stress the *Wanderjahre*'s utopian vision of a more democratic distribution of land, and they also highlight the *Wanderjahre*'s expansive geographic purview (at one point in the novel, Wilhelm considers moving to North America to found a utopian commune with the Bund's assistance). For example, the radical activist Ludolf Wienbarg argued in 1835 that the *Wanderjahre* joined Goethe's discussion of emergent *Weltliteratur* to a revolutionary internationalism. Wienbarg's reassessment of the *Wanderjahre* is a historical link that made it possible for Goethe's term *Weltliteratur* to resurface prominently, just a few years later, in Marx and Engels's *Communist Manifesto* (1848).[27] These early socialist-utopian readings of the *Meister* novels – and of the *Wanderjahre* in particular – are little known, but they afford important insights into the consolidation of the radical bildungsroman as a genre as well as into the emergence of the idea of socialist *Weltliteratur*. To get a better grasp on these left debates, I will begin by sketching out a brief genealogy of this politically progressive criticism in the 1830s and 1840s.

---

25 Gregorovius and Grün also stress the novel's continuity with other late works by Goethe. On the second part of *Faust*, see *Göthe's* Wilhelm Meister, p. 85; and Grün, *Ueber Göthe*, p. 286. The most prominent anglophone statement of this position came some 150 years later, in Marshall Brown's *All That Is Solid Melts into Air: The Experience of Modernity* (London: Verso, 1983).

26 Gregorovius, *Göthe's* Wilhelm Meister, p. 18. The *Lehrjahre*'s concern with interiority, Gregorovius concluded, had looked back to the eighteenth century, whereas the *Wanderjahre* was looking ahead to the social(ist) concerns of the nineteenth (p. 15). What was necessary was therefore an 'unbiased interpretation of the *whole* of *Wilhelm Meister*' (p. 13). This point is echoed in Alexander Jung's *Goethe's* Wanderjahre *und die wichtigsten Fragen des 19. Jahrhunderts* (Mainz: Kunze, 1854).

27 I will return to this point in a moment. See Ludolf Wienbarg, 'Goethe und die Weltliteratur', in Wienbarg, *Zur neuesten Literatur* (Mannheim: Löwenthal, 1835), 1–33. On the activation of Goethe's term by revolutionaries in the 1830s, see Hartmut Steinecke, '*Weltliteratur*: Zur Diskussion der Goetheschen Idee im Jungen Deutschland', in Joseph A. Kruse and Bernd Kortländer (eds), *Das Junge Deutschland: Kolloquium zum 150. Jahrestag des Verbots vom 10. Dezember 1835* (Hamburg: Hoffmann und Campe, 1987), pp. 144–72; and Patrick Fortmann, 'World Literature Turns Political, 1835/36: The Early Afterlife of Goethe's Pronouncement in German Cultural-Politics and in the Young Germany Movement', *Goethe Yearbook* 26 (2019): 217–32.

The German writer and public intellectual Karl August Varnhagen von Ense deserves to be known as the first theorist of the radical bildungsroman. Born in 1785, Varnhagen served as Prussian envoy to the Congress of Vienna, but after 1815 his democratic leanings and Saint-Simonism increasingly got him into trouble with Europe's resurgent autocratic elites. His opposition to the July Monarchy, which was dominated by Napoleonic elements and the *haute bourgeoisie*, is well-documented ('I profoundly detest this crowned schemer [the monarch Louis Philippe] and his miserable ministers'[28]), and he accordingly welcomed the revolutions that swept Europe in the 1840s as harbingers of broader emancipatory struggles.

Varnhagen's early review of the *Wanderjahre* is *the* central critical text in the bildungsroman's early socialist history. Goethe had died in 1832, and Varnhagen's article appeared the same year in the final issue of Goethe's influential periodical *Über Kunst und Alterthum*. Varnhagen's programmatic account of the *Wanderjahre* rather than the *Lehrjahre* is significant because it reminds us that the exclusive focus on the earlier novel has produced a blinkered view of the genre as a whole. Varnhagen points out that the *Wanderjahre*'s attention to social utopianism, global movement ('wandering') and the space available for democratic organizing marked a break with narrowly nationalistic agendas and spoke to the budding socialist movements of his day.[29] Central to this shift is Goethe's decision to replace the *Lehrjahre*'s aristocratic Turm Society, which gently steers Wilhelm towards reintegration with the national community, with a democratic 'League' (Bund) that organizes utopian social experiments in North America. In Varnhagen's account, the *Wanderjahre* invites a radical rereading of the *Lehrjahre*: Goethe's later book renders legible the earlier novel's attention to the monopolization of land by aristocratic and capitalistic elites as well as its focus on the conditions of class struggle and alienation that arise under the current socio-economic order ('a bourgeois can earn wealth and respect but his personality is lost in the process,' Wilhelm notes in the *Lehrjahre*: 'He is

28 Varnhagen, 'Brief an Rahel Varnhagen, 20 March 1848', unpublished autograph letters auctioned in 2019, bonhams.com, last accessed 20 September 2020.

29 'I have been rereading the *Wanderjahre*,' Varnhagen noted in his last letter to Goethe: 'The novel invites comparison with St Simonism . . . which I trust will soon make political inroads into Germany.' See Karl August Varnhagen von Ense, 'Brief an Goethe, 28 December 1831', in *Briefe an Goethe*, vol. 2, ed. Karl Robert Mandelkow (Hamburg: Wagner Verlag, 1968), pp. 597–8 (597). Varnhagen's exploration of the *Wanderjahre*'s Saint-Simonism is echoed in Gregorovius's *Göthe's* Wilhelm Meister, pp. 79–80.

not allowed to ask: what are you? But only: what do you own? . . . The bourgeois self lacks harmony: by proving himself useful in one respect only, he must neglect everything else').[30]

In pursuing his revisionary project, Varnhagen engages in a double manoeuvre: first, he finds in Goethe's work ample evidence of the liberatory 'shattering and vanishing of old forms of life' (*die Zerrüttung und Auflösung der alten Lebensformen*) brought about by the French Revolution; but he also positions the *Wanderjahre* as the central literary work of its own *vorbereitende Epoche* (that is, an era that helps to 'pave the way' for a democratic future).[31] Varnhagen's essay begins by identifying two central ideas in the *Wanderjahre*: Goethe's observation that in Europe all habitable land has come into the possession of aristocratic landowners and capitalist entrepreneurs (*wie die Erde . . . überall schon in Besitz genommen sei*, 533); and his recognition that under the current socio-economic dispensation, happiness and self-realization are denied to most people (*dem Menschen . . . so manches Mögliche versagt worden*, 533). What Varnhagen identifies here, and what he continues to explore over the course of his review essay, are the conditions of economic exploitation and social alienation that characterized Europe in the opening decades of the nineteenth century – a period that Goethe's *Wanderjahre* unambiguously associates with the early stages of industrialization. Goethe, Varnhagen points out, is keenly attuned to the squalid 'living conditions' endured by 'proletarians, slum-dwellers, and the oppressed' (*Proletarier, Verwahrloste und Bedrückte*, 535). As Varnhagen notes, the *Wanderjahre* helps us see that these radical ideas were already central to the *Lehrjahre* and to other texts by Goethe: Goethe's early work 'showed the inner urge for a different life, one which struggles [*unruhig kämpft*] against present social conditions' (544). It is this aspect of the bildungsroman – the fact that it keeps 'its eye set on a rich unalienated future' (546) – that sets Goethe's writing apart from the post-1815 apologists of the socio-economic status quo. Instead of denouncing the radical promise of the French Revolution, Goethe's bildungsromane throw into sharp relief the harsh contradictions and irredeemable defects of the existing social order. Accordingly, the bildung that is described in the two

30 Goethe, *Lehrjahre*, p. 291.

31 Varnhagen, 'Im Sinne der Wanderer' ['In the Spirit of the Wanderers'], *Über Kunst und Alterthum* 6 (1832): 533–51 (542, 540). Subsequent references are given parenthetically. For further commentary on Varnhagen's text, see my introduction to 'In the Spirit of the Wanderers', *PMLA* 138.1 (2023): 102–9.

volumes of *Wilhelm Meister* is not the individual protagonist's slow (re)integration into a pre-existing organic community but rather a collective and future-directed political formation ('a higher formation [*höhere Bildung*]', 541) that grows directly from 'the contradiction between two epochs', one receding and one emerging (541).

What does this bildung entail? Goethe's *Wanderjahre* contains several key chapters that are devoted to a group of characters who try to escape the twinned limitations of contemporary life in Europe – the enclosure of land and the total alienation from social life experienced by 'proletarians, slum-dwellers, and social outcasts' – by emigrating to America. In Goethe's novel, America names not a bounded nation but a radically open geographical space where new and collective experiments in living (which Goethe imagines with help from Robert Owen's utopian-socialist writings) become possible. In the *Wanderjahre*, these communities symbolize a democratic future in which the realization of individual and collective freedom takes priority over questions of national and ethnic belonging. Varnhagen takes up these ideas when he discusses Goethe's critique of the present 'artificial world' (*künstliche Welt*, 545) that is 'everywhere divided by boundaries' (*überall von Schranken durchschnitten und abgetheilt*, 545). In stark contrast to twentieth- and twenty-first-century critical readings that associate the bildungsroman with the idea of national closure, Varnhagen mobilizes the utopian, future-directed and internationalist potential of this still-fledgling genre. Work and bildung are here imagined as connected and fundamentally collective projects (*die reiche Aussicht einer in Arbeit und Bildung fortschreitenden Menschheit*, 550). Eventually, however, Varnhagen forcefully concludes, the bildungsroman's artistic attention to egalitarian forms of life will need to translate into concrete political action: Goethe's 1829 bildungsroman instructs its readers to become 'wanderers' and to join the collective struggle for a better future ('the judgments and insights to be gained [from the *Wanderjahre*] will only be fruitful to those who are prepared to travel, explore, and work tirelessly', 551).

Finally, Varnhagen's landmark essay also insists that it is the *Wanderjahre*'s highly ambivalent generic affiliations that render it attractive to socialist authors. Recent critics of the *Wanderjahre* have reminded us that Goethe's novel 'has always posed classificatory challenges to literary scholars' – a situation exacerbated by the fact that portions of Goethe's text had 'appeared in different versions in various early nineteenth-century print formats over the course of two decades during Goethe's lifetime, from the newspaper to the miscellany to the novel to the collected edition'.[32] When the *Wanderjahre* is read in light of its complex medial and print history, it can easily resemble 'a formless grab bag'[33] – a text marked by a 'disjointed design' that necessitates a 'redescription of the novel as an "aggregate", "collection" or "archive"'.[34] The *Wanderjahre*'s uneven genesis led Goethe's early editors not to reprint the two collections of aphorisms ('Im Sinne der Wanderer' and 'Aus Makariens Archiv') that had featured so prominently in the book's first edition: the experimental nature of these aphorisms threatened to unsettle the closed narrative form of the bildungsroman codified by the *Lehrjahre*. By borrowing the title of one of these collections ('In the Spirit of the Wanderers') for his review essay, Varnhagen pushes back against the tendency to dismiss the *Wanderjahre* as a generic 'grab bag'. The *Wanderjahre*'s formal openness, Varnhagen insists, is in truth its most important artistic and political feature. The book's fragmented and wandering plotlines mirror the errant hopes and frustrations of the struggle for a better world.

Varnhagen's essay helped to energize further socialist readings of Goethe's novel, including two book-length studies by the 1848 revolutionaries Grün (whose book, in turn, provoked an extended response by Marx and Engels) and Gregorovius.[35] But Varnhagen's influence also extended beyond Germany: in the 1840s and 1850s, he corresponded about Goethe with Thomas Carlyle (the first English translator of *Wilhelm Meister*) as well as with the Goethe enthusiasts George Eliot and her partner George Henry Lewes. Crucially, these later readings share the universalist aspirations of Varnhagen's inaugural account of the *Wanderjahre*. These critics recognize that the three terms in Varnhagen's description of the *Wanderjahre*'s protagonists – *Proletarier, Verwahrloste und Unterdrückte* – are not simply synonymous: each new term in Varnhagen's list is more inclusive than the one that precedes it, thus expanding the field

32 Andrew Piper, 'Rethinking the Print Object: Goethe and the Book of Everything', *PMLA* 121.1 (2006): 124–39 (129).

33 Frederick Amrine, *Goethe and the Myth of the Bildungsroman: Rethinking the* Wilhelm Meister *Novels* (Cambridge: Cambridge University Press, 2020), p. 1.

34 Carlos Spoerhase, *Das Format der Literatur: Praktiken materieller Textualität zwischen 1740 und 1830* (Göttingen: Wallstein, 2018), p. 546.

35 For Marx and Engels's no-holds-barred attack on Grün's utopian-socialist reading, see *Marx-Engels Werke*, vol. 4 (Berlin: Dietz, 1971), pp. 222–47. Varnhagen variously commented on the radical sympathies he shared with Grün during those tempestuous years of 1848–9. See, for example, Varnhagen, *Journal einer Revolution, Tagesblätter 1848–49*, ed. Hans-Magnus Enzensberger (Nördlingen: Greno, 1986), p. 210.

of subject positions that are eligible for inclusion in the radical bildungsroman. As will become clear in later chapters, Varnhagen's expansive understanding of the genre – its attention to *Proletarier* as well as to the larger social groups of *Verwahrloste* and *Bedrückte* – echoes through the history of the radical bildungsroman. This means that the particular (early Soviet) inflection of the genre – which fetishizes a narrowly identitarian category of *the proletariat* and which takes this proletarian identity to be (ideologically, economically, artistically) normative across a wide range of conjunctures and geographical contexts – will actually be quite marginal to the larger body of literary and cinematic work I explore in this book. The genre's particular 'commitment to foregrounding the predicaments and agency' of particular (disenfranchised) subjects, to borrow a phrase from the literary scholar Nivedita Majumdar, is 'not only consistent with the acknowledgement of underlying universalisms but is in fact untenable without it'.[36]

Weltliteratur and World Revolution: From Goethe to Marx

Turning to the immediate intellectual afterlives of Varnhagen's account in the 1840s can help us describe the basic formal parameters of the radical bildungsroman, and it also clarifies the genre's contribution to an emergent socialist *Weltliteratur*. Grün (born in 1817) had held anarchist sympathies well before the revolutions of 1848–9, and when these political leanings became known to the Prussian government, he was forced into exile in France. Returning to Germany in 1848 with the intention of joining the revolutionary movement, Grün briefly settled in Trier, Marx's birthplace, before being once more expelled by the Prussian authorities. Gregorovius, although temperamentally less likely than Grün to engage in insurrectionary acts of street fighting, had supported the democratic movement of 1848–9 as a publicist and organizer of a democratic club in his hometown of Königsberg. In the late 1840s, Grün and Gregorovius both wrote studies of Goethe, with Gregorovius's book being dedicated specifically to the *Meister* novels. Both books emphasize that, in the *Wanderjahre*, Goethe's attention shifted from 'bildung of the individual human' to the 'reconstruction of society as a whole'.[37]

36 Nivedita Majumdar, *The World in a Grain of Sand: Postcolonial Literature and Radical Universalism* (London: Verso, 2021), p. 10.

37 Grün, *Ueber Göthe*, p. 270.

Central to this shift, Grün and Gregorovius contend, are the Oheim's fervent critique of private property and his commitment to the establishment of utopian communities in North America. As Grün observes, the 'governing principle of the world' (*Prinzip der Welt*) envisioned in *Wanderjahre*

> is socialism – communism even. We may use this word now that the German public begins to recognize the significance of this world-wide movement [*Weltbewegung*] . . . Communism's insistence on the inviolability of the individual is the true socialism. We will no longer let our view of the world be distorted by plump comforts of private property, not even for a moment. The reality of humanism, the true humanism, is nothing but communism itself, the community of all in work and enjoyment. The Oheim's estate is organized on socialist principles, the plan to create a commune in North America even deserves to be called *communist*.[38]

Taking his cue from Henri de Saint-Simon and Pierre-Joseph Proudhon, Grün argues that communism will address the needs of *all* members of society equitably. Gregorovius and Grün also stress that the *Wanderjahre*'s attention to bildung – to the talents and abilities of unique individuals – resists the reduction of 'individuality' (*Individualität*) to mere economic self-interest that takes place in the 'egotistically depraved society' of the present.[39] The radical bildungsroman gives us glimpses of life after capitalism: in the *Wanderjahre* 'characters undergo bildung [bildung] by attaining a richer life, and they live by attaining a fuller bildung.'[40] As Grün notes, this growth of a socialist personality involves the shedding – the 'unlearning' (*Rückbildung*) – of an earlier self that was formed by bourgeois society.

In the *Meister* books, this process of 'unlearning' never gives way to an anti-foundational vertigo in which selfhood as such is dissolved: in Goethe's novels, the bildung of the socialist self is carried out by the Turm Society and the Bund – two groups whose fundamental wisdom in guiding the protagonists towards self-realization is never questioned. For Grün and Gregorovius, Goethe's bildungsromane come to occupy

38 Ibid., p. 278 (emphasis in original).

39 Ibid., p. 258. On this point, see also Patrick Eiden-Offe, *The Poetry of Class: Romantic Anti-Capitalism and the Invention of the Proletariat*, trans. Jacob Blumenfeld (Leiden: Brill, 2023).

40 Ibid., p. 270.

the same role of *Erzieher* ('educator') that is attributed to the Turm and Bund in the *Meister* novels. 'We happily embrace this education [*Erziehung*],' writes Grün, 'but [its principles] finally point beyond the *Meister* novels and call for the reconstitution of society.'[41] The *Meister* novels, Grün opines, can help to reinvigorate a socialist movement that had devolved, by the 1840s, into a politically inert and anti-revolutionary middle-class '*juste milieu*'.[42] By pointing out what contemporary socialists stand to learn from Goethe's novels, Grün and Gregorovius suggest that the radical bildungsroman can become a formative political force in its own right. Whereas the Oheim's socialism remains largely theoretical, the aim of the radical bildungsroman is to 'make our convictions socially effective . . . to make humanism real': by contributing to the reader's own political bildung, the genre's humanist universalism evinces an 'uncompromising commitment to socialism and communism' (*entschiedener Sozialismus und Kommunismus*) that goes well beyond the Oheim's theorizing.[43] 'Prudence and prohibitions are of no use to an enterprise such as ours,' notes one of the members of the Bund: 'it is necessary to make a completely new start.'[44] The socialist bildungsroman's formal structure – its ability to constellate elements of the bourgeois bildungsroman into new narratives that convey the 'unlearning' of an earlier bildung as well as the halting emergence of a new (socialist) one – is central to the genre's pedagogical work. 'In recent socialist debates,' Grün complained, 'aesthetic questions play only a subordinate role – they are hardly ever spoken of.'[45] Taking their cue from Varnhagen, revolutionary thinkers such as Gregorovius and Grün sought to remedy this situation by demonstrating that the genre of the bildungsroman was capable of doing political work.

The political thrust of Varnhagen's, Grün's and Gregorovius's revisionary accounts is fundamentally aspirational – after all, their readings predated the historical emergence of the radical novel of formation from the second half of the nineteenth century onwards. These early essays were accordingly able to claim for literature a level of political agency that later radical bildungsromane (with the possible exception of Chernyshevsky's *What Is to Be Done?*) would struggle to attain. Even so, these early socialist readers of the *Meister* novels

41 Ibid., p. 278.
42 Ibid., pp. 289–90.
43 Ibid., p. 291.
44 Ibid., p. 332.
45 Ibid., p. v.

succeeded in identifying aspects of the Goethean novel of formation that came to define the genre's socialist variant over the next 150 years. For example, Gregorovius opens his study by noting: 'The human being of our age is closely related to Wilhelm Meister . . . From the heights of the consciousness which he has attained after a slow process of development, he can now purvey with astonishment the results of all his errors and previous bildung [*seiner Irrtüme und Bildungsphasen*] and finally grasp his true aim and destiny.'[46] According to Gregorovius, the defining feature of the present 'age' (*Zeitalter*) is the attempt to break open the encrustations of bourgeois society in order to build a more just social world.[47] In a chapter entitled 'Die Emancipation des Subjekts', Gregorovius gives additional conceptual edge to this process by distinguishing between the *Verbildeten* of capitalist society – that is, individuals who have undergone a process of bourgeois 'mis-bildung' (*Verbildung*) – and those who are engaged in the struggle for a new social order. The latter group, Gregorovius comments, 'hope that their new bildung will provide them with something more worthwhile than recipes on how to get rich'.[48]

If the essays and books by Varnhagen and other critics give us a sense of the broad contours of the radical bildungsroman, they also indicate the internationalist aspirations these critics associated with the genre. On the first page of his book, Gregorovius expressed the hope that Goethe's *Wanderjahre* would contribute to a collaborative, open-ended and future-directed process of *Weltbildung*.[49] The term *Weltbildung* captures the internationalist dimension of bildung that socialist critics of the 1830s and 1840s found in the *Wanderjahre*, but it also resonates with the geographically inclusive tradition of the radical bildungsroman that I map out in this book. Many radical thinkers of the period were writing about the bildungsroman's potentially global reach and its

46 Gregorovius, *Göthe's* Wilhelm Meister, p. 2.

47 Moretti, *Way of the World*, p. 5.

48 Gregorovius, *Göthe's* Wilhelm Meister, p. 67. Lukács's essay '*Wilhelm Meister's Apprenticeship*' (1936) briefly alludes to these debates of the 1830s and 1840s. Lukács's essay is legible as a product of the Popular Front period of the mid-1930s, and it helpfully complicates the terms on which party-line critics such as Leopold Auerbach were dismissing the 'resignation' preached in Goethe's *Meister* novels. See '*Wilhelm Meister's Apprenticeship*', in *Goethe and His Age* (London: Merlin Press, 1968), pp. 50–67; and Leopold Auerbach, 'A Great Man and a Narrow Philistine (On the Centenary of Goethe's Death)', *International Literature* 2–3 (1932): 122–9.

49 Gregorovius, *Göthe's* Wilhelm Meister, p. 1. The term appears in the first sentence of Gregorovius's book.

ability to contribute to the global political struggle. For example, this understanding also animates Ludolf Wienbarg's attempt to distil from the *Meister* novels the vision of an expansive socialist internationalism. According to Wienbarg, this reading of the *Meister* novels requires a shift in critical perspective: it is not Wilhelm's bildung that forms the heart of the novels' internationalist vision – instead, it is Mignon, the frail orphan child, whose erratic wanderings and pan-European pidgin come to symbolize the socialist 'longing' (*Sehnsucht*) for a post-national homeland.[50]

The title of Wienbarg's essay ('Goethe und die Welt-Literatur', 1835) explicitly associates this aspirational internationalism with Goethe's concept of *Weltliteratur*. Wienbarg's use of the term is echoed by other critics of the period (including Grün's 1849 study), and it demonstrates the radical political charge that Goethe's concept came to carry in the heated environment of the 1830s and 1840s.[51] In mobilizing the term *Weltliteratur* for their socialist projects, these critics were responding to Goethe's insistence 'that for "world literature" to become fully effective the category [would] need sustained engagement and debate'.[52] But the term's fascinating early reception history also acts as a bridge that helps to explain how the concept of *Weltliteratur* reached Marx and Engels, who prominently invoked the term in their 1848 *Communist Manifesto*. In the *Manifesto*, Marx and Engels discuss the emergence of *Weltliteratur* as a cultural symptom of the global expansion of capital:

> In place of the old wants, satisfied by the production of each country, we find new wants, requiring for their satisfaction the products of distant lands and climes. In place of the old local and national seclusion and self-sufficiency, we have intercourse in every direction, universal inter-dependence of nations. And as in material, so also in intellectual

50 Wienbarg, 'Weltliteratur', p. 11. The *Lehrjahre* had invited such allegorical readings by contrasting childhood with the '*Überbildung*' (the 'excessive or artificial bildung') of contemporary society (*Lehrjahre*, pp. 518–19). The *Wanderjahre* looks back nostalgically to the Mignon of the *Lehrjahre*, associating her with the 'passionate transgression of boundaries' ('leidenschaftlich über die Grenze gerissen'; *Wanderjahre*, p. 239).

51 For Grün's comments on *Weltliteratur*, see *Ueber Göthe*, pp. 311–16. The idea of *Weltliteratur* had also featured in the *Wanderjahre* itself, notably in the collection of aphorisms entitled 'Aus Makariens Archiv' (*Wanderjahre*, pp. 483, 478).

52 Stefan Hoesel-Uhlig, 'Changing Fields: The Directions of Goethe's *Weltliteratur*', in *Debating World Literature*, ed. Christopher Prendergast (London: Verso, 2004), pp. 26–53 (36).

> production. The intellectual creations of individual nations become common property. National one-sidedness and narrow-mindedness become more and more impossible, and from the numerous national and local literatures, there arises a world literature [*Weltliteratur*].[53]

In a gloss on this passage, the literary scholar Martin Puchner observes that Marx and Engels's use of the term *Weltliteratur* 'no longer imagines the quaint, local market of talented German translators, but a global one that ends up turning against the very existence of the nation-state'.[54] Whereas Puchner (following Marx and Engels) treats global modernity as broadly synonymous with the expansion of capitalism, Wienbarg and other socialist critics of the 1830s and 1840s position Goethe's *Wanderjahre* as the harbinger of an alternative global vision and counter-hegemonic 'aesthetico-social movement' (*ästhetisch-sociale Bewegung*): the expansive solidarities and collectivities that we are shown in the *Meister* novels, Wienbarg contends, point towards a future internationalist 'world league' (*Weltbund*) and egalitarian 'world society' (*Weltgesellschaft*).[55] By the same token, later authors of radical bildungsromane worked to free the concept of world literature of its historical association with the inequalities of bourgeois-capitalist exchange, reclaiming it for a left mode of literary production that can cut across such structural asymmetries.[56]

In these pre-1848 debates, as in the 200-year literary counter-tradition I chart in this book, *Welt* signifies the fully internationalist horizon of a future socialist politics. Taking its cue from these debates, my book seeks to restore to the term *Welt* – in collocations such as *Weltbewegung* as well as in the less conspicuously political *Weltliteratur* – the intensely aspirational charge with which early socialist readers invested it. The literary connections and cross-fertilizations that make up the history of

53 Engels/Marx, *Manifesto of the Communist Party*, trans. Samuel Moore, marxists.org, accessed on 11 August 2021.

54 Martin Puchner, *Poetry of the Revolution: Marx, Manifestos, and the Avant-Gardes* (Princeton: Princeton University Press, 2006), p. 50.

55 Wienbarg, 'Weltliteratur', p. 21. Wienbarg recalls the language of the *Wanderjahre* itself, which had described the 'Weltbund' as 'unity without division, without struggle; its principles shared by all' (*Wanderjahre*, p. 391).

56 As Aamir R. Mufti explains: 'In its historically received forms . . . world literature is fundamentally a concept of exchange (and, as Marx and Engels understood, a concept of bourgeois society) – that is, a concept that recodes an opaque and unequal process of appropriation as a transparent one of supposedly free and equal interchange and communication.' See Mufti, 'Orientalism and the Institution of World Literature', *Critical Inquiry* 36 (2010): 458–93 (488).

the radical bildungsroman yield a map of the socialist International that does not correspond neatly to state-sanctioned political ideologies or to Cold War–style hemispheric alignments. The lines of influence that constitute the genre cut across such tidy divisions – they create an unexpected vicinity between historical moments that seem to have little in common at first glance. For Wienbarg – as for Varnhagen, Gregorovius and Grün – the Bund of the *Wanderjahre*, rather than the *Lehrjahre*'s aristocratic Turm, becomes the emblem of this piecemeal process of internationalist integration: 'following the completion of his individual-humanist bildung, [Goethe] lets Wilhelm *wander* so that his new and global travels [*Weltreisen*] may teach him how his abilities, which were previously limited to the sphere of bourgeois [*bürgerlich*] life, may be translated into active social work [*werkthätig eingreifend*]'.[57] The radical bildungsroman, these socialist critics hoped, would form part of a nascent *Weltliteratur* capable of supporting socialism's new *Weltbewegung* (Grün) and *Weltgesellschaft* (Wienbarg). In doing so, the genre also answered Marx and Engels's call in the *Communist Manifesto* to replace literature's 'purely literary aspect' with a new concern for art's political utility.[58]

The attempt to make the radical bildungsroman do political work – to harness this key genre of left *Weltliteratur* to the revolutionary ends of socialism's *Weltbewegung* – subjected it to considerable artistic pressures. Rather than producing stable political allegories, I argue, novels in the genre think through the process of allegorization itself: they attempt to work out how individual experiences of resistance can be aggregated into a larger movement. The radical bildungsroman is a meta-political genre insofar as it explores how a left International might emerge from a diverse range of more localized struggles. Moreover, because the genre shares the nineteenth-century bildungsroman's interest in producing a reflective understanding of the relationship between self and world, it does not fit neatly into the category of overtly political didactic or activist art. Taken together, my later chapters will suggest that the radical bildungsroman developed a set of aesthetic strategies that were intended to bridge the gap between individual and collective, historical particularity and universality. And, as we will see, for a few of the writers I explore here, the transnational

57 Gregorovius, *Göthe's* Wilhelm Meister, p. 96. This process, Grün observes, will involve the 'total erasure [*Tilgung*] of titles and private property' (*Ueber Göthe*, p. 78).

58 For this critique of *rein literarisches Aussehen*, see S. S. Prawer, *Karl Marx and World Literature* (London: Verso, 2011), p. 123.

history of the radical bildungsroman itself came to stand in as an image, or consolatory vision, of the socialist International: 'some scattered names survived', in Weiss's phrase, 'with which we, in our isolation, long associated a tradition'.[59]

Grün's and Gregorovius's reflections on the socialist struggle in the *Meister* novels – notably their comments on Goethe's vision of a disalienated future and on the attainability of a society organized on democratic and cooperative principles – coalesce around the idea of *work*. In emphasizing the centrality of work to socialist politics, Grün's and Gregorovius's thinking aligns seamlessly with a good deal of mid-nineteenth-century socialist thought, including Saint-Simon's and Charles Fourier's. 'Real-life individuals who act on the hope of building a new social order find their aspirations embodied in the figure of the Abbé,' observes Gregorovius: '[the Abbé's] central doctrine – the maxim of the dignity of work [*Arbeit*] – is also voiced by the most practical-minded character of all, Jarno [a leading member of the Turm]'.[60] Gregorovius proceeds to assert that work is the foundational constituent of social being because it renders intelligible the collective desire for social freedom and equality:

> The principle of equality can only be translated into political action under two conditions. First, the freedom of work and the participation of all in work . . . Work is unfree and inhuman if it does not embody the unity of self-determination and the material determinations of life, the harmony of the ideal and the material. [Second,] all members of society are recognized as workers, each according to his own manner, nature, and skill; and none need envy any of the others since all have chosen their work freely and consciously . . . There will be no capitalist freeloaders . . . Each will work for himself and for all others.[61]

As Grün had concluded in 1848, Goethe's bildungsromane provided 'fuel for a global conflagration' (*Zündstoff zu einem Weltbrand*). The laboriousness of the socialist struggle meant that even the most well-intentioned 'idealism' – with its 'belief in the centrality of the category of the *human*' (*menschlichen Wesen*) – would have to give way to the

59 Weiss, *Die Ästhetik des Widerstands*, 3 vols (Frankfurt: Suhrkamp, 1983), 1:33; *The Aesthetics of Resistance*, 3 vols (Durham, NC: Duke University Press, 2005–25), 1:27.

60 Gregorovius, *Göthe's* Wilhelm Meister, p. 292.

61 Ibid., p. 196.

hard work of the revolutionary struggle and the new political 'praxis of the masses'.[62] As I explain in the remainder of this introduction, the genre of the radical bildungsroman foregrounds precisely the laboriousness of the political struggle – its reliance on multiple coordinated acts of resistance and solidarity, rather than on historical master-teleologies or the belief in a unified historical subject (such as the revolutionary proletariat).

The Work of Bildung: Theorizing the Left Bildungsroman

The importance of *work* in Grün's and Gregorovius's socialist accounts of the *Wanderjahre* may seem unremarkable – after all, the socialist tradition has always given special attention to the conditions of work under capitalism, as well as to the possibility of work's future disalienation. It is also true that the centrality of work to the radical bildungsroman originated in the utopian-socialist milieus of the 1830s and 1840s in which Wienbarg, Grün, Varnhagen and Gregorovius moved. However, it is important to point out that this attention to work is not limited to these early accounts but that it acts as a shared DNA across most of the political novels I explore in this book. This section of the Introduction will turn to a series of initial examples to indicate that the concept of *work* helpfully limns central features of the socialist bildungsroman: first, it helps us articulate the genre's aspirational attention to the idea of non- and postcapitalist forms of coexistence; and second, it captures the genre's tendency to figure the socialist struggle itself in terms of work's human-scale teleologies. Work figures in the diegesis of these texts (that is, at the level of their representational content), but it crucially also affords a general structuring principle, or deep grammar – what I will call, along with Lukács, work's *Modellcharakter*.[63] This deep grammar governs how these texts think about the nature of the socialist struggle as well as, more abstractly, about the ability of individuals to negate existing structures and build a new social world.[64] Work,

62 Grün, *Ueber Göthe*, p. 295 (emphasis in original).

63 Lukács, *Zur Ontologie des gesellschaftlichen Seins*, vol. 2 (Berlin: Luchterhand, 1986), p. 12.

64 As feminist and autonomist scholars have pointed out, centring the logic of work in this way runs the risk of reproducing 'the productivist glorification of work (even socialist or unalienated work)'. See Kathi Weeks, *The Problem with Work: Feminism, Marxism, Antiwork Politics, and Postwork Imaginaries* (Durham, NC: Duke

understood in this sense, becomes central to the radical bildungsroman's internationalist vision, and it helps to anchor what Ngũgĩ calls the genre's 'universalist tendency' as *Weltliteratur*.

Of course, the work-like quality of the socialist struggle has not gone unnoticed by previous critics and activists. For example, it is captured in what is arguably the first attempt to identify the radical bildungsroman as a global genre: Lukács's 1956 essay 'Critical Realism and Socialist Realism'. In this essay, Lukács offers a tantalizingly brief discussion that sheds light on the powerful allure that the bildungsroman held for socialist writers.[65] Lukács draws attention to the important 'autobiographical' dimension of many radical bildungsromane: the genre, he notes, has historically provided authors with a medium in which they can work through experiences of the political struggle (111). While Lukács's *Theory of the Novel* had focused almost exclusively on the nineteenth-century bourgeois novel of formation by describing the protagonist's bildung as 'the fruit of a rich and enriching resignation', his later essay submits that 'in socialist society the situation is different' (112). In the bourgeois bildungsroman, 'society emerges triumphant, in spite of the hero's struggles', but in its socialist counterpart, 'the process [of formation] begins with resignation and leads on to active participation in the life of the community' (113). As Lukács makes clear, the process by which the individual's 'isolation gives way to an increasing involvement with the new social forces' (113) entails work-like processes of unlearning and remaking as experiences of alienation slowly give way to the struggle for a postcapitalist future.

Lukács's fragmentary discussion of the radical bildungsroman suggests that work – understood as an intentional and future-directed activity – can provide a useful general heuristic for the literary historiography of the left bildungsroman. Scenes that dramatize the experience of work

University Press, 2011), p. 103. According to these critics, Marxists who believe that the enrichment of subjectivity is contingent on the category of work fail to recognize that this very category is also complicit with diverse types of (gendered, racialized, ecological) violence. Subsequent chapters will discuss how feminist and anti-colonial authors tested the limits of the category of work in their novels. It should become clear that Lukács's view of the socialist bildungsroman in his 1956 essay was much too optimistic, as the genre undertook to register the frustrations, setbacks and dead ends of the socialist struggle.

65 Georg Lukács, 'Critical Realism and Socialist Realism,' in *The Meaning of Contemporary Realism* (London: Mellon, 1963), pp. 93–135. Subsequent references are given parenthetically. I discuss Lukács's essay at greater length in 'Toward a History and Theory of the Socialist Bildungsroman', *Novel* 48.2 (2015): 167–89.

constitute the gravitational centre of many radical bildungsromane, and they are also integral to the intertwined modes of self-making and world-making that the genre imagines. Consider, for example, the following passage from Nikolay Chernyshevsky's *What Is to Be Done?*, an early exponent of the radical bildungsroman that I will return to in Chapter 1. Chernyshevsky's novel centres on the story of Vera Pavlovna, who escapes her parental home and an arranged marriage in the hope of securing some measure of freedom for herself. Vera soon meets a group of free-thinking radicals, and she becomes swept up in the revolutionary ferment of the mid-nineteenth century. The novel's programmatic vision of a vanguard that is plotting a course for future revolutionary action had a formative political influence on Lenin, Georgi Plekhanov, Alexandra Kollontai and other leading Bolsheviks in the early twentieth century. In one of the visionary dreams that make up central parts of her bildung narrative, Vera participates in a conversation with the medical student Lopukhov and his friend, the materialist Aleksei Petrovich. Standing next to a waterlogged patch of field, the three discuss 'what is to be done' to ameliorate the rotten 'condition of this field'.[66] The problem, Lopukhov notes, is the 'stagnation of the elements': 'You see, the water has no outlet; therefore it stagnates and putrefies.' Aleksei replies:

> Yes, the absence of movement is the absence of work . . . because in an anthropological analysis work constitutes the fundamental form of movement which provides the basis and content of all other forms: recreation, relaxation, amusement, enjoyment. Without work to precede them, these other forms have no reality. And without movement, there's no life, that is, no reality, because the dirt is phantasmic, putrid. Until very recently no one knew how to restore such fields to health; but now a method has been discovered. It's called 'drainage'. Excess waste is channelled off into ditches, leaving only the required amount. And this water is kept in motion; thus the field acquires its reality. But until this method is applied, the dirt remains phantasmic, that is, stagnant; it can't produce any healthy vegetation. (182)[67]

While he was writing *What Is to Be Done?*, Chernyshevsky was famously

66 Nikolay Chernyshevsky, *What Is to Be Done?*, trans. Michael R. Katz (Ithaca, NY: Cornell University Press, 1982), p. 182.

67 Chernyshevsky's Russian original uses труд (work; labour). For purposes of clarity, I have chosen *work* to render this Russian term and to differentiate it from наемный труд (the word more commonly used for *wage labour* in Russian translations of Marx's and Engels's writings).

forced to resort to coded language to avoid censorship (or worse) at the hands of the Russian authorities, and in this passage 'work' acts as a symbolic placeholder for revolutionary action. But the representation of revolutionary practice as a type of work also resonates with the rest of the novel, which tends to depict the realization of radical political goals not in terms of some sublimely singular revolutionary event but rather as a tortuous process of deliberation, discussion and strategizing. Put in Aleksei's more abstract philosophical language, the work of revolution appears as a 'fundamental' and 'anthropological' act – as the work-like imposition of intentional structure and teleological movement onto the fixed mechanical laws of nature.[68] Chernyshevsky's young revolutionaries are equipped with a special technocratic knowledge that enables them to subjugate nature and topple Russia's ruling elite in one fell swoop.

Contemporary readers will rightly feel uncomfortable with Chernyshevsky's attempt to frame the human domination of non-human nature as a metaphor for the socialist struggle. The disastrous ecological consequences of drainage – a technology used to open up fresh soil for habitation and cultivation – are clearer to us now than they were to the novel's original audience: 'Nature is today more than ever conceived as a mere tool of man,' Max Horkheimer was able to write in 1947; 'It is the object of total exploitation . . . Man's boundless imperialism is never satisfied.'[69] It should be clear, then, that, in centring the category of *work*, I merely wish to propose it as a useful exploratory heuristic for the theory and history of the left bildungsroman. What we can glean from Chernyshevsky's novel – and from the literary history of the radical bildungsroman more generally – is a richer understanding of revolutionary praxis as a work-like (slow, elongated, gradual) achievement. In these novels, revolution – the building of a new world that will be more hospitable to human needs – typically takes the form of a laborious and uncertain process of construction.

The nature of this type of radical work can still be articulated using terms set by Hegel and Lukács, provided we no longer understand *work* to be the expression of the subject-protagonist's desires for advancement in the world but as one of the forms taken by the subject's attention to,

68 On this 'anthropological' dimension in Chernyshevsky's thought, see his 'The Anthropological Principle in Philosophy', in *Selected Philosophical Essays* (Moscow: Foreign Languages Publishing House, 1953), pp. 49–135.

69 Cited in Andreas Malm, *Corona, Climate, Chronic Emergency: War Communism in the Twentieth Century* (London: Verso, 2020), p. 171.

and concern for, the world itself. In *The Phenomenology of Spirit*, Hegel gestures towards the type of concern that can find articulation in work. He associates it with the figure of the toiling and disenfranchised 'bondsman' – one of the antecedents of the 'proletarians, slum-dwellers, and oppressed' identified by Varnhagen – rather than with the 'lord's' single-minded desire for domination and control:

> Through work . . . the bondsman becomes conscious of what he truly is. In the moment which corresponds to desire in the [lord's] consciousness, it did seem that the aspect of unessential relation to the thing fell to the lot of the bondsman, since in that relation the thing retained its independence. Desire [in the lord] has reserved to itself the pure negating of the object . . . But that is the reason why this satisfaction is itself only a fleeting one, for it lacks the side of objectivity and permanence. Work, on the other hand, is desire held in check, fleetingness staved off; in other words, work forms and shapes [*bildet*] the thing. [I]t is precisely for the worker that the object has independence. This . . . formative *activity* is at the same time the individuality or pure being-for-self of consciousness which now, in the work outside of it, acquires an element of permanence.[70]

It is possible to extract from this dense passage an alternative model of bildung – a type of formation that resembles an open-ended process of material work rather than the kind of seamless fusion of subject and object, self and world, that previous critics (such as Moretti and the early Lukács) have described as the bildungsroman's ideological solution to the contradictions of bourgeois society. This alternative model of bildung entails the rebuilding (*Neubildung*) of the world and of our relationship to it, rather than the self-actualization of an imperious subject that acquires mastery by subjecting the world to its desires. What gets reconstituted (*gebildet*) in this process of bildung is not only a subject but also an object, not just a rich inner self but also a collectively shared world. In a comment on Hegel's *Phenomenology*, the philosopher Susan Buck-Morss has fittingly described this passage as anticipating 'the universal realization of freedom' – a project that is radically egalitarian not merely in a philosophical but also in a political sense.[71]

70 G. W. F. Hegel, *Phenomenology of Spirit*, trans. A. V. Miller (Oxford: Oxford University Press, 1977), p. 118 (emphasis in original).

71 Susan Buck-Morss, 'Hegel and Haiti', *Critical Inquiry* 26.4 (2000): 821–65 (852). Glossing the same passage from the *Phenomenology*, Buck-Morss adds that 'Marxists have interpreted the slave's coming to self-consciousness as a metaphor for

By framing the realization of the bondsman's desires as a sequence of work-like acts, Hegel's passage suspends the belief that the actions of individuals are preordained by macro-historical patterns of movement. As the political theorist George Ciccariello-Maher notes, this belief is sometimes attributed to a caricatured version of 'Hegel, and a conservative Hegel at that' – it rests on the idea that dialectical movement is something that 'happens to us and acts upon us, in which we are enmeshed whether we know it or not, unconsciously doing the grand work of history'.[72] By contrast, the emphasis on individual work-like acts stresses precisely the importance of concrete material practice. As Ciccariello-Maher explains, this attention to the laboriousness of social struggles gives 'a wholly new meaning' to the dialectic, namely 'that of pressing subjectively forward in collective combat . . . without any certainty whatsoever that a better world will be the inevitable result'.[73] Strictly speaking, this type of work can never be completed: first, because the object-world's sheer materiality resists and reconstitutes the subject's designs and desires; and second, because the open-ended relationship of self and world that this type of bildung models for us does not come to rest in the kind of pre-established 'stable system of [social] relationships' that Moretti identifies with the bildungsroman's political vision.[74] As Hegel suggests in the passage just cited, work produces a particular type of self-knowledge on the part of the subject: workers learn to recognize themselves as deficient subjects whose formation is 'permanent[ly]' incomplete and who paradoxically discover in the recalcitrant materiality of things a model for their own 'independence'. The position of the worker/bondsman remains poignantly ambivalent (Hegel might as well have asked Sisyphus, this 'proletarian of the gods', to take inspiration from the independent being of his boulder!):[75] on the one hand, the worker's/bondsman's 'desire' is 'held in check' by the sheer resistance of the material object-world; on the other hand, it is precisely the worker's/bondsman's separation from this world – his recognition of 'his own

the working class's overcoming of false consciousness: the class-in-itself becomes for-itself. But they have criticized Hegel for not taking the next step to revolutionary practice. I am arguing that the slaves of Saint-Domingue [in the Haitian Revolution of 1791–1804] were, as Hegel knew, taking that step for him' (848, fn. 84).

72 George Ciccariello-Maher, *Decolonizing Dialectics* (Durham, NC: Duke University Press, 2017), p. 14.

73 Ciccariello-Maher, *Decolonizing Dialectics*, p. 14.

74 Moretti, *Way of the World*, p. 55.

75 For Camus's description of Sisyphus as the 'proletarian of the gods, powerless and rebellious', see his *The Myth of Sisyphus* (London: Penguin, 2005), p. 117.

independence' – that serves as a prefiguration of future emancipation.

Before proceeding, it is worth pausing briefly for some terminological clarification. Underlying my theoretical remarks in this chapter is the conviction that Marxist literary historians need to differentiate *work* from the related but distinct concept of *labour*. Whereas the ontological category of work implies the twinned processes of *exteriorization* (the externalization of the worker's skills, abilities, talents and so on) and *objectification* (the worker's shaping of the material world), the term *labour* captures the specific historical conditions that define the commodified character of work under capitalism (that is, labour's aspect as a 'real abstraction').[76] The writers who contributed to the genre of the radical bildungsroman were not blind to the momentous reconstitution of work as *labour* that took place over the course of the nineteenth and twentieth centuries. Indeed, most of the novels I explore in this book are fully cognizant of the specificity of *labour* as a category of social domination under capitalism. In holding on to the category of *work*, then, I do not intend to deny *labour*'s evident analytic importance – rather, I mobilize the term because it opens up a route into the artistic organization and conceptual infrastructure of the (radical) bildungsroman tradition itself.

The concept of *work* has been central to a good deal of scholarship on the bildungsroman, but so far, it has been invoked exclusively to describe the ultimate reintegration of the youthful tearaway into bourgeois society's regime of economic productivity. For example, Moretti notes that the *Lehrjahre* celebrates Wilhelm Meister's return to the bosom of the community by showing that his work 'enhances not having but rather being': 'In this second sense, work is fundamental in *Meister* . . . It is an unequalled instrument of social cohesion, producing not commodities but "harmonious objects", "connections". It gives a homeland to the individual. It is always *concrete* work.'[77] The *Lehrjahre*'s idiom of 'meaningful work', Moretti points out, acts as an ideological

76 Alfred Sohn-Rethel, one of the principal theorists of real abstraction, notes that, under the regime of abstract labour, the postulation of a distinctly human bildung implies a category mistake: 'The self-identification of man as a subject, the discovery of the human, amounts to the anthropomorphizing of a purely reified relation [*Vermenschlichung des Verdinglichten*].' See *Warenform und Denkform* (Frankfurt: Europäische Verlagsanstalt, 1971), p. 81.

77 Moretti, *Way of the World*, p. 29 (emphasis in original). In a related vein, Marc Redfield finds that 'the movement of "education" in the *Wanderjahre* comprises a progression from inwardness to action and from theory to praxis.' See Redfield, *Phantom Formations*, p. 99.

smokescreen that blinds us (as much as Wilhelm himself) to the macro-historical dynamic of capitalism that reduces work to fungible wage labour. The *Lehrjahre*, in other words, masks capitalist exploitation by offering a nostalgic vision of *work* as an inherently significant activity that closes the gap between the individual's needs and desires on the one hand and the reproduction of society on the other. By contrast, the radical bildungsroman effects a series of displacements that open up this grammar of work to critique and that make it amenable to an alternative range of speculative and utopian elaborations. Subsequent chapters will inventory the ways in which the socialist bildungsroman formulates substantive critiques of capitalist society and how these critiques serve to direct the trajectories of individual and collective bildung towards a postcapitalist future. At this point, I will only gesture towards a few short scenes that help to make explicit the genre's particular reliance on work in this sense.

The novels of the Kenyan author Ngũgĩ wa Thiong'o illustrate how the bildungsroman's idiom of work came to be mobilized by authors committed to the global left. Ngũgĩ's early bildungsromane of the 1960s – notably *Weep Not, Child* (1964) and *A Grain of Wheat* (1967) – sometimes seem to appeal to the idea of work as an activity that is characterized by the inherent meaningfulness Moretti describes with a view to Goethe's *Lehrjahre*. *A Grain of Wheat*, for instance, closes with a description of the hospitalized protagonist Gikonyo as he dreams of celebrating his return home by carving a richly ornamented stool. Earlier in the novel, Gikonyo was imprisoned by the British, who suspected him of participating in the Mau Mau rebellion against British colonial rule. Following his imprisonment, Gikonyo has struggled to reclaim a place in his former community, and he now imagines that his carving of the stool will enable him to express his hopes for a restored family that includes himself, his estranged wife Mumbi and Mumbi's child from an extramarital affair:

> At first it was a small flicker, the sort he used to feel at the sight of wood. Then, as he thought about it, he became more and more excited and his hands itched to touch wood and a chisel. He would carve the stool now, after the hospital, before he resumed business, or in-between the business hours. He worked the motif in detail. He changed the figures. He would now carve a thin man, with hard lines on the face, shoulders and head bent, supporting the weight. His right hand would stretch to link with that of a woman, also with hard lines on the face. The third figure

> would be that of a child on whose head or shoulders the other two hands of the man and woman would meet.[78]

Artistic work offers an imaginative fulfilment of Gikonyo's longing for a family, but it also allegorizes – in the form of an imaginary projection – his hopes for a unified and revitalized post-liberation Kenya. The type of non-alienated and nation-centric work that Ngũgĩ pictures here is mirrored in several other scenes that show Gikonyo tilling the soil to prepare it for further cultivation. In *A Grain of Wheat*, as in his slightly earlier bildungsroman *Weep Not, Child*, Ngũgĩ asks us to see such agricultural and artistic work as an attempt to open up an independent future for the nation: 'at last his way seemed clear. The land needed him, and God had given him an opening so that he might come back and save his family and the whole country.'[79] This understanding of work – with its organicist and natalist connotations – can seem politically reactionary, unless we are attuned to the echoes of Chernyshevsky's revolutionary reframing of work that reverberate through these scenes: 'The black folk of Kenya in their struggle to be free,' Ngũgĩ's narrator informs us, can take inspiration from the 'wonderful story of what once happened in Russia.'[80] The language of *work* creates an imaginative wedge that makes it possible for Ngũgĩ to position the October Revolution of 1917 and the agrarian socialism of the Russian Narodniks as historical models for the revolutionary agency of the Kenyan peasantry.[81] The same language made it possible for his later and more overtly left-wing novel *Petals of Blood* (1977) to imagine insurrectionary violence itself as a type of work – what Achille Mbembe, drawing on Frantz Fanon, calls the function of revolutionary violence as a generative 'practice . . . invested

78 Ngũgĩ wa Thiong'o, *A Grain of Wheat* (London: Penguin, 2002), pp. 241–2.

79 Ngũgĩ wa Thiong'o, *Weep Not, Child* (London: Penguin, 2012), p. 116.

80 Ngũgĩ, *Grain of Wheat*, p. 105.

81 In making this historical link, Ngũgĩ – like several other artists discussed in this book – was able to take inspiration from Marx's later letters to Vera Zasulich, in which he entertained the idea that Russia might be able to advance to socialism by way of the peasant commune rather than passing through the stage of industrial capitalism. 'As Marx learned from Chernyshevsky,' Massimiliano Tomba observes, 'historical jumps were possible and Russia did not have to go through the process of capital accumulation that had taken place in Europe.' See Massimiliano Tomba, *Insurgent Universality: An Alternative Legacy of Modernity* (Oxford: Oxford University Press, 2019), p. 6. On Marx's late thinking about peasant communes, see Teodor Shanin, *Late Marx and the Russian Road: Marx and the Peripheries of Capitalism* (London: MRP, 1983).

with positive *formative* features'.[82] As Hegel's discussion of the bondsman's work indicates, the radical praxis that Ngũgĩ allegorizes in the 'desire to carve' does not find unmediated expression in the object but rather undergoes a process of refraction and rearticulation: the worker's desire to remake (*bilden*) the world is transformed in its turn by the material resistance of the object – the piece of wood, the colonizer's violence – that it encounters. Ngũgĩ's understanding of work, I point out in Chapter 3, also prompted him to recalibrate the structure of the bildungsroman itself. As Ngũgĩ insisted in a different context, it did not suffice simply to 'blackanize the personnel' of the European novel form: instead of focusing on the psychological and emotional rewards of the protagonist's 'rich and enriching resignation' (as the bourgeois bildungsroman had done), the radical bildungsroman must figure work as a progressive and transformative struggle, as a teleologically oriented and emancipatory revolutionary praxis.[83]

As the case of Ngũgĩ indicates, the process of formation that we encounter in the left bildungsroman does not involve the relinquishing of teleology as such. In this respect, the radical bildungsroman differs from forms of anti-colonial writing that hope to expunge any and all structures and ideological presuppositions associated with the Western tradition: this body of anti-colonial writing, observes the literary scholar J. Daniel Elam, involves a purely 'negative dialectical movement . . . a *falling-away* from the teleology of achievement'.[84] By contrast, the tradition of the radical bildungsroman entails the partial rearticulation of teleology in terms of the work-like immanence of the socialist struggle. The reconstitution of subject and object through the formative process of work, which Hegel's discussion helped to bring into focus, is fundamental to this basic generic configuration as well as to the left bildungsroman's historical development: while the nineteenth-century bourgeois

82 Fanon's articulation of violence as a type of formative work is discussed in Achille Mbembe, *Critique of Black Reason* (Durham, NC: Duke University Press, 2017), pp. 166–7, and in George Ciccariello-Maher's *Decolonizing Dialectics* (Durham, NC: Duke University Press, 2017), pp. 47–73. Pertinent to the passage from *A Grain of Wheat* I cited previously, Fanon also explores the radical implications of traditional 'artisanship' (such as carving) under conditions of decolonization: 'By bringing faces and bodies to life, by taking the group . . . as creative subject, the artist inspires concerted action.' See Frantz Fanon, *The Wretched of the Earth* (New York: Grove Press, 2004), p. 175.

83 Ngũgĩ wa Thiong'o, 'Author's Note', in *Homecoming: Essays on African and Caribbean Literature, Culture, and Politics* (London: Heinemann, 1972), p. xvi.

84 J. Daniel Elam, *World Literature for the Wretched of the Earth: Anticolonial Aesthetics, Postcolonial Politics* (New York: Fordham University Press, 2021), p. 113 (emphasis in original).

bildungsroman evoked (*pace* Lukács) the image of an 'earthly home', the genre's radical variant indicates that the political struggle involves a continued deferral of the desired (socialist) future. The socialist bildungsheld, in these texts, finally comes to understand that there is 'no home but the struggle'.[85]

Marxist Humanism and the Antinomies of Radical Bildung: Teleology, Agency, World-Making

The history of the left bildungsroman centres work-like intentional agency and the category of the human in ways that will seem problematic (or quite simply unfashionable) to many contemporary readers. In the remainder of this introduction, I want to meet such objections halfway by offering a sense of the remarkable complexity of the genre's humanist and universalist commitments – and of the radical bildungsroman's ability to reckon with the internal contradictions of these commitments. As a way of conceptualizing the genre's internal artistic logic, I will temporarily shift into a more theoretical register by borrowing from the language of mid-twentieth-century Marxist thought.

The radical bildungsroman, as I present it here, is marked by a series of tensions that result from the internal friction between the genre's idealist heritage – its emphasis on the self-actualizing individual; its attention to the human agency embodied in work; its novelistic concern with slow processes of maturation across time – and its principled political commitment to the materialist analysis of socio-economic inequalities and to a vision of collective revolutionary change. In the history of radical thought, the body of work that tries to accommodate these antinomical sets of allegiances has gone by the name of *Marxist humanism*. Tracing its origins to Marx's early *Economic and Philosophical Manuscripts* (a text that famously was not rediscovered and published until the 1930s), the vital current of mid-twentieth-century Marxist humanism succeeded in keeping Marxist modes of social inquiry alive even after the excesses of Stalinism had tarnished them.[86] The radical

85 *No Home But the Struggle* is the title of the third volume of Upward's *The Spiral Ascent*, one of the most important bildungsromane to emerge from the British left's mid-century love affair with communism.

86 It did so not just in Europe and the US. For example, the writings of the Guyanese historian and political activist Walter Rodney offer footholds for an African socialism centred, like the radical bildungsroman, around a 'humanizing' conception

bildungsroman can be fruitfully understood in the light of this intellectual tradition.[87] In what follows, I explicate some of the radical bildungsroman's constitutive tensions by turning to a key document of Marxist humanism, Lukács's unfinished *Ontology of Social Being*. Lukács's ontology can help us grasp the deep grammar of work that structures the radical bildungsroman; it also sheds light on some of the literary-critical problems raised in subsequent chapters.

The *Ontology* stands as one of the towering achievements of twentieth-century Marxist humanism, alongside the work of other well-known thinkers who were Lukács's juniors (and who were influenced by him), such as Ágnes Heller, Ferenc Fehér, C. L. R. James, Raya Dunayevskaya and István Mészáros. Lukács's *Ontology* can be read as a supplement to – or as a sustained philosophical elaboration of – his earlier fragmentary comments on the genre of the socialist bildungsroman in the 1956 essay 'Critical Realism and Socialist Realism'. Indeed, there is a case to be made that Lukács's main contribution to the theory of the radical bildungsroman comes not in his celebrated work on aesthetics (for example, in *The Theory of the Novel*) but in his magisterial but only partially translated *Ontology*. The Marxist-humanist attention to work was intended to open up new ways of thinking about human-scale teleologies (as opposed to the eschatological macro-teleologies of communist history) and about the status of individuality (as opposed to the metasubject of the revolutionary proletariat). Recentring debate around Marxist humanism's attention to work creates important new directions for the literary historiography of the radical bildungsroman: in contrast to the genre's bourgeois variant, in which reality appears frozen into a type of second nature (so unalterable and solid that social 'meaning . . . has become an ontological *fact*'[88]), Lukács's turn to the ontology of work serves precisely to undo the naturalization of values into facts in order to suggest how things might be otherwise.

---

of work: 'man's consciousness is formed in the intervention in nature; nature itself is humanized through its interaction with man's labour'. Walter Rodney, 'Marxism and African Liberation', in *Decolonial Marxism: Views from the Pan-African Revolution* (London: Verso, 2022), pp. 33–51 (37–8). The Coda offers some additional context and commentary on Rodney's claim.

87 It should be clear that I turn to Marxist humanism as an explanatory framework and not as a narrowly historical point of reference. The novels I discuss in subsequent chapters respond to disparate historical conjunctures and only a small number of them could be shown to engage in sustained or explicit dialogue with the historical body of mid-century Marxist-humanist thought I outline in this section.

88 Moretti, *Way of the World*, p. 55.

The *Ontology* is, arguably, the least well studied of Lukács's major books, partly because its attempt to present work as the foundational category of social being has seemed anachronistic – or even politically naïve – to many contemporary commentators. However, discussion of the *Ontology* has also been hamstrung by a number of additional factors that are worth paying attention to. For one, the English translation of the *Ontology* that has been available for some decades is incomplete: it contains only a few short sections from this monumental two-volume work, and it omits Lukács's most programmatic statements of his position – as a result, it tends to obscure the overarching aims of his book. Second, and more pertinent to the present context, the English translation of the *Ontology* uses the term *labour* in all instances where Lukács opts for the German term *Arbeit*. While the word *Arbeit* can indeed refer to both *work* and *labour* in the senses sketched out here, the translation's choice of *labour* obscures the fact that the *Ontology* specifically seeks to displace the analytic hegemony of *labour* as an economic category in favour of the ontological valences of *work*: 'All those determinations which we shall see to make up the essence of what is new in social being are contained *in nuce* in work,' Lukács observes: 'Thus work can be viewed as the original phenomenon, as the model for social being.'[89] Readers of the English translation are bound to miss this important conceptual pivot. Yet, as Lukács himself points out, the ontology of work provides a powerful analytic tool precisely because it allows for the subject-object dialectic to be articulated across a number of different levels of socio-cultural analysis (including the level of literary and artistic production).

The *Ontology* begins with a lengthy discussion that seeks to demonstrate the interest that both Hegel and Marx took in the ontological aspects of work. It is only in the second (largely untranslated) volume of

89 Lukács's German text regularly deploys the more technical term *Lohnarbeit* ('wage labour') to avoid this terminological confusion.

The portions of Lukács's two-volume *Ontology* that have been translated into English comprise three volumes: *The Ontology of Social Being: 1. Hegel*; *The Ontology of Social Being: 2. Marx*; and *The Ontology of Social Being. 3. Labour* (all: London: Merlin, 1978). Inexplicably, the programmatic reflections that open Lukács's *Ontology* ('Prinzipienfragen einer heute möglich gewordenen Ontologie'– 'Foundational questions concerning a newly possible ontology' [*Ontologie* 1: 7–324]) still await translation. To facilitate reference, I will give volume and page numbers for the German text (*Zur Ontologie des gesellschaftlichen Seins*, vol. 1 [1984] and vol. 2 [1986], Berlin: Luchterhand), as well as, where available, for the English translation. Here: *Ontologie* 2, p. 10; *Labour*, p. v. In accordance with Lukács's own usage, all quotations from the English translation will tacitly substitute *work* for *labour*.

the *Ontology* that Lukács presents the speculative core of his own project. Here, the argument proceeds by way of analogies between different levels of social analysis (the metabolism of work; patterns of human interaction; and finally, complex institutions of social organization). Lukács contends that all these levels mirror the underlying structure of work insofar as they are organized according to intricate and interwoven series of teleological positings.[90] Lukács illustrates the teleological character of work by citing a passage from volume 1 of Marx's *Capital*:

> At the end of every work process [*Arbeitsprozess*], a result emerges which had already been conceived by the worker at the beginning, hence already existed ideally. Man [*sic*] not only effects a change of form in the materials of nature; he also realizes his own purpose in those materials. And this is a purpose he is conscious of, it determines the mode of his activity with the rigidity of a law, and he must subordinate his will to it.[91]

Lukács provides the following gloss on Marx's passage:

> This spells out work [as a] key ontological category. Through work, a teleological positing is realized within material being, as the rise of a new objectivity. The first consequence of this is that work becomes the model [*Modellcharakter*] for any social practice, for in such social practice – no matter how ramified its mediations – teleological positings are always realized, and ultimately realized materially. Certainly, as we shall go on to see, this model character that work has for the actions of man in society should not be overstretched in a schematic way; yet it is precisely consideration of the most important distinctions that shows the essential ontological affinity, for these very distinctions reveal how work can serve us in understanding other social-teleological positings because it is their original form as far as being is concerned. (*Ontologie* 2, p. 12; *Labour*, p. 3)

90 The *Ontology* sometimes oscillates between a genealogical account of work, which aims to show that even the most highly evolved forms of social being ('from everyday conversation' to 'the economy'; *Ontologie* 2, pp. 12–13; *Labour*, p. 3) are elaborations of the elementary category of *work*, and a mode of homological or analogical argument that sets up work as an exploratory model rather than as a determinate historical origin. Lukács's failure to distinguish clearly between these two lines of argument has been found unsatisfactory by many critics, but it need not concern us here.

91 The passage appears in Marx, *Capital*, vol. 1 (Harmondsworth: Penguin, 1990), p. 285.

Lukács directs our attention towards a (broadly Aristotelian) understanding of human action as intentional and goal-directed, and he insists that this elementary understanding of work continues to be residually present even in Marx's mature works. The aim of this analytic shift, Lukács explains, is to explore the 'forms of appearance of the specifically human way of life [*menschliche Lebensführung*] that arise from work and must thus be comprehended ontologically and genetically on this basis, no matter how far-reaching their mediations'.[92] Lukács's revisionist enterprise recalls Chernyshevsky's programmatic postulation of 'work' as a basic ('anthropological', 'fundamental') category that introduces teleological movement into the closed causalities of nature. Work, Lukács agrees, marks 'a qualitative leap in the humanization of man, which is something radically new vis-à-vis the whole of nature' – and while 'nothing has changed in the natural causal process itself', it 'can now be transformed into a process that is posited by us, and in this sense – but only in this – it ceases to operate as something "blind"'.[93]

It would be easy to dismiss Lukács's ontological assumptions (as many critics have done) because they appear to ignore the important historical permutations that work has undergone. According to this view, Lukács can be accused (in the words of the Marxist theorist Moishe Postone) of failing to address *labour* as the proper 'object of the critique of capitalist society': it is *only* labour, Postone insists, that enables 'the analysis of the commodity and capital – that is, the quasi-objective forms of social mediation constituted by labor in capitalism'.[94] If we follow Postone's line of argument, Lukács's ontological conception of

92 Lukács, *Ontologie* 2, p. 87; *Labour*, p. 99.

93 Lukács, *Ontologie* 2, pp. 102–3; *Labour*, pp. 119–20. Lukács credits Hegel with 'discover[ing] the real ontological form of the teleology of work'. According to Lukács, Hegel demonstrated that 'a real ontology of social being is not possible without a contrasting of natural causality and work teleology'. See Lukács, *Ontologie* 1, p. 508; *Hegel*, pp. 53–4.

94 Moishe Postone, *Time, Labor, and Social Domination: A Reinterpretation of Marx's Critical Theory* (Cambridge: Cambridge University Press, 1993), p. 6. Postone helpfully distinguishes his own '*critique* of labor' from a type of 'transhistorical' ontology that recalls Lukács's late work. Postone criticizes the latter position '[b]ecause, in this view, labor constitutes the relationship between humanity and nature, it serves as the standpoint from which the social relations among people can be judged: Relations that are in harmony with labor and reflect its fundamental significance are considered socially "natural". The social critique from the standpoint of "labor" is, therefore, a critique from a quasi-natural point of view, that of a social ontology' (ibid., p. 65 [emphasis in original]).

work – including his emphasis on the role of work in the development of the subject's self-consciousness[95] – needs to be rejected, because it does not come to terms with (wage) labour as a category of social domination under capitalism. Yet, despite the criticisms that have been brought against it, Lukács's philosophical account of work deserves attention, not least because its contradictions mirror the constitutive tensions of the genre of the radical novel of formation.

Like much Marxist-humanist thought of the mid-twentieth century, Lukács's *Ontology* can be read as a highly mediated response to the problems that were raised for socialist praxis by the historical tragedy of Stalinism and the ossified rigidities of Soviet political dogma.[96] In addressing this crisis, Lukács's *Ontology* pursues several interrelated aims:

- first, it seeks to reclaim a rich *multiplicity of teleologies* against the notion of a single historical master-teleology;
- second, it aims to reassert *individual agency* vis-à-vis the idea of transpersonal spirit or some unitary subject of history;
- third, it makes room for a vision of *work as a form of creative human world-making*.

The radical bildungsroman echoes these Marxist-humanist aspirations, but the genre also retains a hard-wired commitment – full-blooded in some texts and residual, melancholic or nostalgic in others – to the very ideas that Lukács's *Ontology* sets out to criticize and revise, including the vision of a collective revolutionary subject and the belief in an overarching historical teleology directed towards the realization of communism. Together, these competing commitments make up the antinomical structure of the socialist bildungsroman. It is worth exploring each of these commitments in a little more depth.

First, Lukács's *Ontology* insists on the need to reclaim a space for human-scale teleologies outside the macro-teleologies posited by a certain version of Marxist science: 'It is sufficient to stress,' Lukács writes, 'that our [theoretical] conceptions do not just reject any generalized form of teleology in inorganic and organic nature, but also in society, and confine its realm of validity to the particular acts of human social

95 Lukács, *Ontologie*, 2, pp. 661–3.

96 'The renovation [*Erneuerung*] of Marxism that is needed', Lukács declares early on in his study, 'requires a well-founded and founding ontology' (*Ontologie* 1, p. 515; *Hegel*, p. 61).

conduct of which the most significant form and model is work'.[97] As Nicolas Tertulian explains, Lukács aims to bring teleology down to a smaller scale by introducing into the blind 'causality of nature' a form of 'finalistic activity, which erupts with the appearance of work, the ramified nucleus of social life'.[98] To be sure, for Lukács, the teleological character of work does not signify anything as simple as the realization of a fixed blueprint. Instead, as Hegel had suggested in the passage from the *Phenomenology* I quoted previously, intentionality itself is reconstituted in the encounter with a material world that resists the subject's desires. As such, the teleology of work, according to Lukács, 'remains ambiguously premised on the manifestation of an end that might or might not be achieved in a fashion corresponding to an original design'.[99] This understanding of work also takes inspiration from the early Marx, who had proposed 'an inherently historical – "open" – teleology which cannot admit "fixity" at any stage whatsoever . . . The "goal" of human history is defined by Marx in terms of the *immanence* of human development'.[100]

The radical bildungsroman, too, presents the fight for a postcapitalist social order as an uncertain process marked by multiple stops and starts rather than as the actualization of a political blueprint. As Lukács observes in 'Critical Realism and Socialist Realism', this attention to the 'immanent' work of social transformation is mirrored in the aesthetic procedures of the radical bildungsroman: whereas nineteenth-century critical realists (for example, Honoré de Balzac or Charles Dickens) had depicted the socialist struggle for a better world only 'from the outside', 'the socialist bildungsroman' was committed to 'describ[ing] the forces working toward socialism *from the inside*'.[101] Examples include the

97 Lukács, *Ontologie* 1, p. 615; *Marx*, p. 74.

98 See Nicolas Tertulian, 'Lukács' *Ontology*', in *Lukács Today: Essays in Marxist Philosophy* (Boston: Reidel, 1988), pp. 243–73 (256). Tertulian pointedly adds that the programmatic attention to work was 'utilized by Lukács to question the teleological interpretation of history advanced by those who claimed allegiance to Marx' (246). Dan Blanton agrees that Lukács's ontology constitutes 'a negation in its own right' insofar as it asserts – against any historical macro-teleologies – 'the very possibility of [human] purpose'. See Blanton, 'Judgment and Social Being: Notes on Teleological Positing', *The South Atlantic Quarterly* 119.4 (2020): 725–34 (732).

99 Blanton, 'Judgment', p. 731.

100 This description of the early Marx's thinking is taken from Lukács's student István Mészáros, in his landmark study of alienation: *Marx's Theory of Alienation* (London: Merlin, 2005 [1970]), p. 118.

101 The term 'socialist bildungsroman' is used by Lukács in this context; see 'Critical Realism and Socialist Realism', p. 93 (emphasis in original). Daniel Hartley introduces the helpful term 'proletarian phenomenology' to describe such textual mediations of first-person experience. See Hartley, 'Militant Structures of Feeling:

detached (and typically dismissive) depiction of working-class struggles in 'critical-realist' novels such as Dickens's *Hard Times* (1854), in sharp contrast to the subtle dialectic of diaristic (first-person) and authorial (third-person) voicing that we find in later books such as Lessing's *The Golden Notebook*. Because the radical bildungsroman homes in on the first-hand experiences of revolutionary praxis, it is not usually in the business of speculating about the precise forms that the postcapitalist society of the future will take. The radical bildungsroman is 'an important object of study', Lukács contends, precisely because it renders legible a historical 'transition period' as well as the troubled 'conflicts of allegiance' experienced by individuals undergoing a socialist bildung.[102] By presenting the socialist project '*from the inside*', the novels of formation I explore in this book stage the experiential drama of individuals who are in the process of learning a fundamental truth about the socialist struggle – that far from providing a safe 'earthly home' (or offering the utopian blueprint for such a home), political struggles are characterized by a continually receding telos and a deferral of revolutionary fulfilment.

Second, and related to the preceding point, Lukács's *Ontology* is concerned to delineate a space in which human agency – understood as a form of action that is not fully predetermined by socio-economic factors – can unfold. Socialist fiction has sometimes been reductively identified with the transcendent ideal of the radiant 'New Men' – the unbearably selfless, austere and work-loving heroes who feature in a good deal of early Soviet fiction (Chernyshevsky's Rakhmetov, in *What Is to Be Done?*, had provided the prototype: like a latter-day Orthodox saint, Rakhmetov sleeps on a bed of nails to purify himself). Whereas these New Men were galvanized into life by a singular revolutionary event, socialist novels of formation show us a drawn-out, halting and uneven process of bildung that involves the painful reconstitution of society as much as of subjectivity itself – a process Hegel once described as 'the hard work of formation' (*die harte Arbeit . . . der Bildung*).[103] As I point out in Chapter 2, this work of bildung is made even harder by the fact that the formation of the socialist subject cannot simply replicate

---

Raymond Williams, Claude Lefort, and Workers' Inquiry', in *The Political Uses of Literature: Global Perspectives and Theoretical Approaches, 1920–2020*, ed. Benjamin Kohlmann and Ivana Perica (London: Bloomsbury, 2024), pp. 121–36 (127).

102 Lukács, 'Critical Realism and Socialist Realism', p. 111.

103 Hegel, *Grundlinien der Philosophie des Rechts* (Frankfurt: Suhrkamp, 1986), § 187.

the closed trajectories of the nineteenth-century bourgeois bildungsroman that had reliably delivered a moment of fulfilment and plenitude at the end of the protagonist's long wanderings. This fundamental dilemma helps to explain the left bildungsroman's formal openness. At an extreme, the genre's vision of bildung offers the vertiginous glimpse of a radically anti-foundational bildung that cannot fall back either on historically established patterns of individual formation, or on the imputed authority of a fully constituted collective subject ('the revolutionary proletariat').[104]

This dilemma is mirrored in a good number of radical bildungsromane, notably those that stress the element of autodidacticism demanded of the socialist bildungsheld. The left novel of formation's peculiar resistance to ideological closure, I note in Chapter 4, has sometimes led authors to ask what it would mean to experience the socialist struggle in terms of a radical formlessness – that is, in terms of the lack of historical directionality as such. Lessing's *The Golden Notebook* will feature prominently in Chapter 4, as will Peter Weiss's trilogy *The Aesthetics of Resistance* (*Die Ästhetik des Widerstands*, 1975–81). Weiss's first-person narrator learns that in the process of socialist bildung, 'there was no point of departure, I would have to start with the shapeless [*dem Formlosen*]'.[105] But we can also think of Richard Wright's communist bildung narrative, *Black Boy* (1945/77): Wright's protagonist begins by observing that 'the substance of my hope was formless and devoid of any real sense of direction', only to discover that his later espousal of communism, far from yielding a firm political orientation, catapults him into a new kind of existential uncertainty.[106] Such 'formlessness' – the suspension of the bildungsroman's traditional orientation towards a clear historico-narrative telos – may, at first, seem to apply only to a small number of texts. It will, however, be one of the central contentions of my book that this novelistic attention to moments of formlessness

104 'People,' Lukács agrees, 'are only transformed when they participate in the transformation of reality' ('Critical and Socialist Realism', p. 104). The formal openness of the socialist novel of formation also means that this genre never congealed into anything as coherent as a 'metabildungsroman' – Esty's term for a subgenre that systematically probes the genre's conventional parameters (see *Unseasonable Youth*, p. 13).

105 Weiss, *Ästhetik*, 1:136; *Aesthetics*, 1:117.

106 Richard Wright, *Black Boy: A Record of Childhood and Youth* (New York: Vintage, 2000), p. 260. The passage cited here appears at the very end of the first volume ('Southern Night') of Wright's bildung narrative, which chronicles the protagonist's life in the segregated South – shortly before his escape to the North and his embrace of communism.

throws into relief experiences of perplexity and disorientation that are constitutive of the socialist struggle as such. In sharp contrast to the bourgeois bildungsroman, the left novel of formation does not discount these moments of disorientation as tokens of youthful immaturity that need to be hemmed in or overcome but, rather, treats them as foundational to the experience of the political struggle itself.[107]

Third, by loosening the grip of historical master-teleologies and creating a space for individual growth, the left bildungsroman also makes it possible to reconceptualize work as a constructive and open-ended activity of world-making rather than merely as a category ('labour') of Marxist economic analysis. It is in this sense that the term *work* figures in many radical bildungsromane. For example, in Peter Weiss's semi-autobiographical novels of formation *Leavetaking* (*Abschied von den Eltern*, 1961; literally, 'Farewell to the Parents') and *Vanishing Point*, *work* is linked to the process of artistic creation itself. 'Your attempts to work [*Arbeitsversuche*] will remain barren unless they serve the struggle [*Kampf*] for social change', the narrator is admonished by his friend Hoderer, one of the many mentor figures in Weiss's fictions.[108] In a move that is typical of Weiss's novels, the protagonist experiences his artistic work both as a liberation from the strenuous demands of society and as a tool with which to forge new solidarities outside the conventicles of the Communist Party: 'I had tried to break the final bond to my old life by leaving my parents' home, so as to devote myself to the tasks [*Aufgaben*] at hand. Political and ideological demands seemed insignificant when compared to the work [*Arbeit*] that awaited me.'[109] Weiss's nameless protagonists hope that their art will possess some political 'use value' (*Gebrauchswert*), but their special attention to the daily demands of the socialist struggle also means that these bildungshelden never attain the sense of historical closure and finality that critics like Lukács and Moretti have associated with the bildungsroman's bourgeois archetype.[110] Instead, the governing mood of Weiss's novels is one of hesitation and 'inconclusiveness' (*Entschlusslosigkeit*): 'I saw myself standing in the middle of the whirling snowflakes, and this

107 For Moretti's comments on modernity's 'formlessness', see *The Way of the World*, p. 5. By embracing an aesthetic of 'formlessness', left bildungsromane do not reject the open-endedness that is an artistic mark of modernity but rather try to find alternative political meanings for it.

108 Peter Weiss, *Fluchtpunkt* (Frankfurt: Suhrkamp, 1965), p. 60.

109 Ibid., p. 15.

110 Ibid., p. 69.

moment had already acquired a certain timelessness, I would stand here forever, facing tasks [*Aufgaben*] I knew I would be unable to accomplish.'[111] What we are given here is not so much a resigned acceptance of political failure but a vision of the political struggle itself that has been transposed into a kind of epiphanic stasis – a realization that the activist's home is only to be found *inside* the vagaries of the struggle for a better world.

To the extent that the radical bildungsroman possesses a future-oriented or utopian thrust, we can find it in the glimpses of disalienation that are held out by the genre, as well as in its sustained attempts to cast the formation of a single individual (or group of individuals) as the image of a coming socialist collectivity. Recent scholarship on the bildungsroman has moved past reflexive critiques of the bildungsroman's conservatism to recover the significant emancipatory charge that resides in the genre's portrayal of free development and self-determined agency.[112] This scholarship shares with Lukács's late ontology a universalist orientation that emphasizes the possibility of non-alienated human agency. 'Work', Lukács notes in the *Ontology*, is 'the starting-point for the humanization of man, for the extension of his abilities': 'We can not investigate here how far these [abilities] remain linked to work even at a later stage [that is, to 'labour' under capitalism]; what matters here is simply this ontological priority' – and he adds that it is 'in and through work that the realm of the human [*Bereich des Menschlichen*] [is] constitute[d]'.[113]

Lukács's tendency to frame disalienation in terms of the individual's capacity for self-determined action – that is, in terms of the locally circumscribed teleologies of work – has made this the most contentious and most maligned aspect of his later Marxist-humanist thinking. In a collaboratively written article, Lukács's former students Ferenc Fehér, Ágnes Heller, György Márkus and Mihály Vajda find particular fault with this feature of Lukács's ontology: 'Alienation, or more precisely alienations, is [in the later Lukács] a category that applies only to individuals, i.e., it is a theoretical category of

111 Ibid., p. 187.

112 For example, Joseph Slaughter, *Human Rights, Inc.: The World Novel, Narrative Form, and International Law* (New York: Fordham University Press, 2007); and Redfield, *Phantom Formations*, p. 43.

113 See Lukács, *Ontologie* 1, pp. 620–1; *Marx*, p. 80. Elsewhere, Lukács explains that his ontology is intended to demonstrate 'how broad a field work gives rise to in the humanization of man [*Menschwerdung des Menschen*]' (*Ontologie* 2, pp. 94–5; *Labour*, p. 109).

personality, but not an historical one.'[114] Fehér, Heller, Márkus and Vajda note that Lukács comes dangerously close to describing work as a fundamentally non-alienated activity, and they accordingly charge him with an overly 'idealist' and individualist understanding of the (cultural, social, historical) category of personhood.[115] The same charge also applies to the bourgeois tradition of the bildungsroman, with its depictions of inherently meaningful craft-like work. By contrast, I want to contend that the radical novel of formation counters such objections by pushing back against dehistoricizing ontologies of work and their individualist bias. As I indicated previously, the friction between an *idealist* conception of work (which views work as the realization, however complex and dialectically mediated, of the subject's self) and a fully *materialist* one (which remains attuned to the role of labour as a means of social domination) is central to the genre of the radical bildungsroman. For example, Weiss's *Leavetaking* repeatedly struggles to disarticulate the protagonist's process of inner bildung (which unfolds during years spent working in factories in rural Sweden) from the '*Werdegang der Ware*' – that is, from the material processes that prepare commodities for the market.[116] In a related vein, Paul Nizan's novel *Antoine Bloyé* (1933) offers us a claustrophobic vision of proletarian existence by focusing on the narrator's father: the father's way of life, Nizan insists, is so thoroughly integrated into the circuits of surplus value extraction that any hope for a liberatory socialist bildung centred around the category of work is ruled out from the start.[117] It is only against this bleak historical backdrop, and in full recognition of the conditions of social alienation, that the left bildungsroman offers us some cautious glimpses of a disalienated life – a life in which the 'absolute working-out [*Herausarbeiten*] of [man's] creative potentialities . . . the unfolding of human abilities and needs' might finally come about.[118] Subsequent chapters of this book will unpack

114 Ferenc Fehér et al., 'Notes and Commentary', *Telos* 29 (1976): 160–81 (180).

115 'Comrade Lukács goes so far . . . as to state: the individual is capable of abolishing his own alienations even independently of his concrete social situation. But this can only mean the transcendence of alienation in consciousness' ('Notes', p. 180).

116 The German term *Werdegang* suggests a progressive and quasi-organic development. See Weiss, *Abschied von den Eltern* (Frankfurt: Suhrkamp, 2007), p. 117.

117 In Nizan's novel, 'personality' (*personnalité*) is conspicuously attributed to machines but not to the workers, who are presented as objectified parts of these machines. Paul Nizan, *Antoine Bloyé* (Paris: Grasset, 1962), pp. 94–5.

118 See Lukács, *Ontologie* 1, p. 620; *Marx*, p. 79.

these tensions further – but they will do so at the level of individual literary works rather than at the more abstract level of philosophical argument. In doing so, I will also explore how radical bildungsromane work to deindividualize the question of emancipatory political action by positioning it in the context of larger collective struggles. This feature helps to explain the genre's ability to accommodate non-hegemonic (female, queer, non-white) subject positions as well as the forms of identity politics that came to the fore in the context of the New Left of the 1960s and 1970s.

Chapter Organization

Revolutionary Subjects is not a simple influence study – it does not ask which socialist writers had read their Goethe and which hadn't. Instead, this book makes a more ambitious conceptual claim: that literary form can be grasped as a medium of historical understanding and universalist political thought in its own right. Accordingly, my discussion centres the specific formal conveyances that cause these novels to cohere into a recognizable literary tradition. Each of my chapters identifies one unifying theme – or overarching historico-conceptual problem – which the texts in this tradition set out to address, ranging from the question of a genuinely socialist modernity (Chapter 1) and the elusiveness of anti-hegemonic bildung (Chapter 2) to the radical de-individualizing of bildung (Chapter 3) and the sobering deferral of socialism's political hopes (Chapter 4).

Chapter 1 ('The Left Bildungsroman's Early History: Genre at Modernity's Periphery') shows that early authors of the socialist bildungsroman, from the 1860s through the early 1900s, aimed to carve out a space for the genre by presenting their novels as critiques of specific (bourgeois) precursor texts. An early work I consider here is Chernyshevsky's *What Is to Be Done?*: while the novel is more widely known for its centring of (male) revolutionary agency, I pay special attention to the novel's female protagonist, Vera Pavlovna, whose political bildung proceeds in stops and starts and involves a complex dialectic of fantastic dream visions and practical political work. I propose that the slow and fitful course of Vera's bildung, which unsettles masculine dreams of revolutionary heroism, marks the novel's real contribution to the emerging tradition of the left bildungsroman. The chapter also explores *Pelle the Conqueror* by the Danish socialist Martin Andersen

Nexø: this novel offers a response to Henrik Pontoppidan's influential *Lucky Per* (1898–1904), a text that figures in Lukács's *Theory of the Novel* as a key exponent of the 'bourgeois bildungsroman'. While Pontoppidan's novel treats individual formation in narrowly economic terms, Nexø's male (Pelle) and female (Ditte) protagonists learn to chart alternative trajectories that point a way beyond existing social constraints. Chernyshevsky's and Nexø's novels illustrate key features of the radical bildungsroman: they emphasize the collaborative (rather than narrowly individual) character of bildung, and they also highlight the pressures of second-order bildung – that is, the socialist revision of an earlier mis-bildung. The fact that these novels speak from comparatively peripheral positions within the capitalist world-system, I argue, gives them particular critical leverage over the forms and conventions of the bourgeois bildungsroman.

Chapter 2 ('Educating the Educator: The Radical Bildungsroman and the Problem of Second Bildung') takes a deep dive into the forms of anti-hegemonic bildung that are imagined by the radical bildungsroman. It starts out from Marx's third 'Thesis on Feuerbach', which insists that the socialist movement will only have a future if it succeeds in 'educat[ing] [*erziehen*] the educator [*Erzieher*] himself'. We can think of this foundational dilemma as Marxism's equivalent of the chicken-and-egg problem: instead of settling the question of radical bildung, Marx asks how anti-hegemonic bildung should proceed if it cannot take recourse to historically established patterns of individual formation. The socialist bildungsroman's attention to the halting process of second-order bildung makes it possible to identify a sizable subset of texts that would otherwise be hard to define as paradigmatic bildungsromane – from Maxim Gorky's ageing female protagonist in *Mother*, Fyodor Gladkov's Gleb in *Cement* (1925) and Jean-Paul Sartre's dissatisfied bourgeois anti-hero Mathieu in *The Roads to Freedom* (*Les Chemins de la libert*, 1945–9) to the autobiographical narrators in Richard Wright's *Black Boy*, Peter Weiss's *Leavetaking* and Karin Struck's *Klassenliebe* (1973). These novels ask according to which (if any) protocols the unlearning of an earlier hegemonic bildung unfolds and how this process is lived and experienced. I argue that this laborious and painful process of unlearning – rather than the radiant vision of an achieved political bildung – was key to the radical bildungsroman's historical emergence. Some bildungsromane in the socialist tradition attribute an autonomous value to youth, while others betray fears that youth might signify the danger of stagnating or frozen development. Yet another group of texts unfolds according to an internal dialectic of phenomenological immersion and critical distantiation that gives equal weight to disorientating first-hand experiences of the socialist struggle *and* to the abstract knowledge gained through retrospection. The process of bildung, as it crystallizes in these novels, involves the recognition that the socialist struggle – when viewed from the inside – can provide few hard-and-fast teleological guarantees.

Chapter 3 ('"Knowledge in Struggle": Collective Formation and Revolutionary Pedagogy') examines novels that put pressure on the (bourgeois) bildungsroman's hardwired commitment to individual growth. These novels indicate that the work of bringing about a postcapitalist world must by necessity be a collective one – accordingly, this future social order is imagined not as a fixed telos but as a process that involves the recognition of shared needs and the forging of new solidarities. The necessity to reformulate the parameters of the bildungsroman in this way arose with particular urgency in the context of new emancipatory movements in the second half of the twentieth century – these included feminist and autonomist demands as well as anti-colonial liberation movements. Novels considered here range from Paul Nizan's writings of the 1930s to Nanni Balestrini's Autonomia novels, and from a set of Maoist-inflected novels and films (by Ding Ling, Li Wenhua and Jean-Luc Godard) to African bildungsromane by Ngũgĩ wa Thiong'o. The revisionary model of anti-individualist bildung that I outline here was first given coherent and programmatic articulation in an important body of pedagogical writings from the mid-century – some of these writings emerged from Maoist traditions, while others grew from Latin American and European schools of critical pedagogy. To the extent that these literary and non-literary works remain committed to a universalist political project, they imagine it not through the problematic figure of the (heroic, male, white) bildungsheld but as the outcome of a series of complex coalitions, as 'a process or condition' irreducible to a single fixed identity.[119]

Chapter 4 ('No Home but the Struggle: The Left Bildungsroman and the Formlessness of History') examines novels that figure the socialist struggle in terms of experiences of directionlessness or homelessness. In these works, the socialist struggle seems uncoupled from a redemptive historical telos, giving way instead to the vision of an endlessly deferred 'earthly home'. Although this view of the socialist struggle may at first sight appear extreme, the association of the political struggle with a deferral of plenitude is in fact one of the

119 Judith Butler, Ernesto Laclau and Slavoj Žižek, *Contingency, Hegemony, Universality: Contemporary Dialogues on the Left* (London: Verso, 2000), p. 3.

defining features of the radical bildungsroman: instead of inhabiting the optimistic, future-directed (Blochian) Not-Yet of the utopian imagination, the genre gives expression to what could be called the negative temporality of the Not-Now, the series of missed historical opportunities and uncertain futures that characterize the socialist struggle. Far from being outliers, then, the novels considered in this chapter give voice to one of the genre's central insights. My discussion ranges from Guido Morselli's novel *The Communist* (1976) and Lessing's *Golden Notebook* to Maryse Condé's *Hérémakhonon* and Weiss's *The Aesthetics of Resistance*. Looking back to my discussion (in the Introduction) of the experimental openness of Goethe's *Wanderjahre*, Chapter 4 shows that experiences of formlessness – and the aesthetic means by which these experiences are articulated in the left bildungsroman – are central to the genre's political vision and provide much of its narrative energy. In contrast to the nineteenth-century bourgeois bildungsroman, which had sought to provide a symbolic form capable of containing the revolutionary changes wrought by modernity, the socialist novel of formation insists on the essential ongoingness of the struggle and on the ways in which subjects are made and unmade – formed and de-formed – by history.

The brief Coda returns to some key themes of the book – the radical bildungsroman's universalist politics, its centring of the human and its experimental retooling of bildung motifs – and carries these themes forward into the present. Drawing attention to a diverse set of texts – by the Combahee River Collective, the Catalan trans theorist Paul B. Preciado and the Jamaican-British cultural scholar Stuart Hall – I suggest that these works capture a key dimension of the political struggle for a new world, namely the experience of existing in a state of in-betweenness, of being caught in the midst of historical contradictions. By lending these questions an acute autobiographical dimension, these texts remind us that the project of radical bildung involves not a single moment of revision, or a crisis-like turning point, but rather the drawn-out transformation of acquired knowledges and modes of thought and feeling, what Hall calls the 'unlearning' of 'the norms in which I had been born and brought up' – 'a long, continuing process of disidentification [that] has shaped my life'.[120]

120 Stuart Hall, *Familiar Stranger: A Life Between Two Islands* (London: Penguin, 2018), p. 3.

1

The Left Bildungsroman's Early History: Genre at Modernity's Periphery

The radical bildungsroman did not enter the world-literary stage fully formed. As the preceding chapter has shown, it made its first spectral appearance in the 1820s and 1830s, in the forward-looking essays of literary critics who predicted that new narratives of development would emerge in response to the revolutionary eruptions of the eighteenth and nineteenth centuries. Even prior to its emergence as a genre from the 1860s onwards, then, the idea of the left bildungsroman had become linked to a radically anti-capitalist vision of *Weltliteratur* – a vision that was deeply rooted in the early and mid-century milieu of political activism and social dreaming that is now typically referred to under the label *utopian socialism*. As I argue in the present chapter, the delayed historical development of the socialist bildungsroman meant that authors working in this nascent genre had to contend with a twofold impulse: on the one hand, the emergence of the genre's socialist variant was marked by a reliance on the specific generic affordances of the bourgeois bildungsroman, as these had begun to materialize from the late eighteenth century onwards; on the other, socialist writers sought to remake these generic parameters so that they would speak to a radically new range of political projects oriented towards an internationalist future rather than the consolidation of the nation-state or more locally rooted communities.

My argument shares with Fredric Jameson and recent world-systems theorists the intuition that the most 'satisfactory semantic meaning of modernity lies in its association with capitalism.'[1] This means that

1 Fredric Jameson, *A Singular Modernity: Essay on the Ontology of the Present* (London: Verso, 2002), p. 13.

novels written at different geographical locations or discrete chronological moments can be understood as responses to a single process of socio-economic modernization, what Jameson has called our 'singular modernity'.[2] Of course, to suggest such deep structural connections is not to claim that modernity is characterized by a uniform set of cultural styles or some kind of artistic monoculture. Because modernity is uneven in its structural effects, Jameson's thesis leaves open space for conjuncturally distinctive responses to the global expansion of capital. By the same token, in the words of Bruce Robbins, the 'world-system' of capitalist modernity does not turn those who inhabit its geographical margins into 'passive objects of their own history and not its authors' – instead, it grants them a crucial measure of agency over the modalities of their collective cultural, political and artistic expression.[3] The two socialist novels I focus on in what follows – Martin Andersen Nexø's *Pelle the Conqueror* and Nikolay Chernyshevsky's epochal *What Is to Be Done?* – are useful cases in point. Because these novels address themselves to modernity's nineteenth-century periphery (Denmark and Russia, respectively), they are uniquely positioned to register the variable speeds of modernization. The egalitarian politics that these novels espouse are therefore not reducible to what Dipesh Chakrabarty has called the 'empty . . . universal and necessary history we associate with capital'.[4] Emerging from the cracks and interstices of the world-system, Nexø's and Chernyshevsky's narrative projects commence the task of imagining counter-teleologies to capitalist modernity. These alternative teleologies picture a process of modernization that leads on to socialism rather than one that proceeds, according to some iron logic, towards the total subsumption of human relations under the law of exchange value.

From a more specifically literary viewpoint, *Pelle the Conqueror* and *What Is to Be Done?* illustrate the tendency of the early left

2 At an extreme, this theory has been taken to suggest a radically decentred understanding of the growth of the capitalist world-system. As the Warwick Research Collective observe, modernity in this sense 'is neither a chronological nor a geographical category. It is not something that happens – or even that happens first – in "the west"'. See Warwick Research Collective (WReC), *Combined and Uneven Development: Towards a New Theory of World-Literature* (Liverpool: Liverpool University Press, 2015), p. 13.

3 Bruce Robbins, 'Blaming the System', in *Immanuel Wallerstein and the Problem of the World: System, Scale, Culture* (Durham, NC: Duke University Press, 2011), pp. 41–63 (48).

4 Dipesh Chakrabarty, 'Universalism and Belonging in the Logic of Capital', *Public Culture* 12.3 (2003): 653–78 (668).

bildungsroman to constitute itself through a process of generic revision. The novels offer two strikingly different paths forward for the radical novel of formation, both of which were taken up by later authors. Whereas Nexø's novel preserves the narrative coherence of the bildungsroman's teleological arc by rearticulating it in a socialist register, Chernyshevsky's book isolates and reconstitutes individual bildung motifs rather than appropriating the structure of the bourgeois bildungsroman wholesale. These formal choices have important implications for the way both novels imagine social change: while *Pelle the Conqueror* pictures such change in terms of a progressive transformational rebuilding, *What Is to Be Done?* dramatizes the promise of revolutionary rupture. These divergent visions of radical change are rooted in Nexø's and Chernyshevsky's different experiences of the political struggle: whereas Nexø was able to imagine a slow transition to socialism (he was a member of the powerful social democratic movement in Denmark and only joined the Communist Party after the First World War), the seemingly impenetrable authority of nineteenth-century tsarism drove Chernyshevsky to adopt a vision of total revolutionary change.

In order to make visible the early socialist bildungsroman's work of generic reinvention and ground-clearing, the present chapter pairs each of these two books with another bildung narrative that Nexø's and Chernyshevsky's novels set out to revise: Henrik Pontoppidan's *Lucky Per* (1898–1904) and Ivan Turgenev's *Fathers and Sons* (1862). Pontoppidan and Turgenev register the perils of (social, scientific, technological) modernization, but they find ways of accommodating themselves to these serious risks and of rejecting the alternative path of socialism. By contrast, Nexø and Chernyshevsky orient their novels towards a specific political goal: the socialist revolution. They also account for the condition of 'wandering' – of migration, exile and homelessness – as a central historical feature and an enabling precondition of revolutionary praxis in the present.

'An almost holy expectation': Pontoppidan's *Lucky Per* and the Exhaustion of Bourgeois Bildung

Born in 1857, Pontoppidan began his literary career as a champion of the extreme naturalism of the late nineteenth-century Modern Breakthrough movement in Denmark – an artistic association that led Pontoppidan to pen unsparing accounts of life among Denmark's impoverished peasantry and growing urban proletariat. By contrast, *Lucky Per* embraces a more capaciously realist aesthetic that gives expression to Pontoppidan's growing optimism that piecemeal (scientific, technological, social) progress will improve the living conditions of the poorest. In the Scandinavian countries, *Lucky Per* has long held canonical status, but the novel's reputation as a quintessential bildung narrative has rarely extended beyond its geographical place of origin. The book's young protagonist, Per Sidenius, is an aspiring engineer whose superabundant talent and raw ambition put him at odds early in life with the strict Lutheran environment of his home and social milieu. Breaking with his family, Per departs for Copenhagen, where he learns about cutting-edge developments in technology and the natural sciences. Per soon begins to draft plans for an infrastructural project of unprecedented scale – a vast system of inland locks and shipping canals that will bring prosperity to his native Jutland by connecting it to the globalizing world without. Per's reluctance to compromise with the political enemies of his grand project finally leads to its failure, but Pontoppidan clearly wants his readers to recognize that Per's hypertrophic ambition – his professed desire to obey only the Nietzschean 'I *will*'[5] – remains unbroken. So powerful is Per's future-directed '*will*' that it even appears to extend beyond his own physical death. As the novel closes, we are made to hear Per's voice from beyond the grave, rendered in the surviving pages of his diary: 'Without the original human urge to develop, without the self-generated power that expresses itself as passion . . . and without that strong, even bold courage to will to be oneself . . . no one reaches freedom. Because of this, I am grateful that I have been living in such a time that calls out to this instinct and strengthens this essential courage . . . I am still a world conqueror' (585). The momentous historical epoch on which Per's diary entry reflects promises to give free rein to the world-making capacities of the enterprising individual. It is precisely this historical prototype of the entrepreneur and self-made capitalist that Pontoppidan models for us in the figure of Per.

The intensity of Per's desire for self-assertion and domination is, in many ways, extreme. Indeed, he seems constitutively incapable of achieving the kinds of social compromise that enable the (re)integration of other bildungshelden into the pre-existing social order. *Lucky Per* thus marks a crucial inflection point in the history of the

5 Pontoppidan, *Lucky Per* (New York: Everyman's Library, 2019), p. 220 (emphasis in original). Subsequent references will be given in the text.

bildungsroman genre – what Lukács, in an extended discussion of Balzac and Pontoppidan in *Theory of the Novel*, called the 'novel of abstract idealism'.[6] In Lukács's usage, *abstract idealism* refers to a will which is so intense that it threatens to transcend completely the constraints of the everyday world. As such, the term describes a fundamental 'incommensurability' between the protagonist's desiring 'soul' and the material 'work' through which this desire seeks to express itself: Per's desire to remake the world according to his inner 'ideal' of perfection exceeds any individual task and accordingly fails to settle into a permanent and stable form. In *Lucky Per* this contradiction between the transcendent force of the individual will and the constraints of social convention manifests in a strikingly innovative use of the bourgeois bildungsroman's guiding trope – the idea of the nation as an 'earthly home' that will serve as a natural vessel or container for the individual's desires.[7] While the novel variously alludes to Per's longing for 'that country of happiness . . . the nation's soul' (34, 110), his ambition finally points beyond the nation and towards a fully interconnected world-system. Because of the sheer scale of this vision, the novel describes it as an as-yet-unrealized 'dream', an unfulfilled 'wealth of fantasy' that chafes against the 'persistent predilection of the tried and tested'. To emphasize the aspirational (or 'idealist') aspect of Per's utopian dreams, Pontoppidan repeatedly compares his protagonist to the Oriental 'Aladdin, a charmed boy on whose Caesar brow God's finger had written, "I come, I see, I conquer!"' (40). When Denmark is measured against the global scope of Per's entrepreneurial ambition, the country itself appears fantastically unreal in its proportions: '"Such a Lilliputian country as Denmark is in itself an absurdity." So little and poor a country is, finally, untenable in our day' (213). The solution, as Per sees it, is that Denmark must be firmly tied into the circuits of globalizing capital: 'We must engender respect by our abundance. The solution will be money, money, and more money' (213). In *Lucky Per*, the anticipatory vision of an emerging global order possesses the transcendent radiance of an 'abstract ideal' whose realization lies beyond the capabilities of any single individual or nation and is instead revealed to depend on the centrifugal logic of capital.

Fredric Jameson has observed that Per's position as a bearer of capital leads to a curious devaluation of the individual and that it thereby

6 Georg Lukács, *The Theory of the Novel* (Cambridge, MA: MIT Press, 1999), p. 97.

7 Ibid., p. 135.

produces an 'exhaustion of traditional narratives': 'once the protagonist knows the great project can be completed, he loses interest, he no longer needs to complete it.'[8] The crisis that Jameson identifies here is partly the crisis of the bildungsroman genre itself – a literary genre that had depended on the protagonist's centrality to the plot and on his (or her) profound sense of vocational commitment. Whereas the nineteenth-century bildungsroman had often sought to contain the energies of modernity by funnelling them into a reassuringly national form, *Lucky Per* gives us glimpses of a world in which capital's centrifugal impulse – its tendency to subsume all human activity in an interminable process of accumulation that David Harvey dubs 'bad infinity' – is granted free rein.[9] By the same token, Pontoppidan presents Per's work as an engineer not as a deeply held vocation but as the narrowly technical command of a type of instrumental rationality. When *Lucky Per* is read in this way, it marks the (structural, if not strictly chronological) endpoint of the nineteenth-century bildungsroman's attempt to present work as the medium of enriching and socially meaningful experiences.

As we will see, *Lucky Per*'s distinctive idiom of technological mastery – 'I am still a world conqueror'; 'I come, I see, I conquer!' – gets remobilized in a strikingly different (socialist) register in *Pelle the Conqueror*, the novel that Nexø dedicated to 'Pontoppidan, the Master'. At certain points in *Lucky Per*, however, Pontoppidan himself – this great prophet of capitalist modernity – seems to acknowledge the gravitational pull of the period's radical socialist politics, as the novel's celebration of technological rationality is experimentally harnessed to a larger vision of progressive social change. In one scene, a vicar challenges Per's absolute belief in technology: 'He told about the hordes of roaming workers, men and women for whom the words "home", "family", "security" and "comfort" already were as good as meaningless' (420). These impoverished and homeless proletarians and migrant workers matter to Per not only because they mirror his own sense of himself as 'a fugitive and a vagabond on earth' – an outcast from the religious home in which he grew up – but because their lives give poignant expression to the contradictions of capitalist modernization. In these scenes, many of which are

8 Jameson, 'Cosmic Neutrality', *London Review of Books*, vol. 33, no. 2 (20 October 2011), lrb.co.uk.

9 David Harvey, *Marx, Capital, and the Madness of Economic Reason* (New York: Oxford University Press, 2018), pp. 173–4. Harvey takes the term from Hegel, who discusses the 'bad infinite' in the *Science of Logic* (Cambridge: Cambridge University Press, 2010), pp. 109–20.

set in the poorest boroughs of Copenhagen, Pontoppidan offers moving descriptions of existential precarity and material deprivation: 'What a despairing lot our time – our great, beautiful, progressive time – has prepared for children in poor circumstances, and how mercilessly little is done on the social side to help them to a humane, a merely natural existence' (517). What is true of Copenhagen is also true of the uneven development of the nation as a whole. In the 'provinces', the narrator reminds us, 'life was still lived virtually unchanged in its worn-out forms': 'The fact was that Copenhagen had taken the wind out of the sails of the country that dwindled more and more to mere outskirts of the capital' (263). The absoluteness of Per's 'I *will*' is here briefly measured against a collective 'New National Project' (307) – the vision of a more egalitarian distribution of wealth and a democratically organized process of modernization that will extend beyond the capital of Copenhagen and into the remoter provinces of Jutland.[10]

This is not to say, of course, that *Lucky Per* presents us with a fully developed socialist alternative to the process of capitalist globalization. Pontoppidan's novel remains unapologetically reformist and its vision of a new and emerging elite of capitalist entrepreneurs is fundamentally at odds with a committed collectivist or genuinely 'revolutionary' political vision (198). Indeed, much of the book's thematic thrust derives from Pontoppidan's attempt to peel away, one by one, the social(ist) pretensions of Per's enterprise. Per's early decision to become an engineer – 'He wanted to be an engineer . . . the real fulfilment of his dream of a proud and free-roaming life' (24) – makes it clear that his chosen profession is intended to afford him a life of comfort and cosmopolitan travel, in sharp contrast to the enforced migrancy of the 'roaming' urban proletarians. The New National Project remains first and foremost 'his *own* project', and his flights of fantasy, which lead him to envision this project in awe-inspiring technical grandeur, are ultimately self-aggrandizing: as the narrator informs us towards the end of the novel, 'the significance of [Per's] plan for the nation's future had disguised his egoism' (470, emphasis in original).[11] The cumulative effect of

10 Pontoppidan's novel shows more sympathy towards the Danish rural peasantry than some of Nexø's novels, most notably *Ditte, Child of Man* (1921), the companion volume to *Pelle the Conqueror*, whose female protagonist is presented as a role model for the new (female) urban worker.

11 In keeping with the deeply anti-egalitarian strain of fairy-tale romance that runs through Pontoppidan's bildungsroman, Per repeatedly imagines himself as one of the elect, as the member of a new bourgeois ruling class – a 'king's son' 'abducted by an itinerant band, sold, and then held in captivity in the parsonage' (14).

Pontoppidan's mode of characterization – whereby the novel progressively reveals the egoism that lies at the heart of Per's vocational choices – marks a significant break in the history of the nineteenth-century bildungsroman: while it is true that *Lucky Per* pays lip service to the formal parameters and traditional themes of the genre, in Pontoppidan's novel this tendency coexists with the decommissioning of these same conventions in favour of a new centrality of fantasy, the visionary and the 'abstract ideal'. The bildungsroman's conventional endpoint is acknowledged as a desirable telos ('All that he personally hoped from this work was that it would make it possible to lead a peaceful, happy, useful life in harmony and consonance with his heart's desire', 483–4), yet the fundamentally anti-social quality of Per's yearning for personal distinction and economic success finally gives rise to a restlessness that resists such attempts at formal closure. It is this structural dilemma or impasse – the visible 'exhaustion of traditional [bildung] narratives', in Jameson's phrase – that called for the differently motivated political solutions offered by the socialist bildungsroman. As I suggest in what follows, Nexø's *Pelle the Conqueror* performs a left critique of Pontoppidan's linking of the bildungsroman and capitalist modernization.

Socialist Modernity: *Pelle the Conqueror*, Cooperation and Internationalism

Lucky Per offers its readers a glimpse of the capitalist 'Man of the twentieth century': Per, we are told, 'was like the first, formless draft of a coming giant race that – as he himself had written – finally could seize, as legitimate masters of the earth, ownership of it and mould it to its needs' (216). Socialist fiction and visual art of the nineteenth and twentieth centuries were eager to invent new and anti-capitalist versions of this 'New Man' trope. Later in this chapter, I will turn to the most prominent character created in this mould – Chernyshevsky's socialist superman Rakhmetov. Strikingly, however, the first socialist novel-project I explore here – the four volumes that make up Nexø's *Pelle the Conqueror* – responds to Pontoppidan's artistic vision by deflating the temptation to create a socialist counter-myth of the New Man.

Like Pontoppidan, Nexø had parted ways with the naturalism of the Modern Breakthrough movement; unlike Pontoppidan, however, Nexø renounced naturalism's pessimistic outlook in favour of a programmatic artistic commitment to socialism rather than a hopeful vision of capitalist modernization. The opening chapter of *Pelle the Conqueror* programmatically draws the reader's attention to the mass of dispossessed migrant workers – Varnhagen von Ense's 'Proletarier, Verwahrloste und Bedrückte'[12] – whose presence is only obliquely acknowledged by Pontoppidan's Per. In Nexø, these impoverished *Verwahrloste* are Swedish emigrants to the Danish island of Bornholm in the Baltic Sea: migrant workers escaping from extreme poverty, they are described as 'strangers' and 'slaves', and their group includes Pelle and his recently widowed father, Lasse.[13] This profound sense of geographical displacement is important because it makes it possible for the young boy Pelle to imagine 'home' as something that is not confined to a particular nation or place:

> His father's words about the best being in store for them, were to him only a feeble expression for a great truth, namely, that the whole world would become theirs, with all that it contained in the way of wonders . . . This was a new world altogether, and Pelle was engaged in making it his own. Not a shred of it he would leave. (10)

In contrast to Per's self-centred ambitions, Pelle's desire to 'conquer' the world by making it more hospitable to those living on society's margins will finally lead him to embrace socialist internationalism. From the beginning of the narrative, Nexø is at pains to emphasize that Denmark is not the paradisiacal new place that Lasse remembers from an earlier visit: Lasse finds the commotion of bodies at the harbour disorientating, and he worries that 'here he was in the midst of all this splendor, and could not even find a humble situation for himself and the boy. He could not understand it' (9). The anticlimax of Lasse and Pelle's arrival on Bornholm helps to establish the novel's overwhelming sense that home is not a place we are free to return to after a period of prodigal 'wandering' but rather a community – a set of human relations – that needs to be actively brought into existence. Similarly, while Pelle's physical appearance ('with bristling hair . . . his hands buried in his trouser pockets', 24) marks him out as a self-confident adolescent, he appears to be not a complete individual – a radiant New Man – but rather one in need of growth and development,

12 See the previous chapter for this quotation ('proletarians, slum-dwellers, and the oppressed') from Varnhagen's early theorization of the bildungsroman: 'Im Sinne der Wanderer' [In the Spirit of the Wanderers], *Über Kunst und Alterthum* 6 (1832): 533–51 (542, 540).

13 Martin Nexø, *Pelle the Conqueror* (New York: Mondial, 2006), pp. 2–3. Subsequent references are given parenthetically.

whose knowledge of the world must still be 'learned by experience' (40). Pelle undergoes a strenuous regime of self-examination and critique. To adapt a phrase by the literary scholar Carolyn Lesjak, for Pelle, 'learning how to see through the kinds of concealments [of capitalist ideology] defines the process of Bildung itself'.[14]

As the novel progresses, it becomes clear that the 'conquering' invoked in the book's title signifies not a singular act of violent domination and subjugation but a process of collaborative building and construction: 'His world was small,' the narrator informs us, 'he had only just begun to create it . . . Beyond that floated raw matter, chaos. But Pelle already found his world immense, and was quite willing to make it infinite' (50).[15] Pelle's 'impatience' vis-à-vis the spectacle of an 'incredibly great world' (215) echoes the entrepreneurial 'restlessness' of Pontopiddan's Per. Pelle temporarily manages to quell his intense 'appetite for the great world' (155) by accumulating money – this brief episode, which is inspired by Pelle's acquaintance with a Bornholm trader, leads him to 'become a capitalist' (81). Quickly, however, the greed bred by trading begins to corrupt Pelle's character, leading him to lash out in blind frenzy at friends who owe him money ('There was hatred in every stroke that Pelle struck, and they went like shocks through his [friend's] body, but he never uttered a cry. No, there was no point in his crying, for the coin he held in his hand took away the pain,' 89). Nexø asks us to recognize that Pelle's initial (capitalist) bildung is, really, an anti-social mis-bildung, before finally placing Pelle on the trajectory towards a more properly socialist formation that proceeds by way of cooperative action and mutual effort rather than individual enterprise.

The first volume of *Pelle the Conqueror* (entitled *Childhood*) recounts Lasse and Pelle's arduous first years in Denmark as well as their difficulties in making ends meet while working on a farm owned by the tyrannical Kongstrup. At the farm, Pelle becomes friends with Danes and Swedes alike, all of whom are suffering equally under Kongstrup's brutal dictatorial regime. A particularly close bond forms between Pelle and Erik, another young Swede, who is regularly

14 Carolyn Lesjak, *Working Fictions: A Genealogy of the Victorian Novel* (Durham, NC: Duke University Press, 2006), p. 93.

15 On this aspect of *Pelle the Conqueror*, see Nicklas Freisleben Lund, Magnus Nilsson and Henrik Yde, 'A Man of the Red World? Martin Andersen Nexø's Journey between Danish Periphery and Soviet Centre', in *The Routledge Handbook of Red World Literature*, ed. Hunter Bivens and Anna Björk Einarsdóttir (Abingdon: Routledge, forthcoming).

harassed for his alleged laziness. Erik becomes Pelle's first political role model when he helps to instigate a revolt against Kongstrup. Even though the insurrection fails and Erik ends up injured and disabled, his instinctive and unwavering opposition to any form of oppression continues to be invoked as a model for Pelle's later socialist commitments. The meeting with Erik helps to establish the key narrative pattern for the novel: in *Pelle the Conqueror*, socialism is not a fixed set of dogmas but something that must be learned dialogically and 'through experience'. As the literary critic Andrew Miller has noted in a different context, Pelle's politics is learned 'not through obedience to . . . codes, but through openness to example – through responsive, unpredictable engagements with other people'.[16] Through his encounters with other characters – young and old, conformist and rebellious – Pelle begins to arrive at a clearer understanding of the dreams of world-conquering that had occupied him ever since his arrival on Bornholm. While his earlier 'childish imagination' (83) had run ahead of reality in the manner of Per Sidenius's utopic abstract idealism (we are told that '[Pelle's] world was supersensual', 83), he now begins to 'examine himself critically' (100): 'He exercised his small mind as he exercised his body . . . It was Pelle's first attempt at obtaining a general survey of himself' (86, 100). It is through Pelle's first-hand experience of solidarity and mutual help among the workers on Bornholm that he attains a more concrete sense of the earthly home that socialism aims to build. There are many scenes in the novel that describe the individual stages of Pelle's socialist bildung. These include a moving scene in which a young man, Niels, dies in a shipwreck and his father receives consolation and support from the rest of the workers' community. This scene culminates in Pelle's growing recognition that it will be his duty to support Lasse in the solitude of old age.

Crucially, the slow and halting process of socialist bildung pictured by Nexø entails not a total renunciation of Pelle's 'childish imagination' but, rather, its rearticulation within a larger collective or communal movement. As we are informed towards the beginning of the novel's fourth volume (*Daybreak*):

> It had always been the lot of the poor man to create worlds out of the void, beautiful mirages which suddenly broke and threw him back even

16 Andrew Miller, *The Burdens of Perfection: On Ethics and Reading in Nineteenth-Century British Literature* (Ithaca, NY: Cornell University Press, 2008), pp. 3–5.

> poorer and more desolate. But this lasted. All the threats of life seemed to be joined together in the bare cell. It was like the dark, underground place in large buildings where the machinery is kept that admits and excludes light and heat to the whole block. There he discovered how rich and varied life is. (702)

The key moments in Pelle's development from youthful dreamer to committed socialist occur in Volume II (*Apprenticeship*) and Volume III (*The Great Struggle*) of the novel. In a striking sequence of scenes that make up the thematic core of the second volume, Pelle experiences the early stirrings of revolutionary consciousness while engaged in work that he finds alienating. Having left Kongstrup, Pelle has secured new employment in a neighbouring town:

> He was disillusioned; the descent from his dream to this naked reality was too great. And a feeling rose within him of dull resentment against this endless labor, which, inexperienced though he was, was yet part of his very being by virtue of the lives of ten, nay, twenty generations . . . But he had not inherited his father's joy in the soil; his thoughts had struck out in a new direction. (257)

The growth of revolutionary consciousness is here pictured as a work-like activity, and it recalls the passages from Chernyshevsky, Ngũgĩ and others that I quoted in the Introduction. This sedimentation of collective memories across several generations eventually breeds, in the figure of Pelle, a desire for revolutionary change: 'He had an irrational longing that something of this kind should happen, something to drive the blood from his heart and make his hair stand on end' (261). This desire is no longer an impulsive or purely individualistic dream of youthful revolt (as in the case of Erik) but an incipiently revolutionary desire for wholescale social change that issues from a longer history of oppression.

In a gesture that is characteristic of the genre more generally, *Pelle the Conqueror* does not picture the attainment of socialist bildung as a clear-cut process by which youthful radical spontaneity is displaced in favour of some more mature type of revolutionary consciousness.[17]

17 On the centrality of the spontaneity/consciousness dialectic to the proletarian novel, see *The Soviet Novel: History as Ritual* (Bloomington: Indiana University Press, 2000), pp. 16–17. I provide further commentary on the radical bildungsroman's attempts to incorporate this dialectic in my discussion of Fyodor Gladkov's 1925 Soviet novel *Cement* in Chapter 2.

Instead, Nexø's narrative enacts a dialectical movement whereby the importance of spontaneity is upheld even at the point when maturity is finally attained: 'I meet young men and my mind inclines to them,' notes Brun, Pelle's aged, working-class friend, towards the end of *Daybreak*, 'but it's like evening and morning meeting in the same glow during the light nights . . . I was born old. I'm only now beginning to feel young' (793–4). The restless energies of revolt must not be hemmed in or deactivated in favour of an allegedly 'mature' resignation vis-à-vis existing social structures. The galvanizing force of youthful revolt is necessary because it pushes political consciousness beyond itself, transmitting an electric current of insurrectionary desire that galvanizes this consciousness and jolts it on towards revolutionary action.

Volume II (*Apprenticeship*) of *Pelle the Conqueror* narrates central aspects of Pelle's bildung – it is here that he learns to resist the temptations of petit bourgeois life by integrating himself into a larger collective revolutionary movement. Depicting the years following his adolescence in rural Denmark, Volume III (*The Great Struggle*) extends Pelle's revolutionary *Lehrjahre* by depicting his immersion in the working-class and socialist milieus of Copenhagen. Volume II closes with a rousing appeal that the narrator seems to address to the character of Pelle himself ('He must go away, far away from here, and live the wandering life', 314). It is this sense of departure and new beginnings that sets the tone for the rest of the novel: 'He felt that what he should now set out upon would be decisive; if he was victorious now, he would conquer eternity,' the narrator observes towards the end of the novel, adding that 'this time it must be either for weal or woe' (659). Pelle's arrival in Copenhagen seems to him to be the arrival in 'quite a new world . . . nothing was the same as at home; here a hundred different things would happen in the course of today' (401). Politically, the key difference between the agrarian labourers of Bornholm and Copenhagen's working class is that the latter 'didn't beg for what they wanted' (403). More than anything else, Per's *Lehrjahre* among the urban proletariat produce in him the ability to 'set to work in practical manner' and in concert with others (430).

In Copenhagen, Pelle embraces trade unionism and is immediately swept up in protests and demonstrations by the city's destitute proletariat. These 'crowds', whose 'thousand-voiced song' seems to Pelle a harbinger of 'the new times that were to come', 'affect him powerfully' by offering a sense of real community (419): 'Here were several thousands of people gathered together for a common object, and it became exceedingly clear to him that he himself belonged to this crowd' (419). These 'masses' seem to him to be involved in precisely the same process of political bildung that he has begun to experience:

> The masses would no longer allow themselves to be held down in stupid resignation. Men who all their lives had plodded their accustomed way to and from their work now stood still and asked unreasonable questions as to the aim of it all. (428)

The centre of Pelle's life in Copenhagen, which lends experiential and emotional depth to these heightened moments of collective insurrectionary activity, is 'the Ark', a collection of dilapidated dwellings inhabited by a combination of proletarians and lumpen outcasts. The 'thousand-voiced song' that so exhilarates Pelle during the demonstrations in Copenhagen is echoed in the polyphonic 'buzzing of the Ark' (483). A collective beehive-like organism rather than just a building, the Ark provides the setting for many poignant moments of solidarity among these social rejects as well as for the sheer exertion of proletarian life in the industrializing metropolis. As the book's central politicized setting, the Ark performs a double function. On the one hand, the novel shows us how a particularly harsh winter decimates the most vulnerable inhabitants of the Ark and how, following a series of spring lockouts, many of those living in the Ark are pushed to the point of starvation. These experiences convince Pelle that national divisions are of only secondary importance when compared with the more momentous division of the capitalist world into capital and labour, into profiteers and the poor. On the other hand, it is at the Ark that Pelle witnesses how residents support and take care of each other despite their desperate living conditions. Pelle himself comes to share an apartment with three orphans, and these children form his initial bond with the larger 'Family' (424) that makes up the fabric of life at the Ark: 'In the Ark everybody liked them, and helped them to keep their secret [that is, the secret that they live by themselves rather than having adult guardians and going to school]' (435).

The bonds that connect the extended 'Family' of the Ark, Pelle understands, are nourished by the 'sustaining strength' of mutual 'trust' (501). Similarly, the Ark's collective organism lends support to Pelle's socialist bildung: 'A greater nature was working within him, with more responsibility, according to his old presentiment. He tested himself, in order to assimilate this as a conviction, and he felt that there was virtue in the idea' (540).[18] Pelle's later bildung differs from the values he imbibed as a child insofar as it is fully conscious and self-determined – it derives its force from his deliberate immersion in the multifarious social ties that make up the Ark's collective. At the same time, and as the language in these passages indicates, Pelle's experiences at the Ark are sometimes elevated to a kind of religiously infused 'magic[al] socialism': these experiences afford glimpses of forces – of 'a greater nature' (540) – that point beyond the merely local and that foreground Pelle's wider kinship with the poor of other cities and other nations.[19] The networks of mutual support in which Pelle participates at the Ark offer him an intimation of socialism's earthly home: they offer a lesson in socialism not as a form of abstract dogma but as a realized ethos or way of life. At the same time, the full historical realization of socialism's larger revolutionary project continues to prove elusive: 'One of their choirs breaks into song: "We are bound for the Land of Fortune!" And where does that land lie? Has any of your watchers seen it? Or was it not merely a deceitful dream, engendered by hunger?' (642).

Owing to Pelle's considerable oratorical talents, he soon becomes president of the Shoemakers' Union and a hero to many of the Ark's inhabitants. The main temptation that threatens to derail his socialist bildung is the seductive lure of a comfortable bourgeois existence. Following his first oratorical successes, the newly wed Pelle feels the attraction of settling into 'his home' (727) with his wife Ellen: 'Home was a conception which was only now forcing its way downward from the middle classes' (595). Pelle's bildung thus remains precarious, and it is only thanks to the ties he has formed with other former inhabitants of the Ark's Family that he is 'spared' the traditional fate of the bourgeois bildungsheld – the altogether more homely life of guarded domestic bliss.

Key portions of *Pelle the Conqueror* are used to set up the intense inner conflict between Pelle's two bildung trajectories. Central to this inner struggle are Pelle's friend, the ardent radical Morten (a key figure

18 Nexø's interest in imagining a vastly extended socialist family carries over into *Ditte, Child of Man*, the 1921 sequel to *Pelle the Conqueror*. However, Nexø achieves this only by reducing the novel's female protagonist to a profoundly gendered, maternal figure: Ditte becomes surrogate mother to a flock of children whose families have proved unable to care for them.

19 For the 'magical' qualities of Pelle's socialist bildung, see Naomi Lebowitz, 'Magic Socialism and the Ghost of *Pelle Eroberen*', *Scandinavian Studies* 76.3 (2004): 341–68.

in Volumes III and IV), and Morten's father (a key protagonist in Volume II, where he is consistently referred to by his nickname 'Great Power'). These two figures represent the better angels of Pelle's bildung. As Great Power reminds Pelle towards the end of *Apprenticeship*, the respectability craved by bourgeois bildungshelden is inaccessible to proletarians like himself:

> Even if I wanted to keep myself decent, what should we gain by it? Can a family get decent lodging and decent food and decent clothing for nine kroner a week? Will the means of a laborer allow him to live anywhere but by the refuse-heaps, where only the pigs used to be kept? (327)

And even Pelle's father, Lasse, who once had high hopes for his son's 'respectability and prosperity', is now 'ashamed' by the conformity of his former desire for social rise (494). The four volumes of *Pelle the Conqueror* derive their narrative momentum from Nexø's simultaneous critique and transvaluation of the concept of 'home'. In a climactic passage towards the end of the novel, Pelle arrives at a newly expansive concept of 'home' that is capable of providing inspiration to the globally dispersed 'Family' of socialists:

> It was high time for a new idea to come and take them on; they had grown weary of this perpetual goose-step; the Movement was running away from them. But now he had come with an idea of which they would never grow weary, and which would carry them right through. No one would be able to say that he could not understand it, for it was the simple idea of the home carried out so as to include everything . . . The world would be like a good, loving home, where no one oppressed the other – nothing more complicated than that. (772)

This new 'idea of home' helps Nexø preserve the bildungsroman's animating narrative energy – the bildungsheld's progress towards an earthly home – while also picturing this home as a future possibility rather than a pre-existing social order to which the protagonist must finally resign himself. Importantly, this future home, of which the Ark offers us an anticipatory glimpse, is imagined not as a stable geographical place but as an unfinished project involving the participation of many: 'In other countries matters were progressing as here, so why not summon all countries to one vast work of cooperation [*én stor samverken*]? Before Pelle was aware, he had included the whole world in his solidarity. He knew now that poverty is international. And he was convinced that the poor man felt alike all the world over' (543). This remark suggests the possibility of an internationalist collective bildung, but it can also be understood to recognize the internationalist horizon of the bildungsroman form itself and its broad geographical portability across many different national contexts.

As I noted in the Introduction, theorists of the bildungsroman have argued that the genre 'stabilizes the bourgeois revolution into a narratable form' by framing the unruly and boundless energies of modernization in terms of the contained structure of the nation-state.[20] By contrast, the socialist bildungsroman reimagines the centrifugal impetus of modernity in a distinctly socialist register by showing that the dramatic inequalities produced by the process of uneven modernization also create footholds for an expansive socialist solidarity. In these novels, the nation-state is figured not as a final telos but as a kind of halfway house – as a vanishing geographical mediator – for the emergence of a fully socialist ethos. 'A murmuring wave passed through the ranks, reaching even to the foreign workers,' Nexø's narrator notes of one political meeting at which Pelle speaks: 'They were infected by the emotion of the others . . . This was solidarity, the mighty, earth-encircling power!' (618). As the novel progresses, and as Pelle considers settling into a more homely existence, it is Morten's youthful restlessness – his unabated desire to engage in revolutionary activity – that comes to embody this alternative (anti-capitalist) modernity: 'Although he himself when a child had sported in the light, yet his mind was saddened by the misery of all those who were dead or fighting in distant parts of the earth; and it was on this fact that the feeling of solidarity must be based' (450).

What is most striking about Nexø's handling of the bildungsroman form in *Pelle the Conqueror* is just how faithful he remains to the basic generic parameters of the genre while infusing them with a distinctly anti-capitalist and anti-hegemonic thrust. In *Pelle the Conqueror*, there is comparatively little of the iconoclastic impulse that characterizes Chernyshevsky's engagement with the bildungsroman – the experimental fragmentation of the bildungsroman into a looser constellation of bildung motifs that would prove such an influential model for the twentieth-century literary history of the radical novel of formation. Much

20 Jed Esty, *Unseasonable Youth: Modernism, Colonialism, and the Fiction of Development* (New York: Oxford University Press, 2013), p. 47.

like the bourgeois bildungsroman, Nexø's novel explicitly presents Pelle's socialist bildung as a process of humanization, disalienation and the reconciliation of the demands of the collective with the needs of the individual. This is what Pelle recognizes just as he is about to leave the Ark to move into a new apartment with his wife Ellen:

> Only now, when he had left the Ark, did he realize that there was something to which he was bidding farewell. It was the cordial community with all his kind, their radiant faith in him, and his own belief in his mission there . . . And could he justify himself for leaving them all in the lurch because of his own good fortune . . . Common cares had made him a man, and the struggle had given him a peculiar and effective strength. (578–9)

As Pelle discovers, it will be his mission to translate his solidarity with the inhabitants of the Ark into a broader and more principled commitment to socialism – a process that will involve a translation of his youthful spirit of revolt into an embrace of revolutionary internationalism. To be sure, this narrative movement is not identical with the bourgeois bildungsheld's conformist relinquishing of personal desires in favour of a pre-existing social community. Instead, it involves the future-oriented vision of a mutually sustaining relationship between self and community.

While Nexø's novel remains remarkably faithful to the overall structure of the bildungsroman, it departs from many of its bourgeois precursors in foregrounding the essentially collaborative and open-ended nature of the project of socialist bildung as well as its orientation towards wholesale social transformation. Throughout Volumes III and IV, *Pelle the Conqueror* stresses the constitutive *collective* dimension of socialist bildung, and it is not difficult to detect in this emphasis on collective bildung an echo of the structures of working-class solidarity that characterized Denmark's strong social democratic movement in the early 1900s. In particular, Pelle's formation proceeds dialectically through numerous conversations with his hot-headed radical alter ego Morten. Whereas Morten asserts the absolute priority of direct action and revolutionary violence ('Revolution is the voice of God, which administers right and justice, and it cannot be disputed', 524), Pelle finds himself defending an alternative set of socialist virtues:

> There was something in all this that did not satisfy him; it was in his nature to create, not to destroy. But if only the poor would, they could

> make society all over again – so Morten had one day said, and the words had never ceased to haunt Pelle's mind. But he could not endure the idea of violent revolution; and now he had found a good way out of his difficulty. He felt convinced that cohesion was irresistible, and that life would undergo a peaceful change. (543)

In *Pelle the Conqueror*, the eruptive mode of social change is associated firmly with the (relatively unchanging and flat) character of Morten. By contrast, the slow evolution of Pelle's 'creat[ive]' abilities is endowed with all the psychological plasticity and depth that the bildungsroman form affords.[21] It is easy to see why this should be the case: given the radical bildungsroman's basic generic parameters – its orientation towards a universalist category of the human; its residual teleological or evolutionary momentum; the foundational belief in the possibility of agential autonomy – the genre can seem paradoxically unaccommodating to the violent disruptions of revolutionary upheaval. As I argue in later chapters, many politically committed nineteenth- and twentieth-century authors sought to modify the bildungsroman's fundamental structure to render it capable of incorporating the experience of revolution – these recalibrations of the genre were intended to open up the bildungsroman to new historical experiences, including the experience of total insurrectionary disruption.[22]

At several points, Nexø's narrative registers the peculiar artistic difficulties that result from the postponement of revolutionary expectations. The case of the clockmaker Anker, who appears in Volume II of the novel, is especially interesting in this regard. The old Anker is associated with various nineteenth-century radicalisms – from Giuseppe Garibaldi's revolutionary nationalism to republican anti-royalism. In 1848, when he was swept up ('like a child', 273) in the enthusiasm that accompanied the dawn of the pan-European revolutions, Anker set himself the task of constructing a clock that would serve as the emblem of the imminent 'new age':

> Now, he said, the new time has begun, and in its honor he intended, in his insane rejoicing, to make an ingenious clock which should show the

21 It is only in *Ditte, Child of Man* and Nexø's later novels that Morten emerges as a rounded revolutionary protagonist in his own right.

22 In this respect, the formally experimental narrative structure of Chernyshevsky's *What Is to Be Done*? offers a clearer antecedent of the long and variegated history of the socialist bildungsroman in the twentieth century.

> moon and the date and the month and year. Being an excellent craftsman, he completed it successfully, but then it entered his head that the clock ought to show the weather as well. Like so many whom God had endowed with His gifts, he ventured too far and sought to rival God himself. (273)

The mechanism of Anker's clock mirrors the well-nigh cosmic ambitions he associates with revolutionary action. Unsurprisingly, given the sheer scale of social change imagined by Anker, he is increasingly worried that contemporary Europe might be incapable of giving birth to such all-encompassing newness: '[His] money he gave to the poor, and he lamented that the new time had not yet arrived' (273). The clock that Anker is in the process of building registers the hopes associated with revolutionary action as well as the difficulty of bringing about its professed telos, a socialist earthly home: 'Fortune disappears, and there are few that have their share of it,' Anker concludes: 'We need the new time very badly' (301). Anker's work becomes an obsession: 'So he sank even deeper into his madness, and however hard Jeppe scolded him and lectured him it did no good. Finally he went so far as to fancy that he was appointed to create the new time' (273). So extreme is his fascination with his 'infallible clock' that it appears no longer as a mere chronicler of revolutionary time but, bizarrely, as the very medium of internationalism's prophetic realization: this clock would not only 'show the time; it would *be* the time' (274, emphasis in original).

Anker's intense affective investment in the construction of the timepiece mirrors Nexø's own recrafting of the bildungsroman genre. Whereas the nineteenth-century bildungsroman tended to foreground what Mikhail Bakhtin calls '*national-historical time*' by allegorizing it in the figure of the bildungsheld, Nexø's novel turns its yearning attention to a wider geographical horizon and an as-yet-unrealized historical goal.[23] As I have suggested, the formal structure of the nineteenth-century bildungsroman was more suited to recording the painful process by which a protagonist adapts to the status quo. By contrast, Nexø wanted the genre to become the medium of new and future-oriented narratives of political becoming – an artistic means of picturing in great experiential depth modernity's movement towards socialism. It is one of

23 Mikhail Bakhtin, 'The Bildungsroman and Its Significance in the History of Realism (Toward a Historical Typology of the Novel)', in *Speech Genres and Other Late Essays* (Austin, TX: University of Texas Press, 1987), p. 52 (emphasis in original).

the foundational paradoxes of the radical bildungsroman that, despite the genre's orientation towards the socialist future, it also allows for a more sobering view of history as an accumulating sequence of missed opportunities. When Pelle asks Anker, 'how goes it with the new time?', Anker replies: 'Not at all well! . . . The pendulums that should keep the whole in motion are failing me . . . They ought to be made of perennial material, but this has got to be invented first' (274). In *Pelle the Conqueror*, as in the radical bildungsroman genre more generally, the socialist world revolution remains the inescapable and longed-for horizon of historical expectation, but instead of offering us the vision of a stable earthly home, the bildungsroman's left variant keeps reminding us of the ongoing travails of the political struggle.

New Men and New Women in Chernyshevsky's *What Is to Be Done?*

As with most of the novelistic protagonists I discuss in this book, Pelle's story depicts a bildung experience that is specific to a particular historical time and place. At the same time, however, this singular experience also doubles as an allegory of the hesitations and setbacks that beset the socialist struggle as such. The socialist recasting of bildung, as it emerges from *Pelle the Conqueror*, is rooted in an understanding that the protagonist's formation must remain incomplete absent socialism's full historical actualization. This explains why Nexø's novel does not feature a radiant New Man – the left equivalent of Pontoppidan's 'coming giant race' – but is populated instead with figures who express the characteristic untimeliness of radical action: crazed dreamers (such as Anker), struggling radicals (such as Pelle) and premature insurrectionists (such as Great Power and his son Morten). The presence of these untimely figures is an index of the artistic difficulties Nexø encountered in imagining radical bildung as a unilinear process: while the novel attempts to forge a connection between Pelle's biographical development as a bildungsheld and the socialist struggle for a better world, the novel is populated with characters who embody a sense of revolutionary time that is significantly more scrambled and complex.

My reading of Nexø's novel has indicated that it was possible for writers to redress the aporias of unfinished bildung by reimagining it as a collaborative and collective process. Nexø's socialist prose epics – from *Pelle the Conqueror* and *Ditte, Child of Man* (1921) to the unfinished trilogy *Morten the Red* (1945), *The Lost Generation* (1948) and

Jeanette (1957) – fall short of this aim to the extent that they imagine bildung (almost) exclusively as a male prerogative. This is true of *Pelle the Conqueror* (where Ellen is sometimes rendered as the sentimental embodiment of 'happiness itself', 650), but it applies most damagingly to Nexø's later novels: Ditte, the female protagonist of Nexø's sequel to *Pelle the Conqueror*, shares Pelle's desire to be part of Denmark's fledgling socialist movement, but she lacks Pelle's intellectual and organizational abilities. As a result, her interiority remains flat and ill-explored, lacking the complexity we find in Nexø's male protagonists – her defining character trait is a stereotypical 'selflessness'.[24] By contrast, the novel I turn to now, Chernyshevsky's *What Is to Be Done?*, offers a more searching exploration of non-hegemonic voices, including that of the book's female protagonist, Vera Pavlovna. Importantly, when *What Is to Be Done?* is compared to *Pelle the Conqueror*, Chernyshevsky's keen attention to marginalized social experiences, combined with his artistically adventurous recalibration of the bildungsroman's formal parameters, gives a much clearer indication of the remarkable generic flexibility that came to characterize the subsequent history of the radical bildungsroman. In Chernyshevsky's case, the experimental quality of the narrative is due in part to the vision of revolutionary change that underpins it. Whereas Pelle's political bildung reflects a recognizably Marxist understanding of historical movement (from rural economy to urban capitalism to communism), Chernyshevsky's view of radical transformation is animated by an interest in historical leaps and discontinuities. This alternative view of socio-political change made it possible for Chernyshevsky to imagine the Russian path to communism as proceeding directly from the rural (peasant) commune, without having to suffer through the intermediary stage of industrial capitalism.[25]

As I point out in later chapters, we can find echoes of this particular version of revolutionary development in the peasantry-centred fiction of Ngũgĩ wa Thiong'o and others. For now, it will suffice to observe that

24 Ditte, writes Nexø, 'did not understand what it was to spare herself': *Ditte, Daughter of Man* (New York: Henry Holt, 1921), p. 295. Like Ellen in *Pelle the Conqueror*, Ditte longs for the domesticity of a familial home – a yearning that puts her at odds with the more (socially, geographically) expansive socialism of Nexø's male protagonists. The portrayal of female characters is even more hostile in *Morten the Red*, *The Lost Generation* and *Jeanette* – Nexø's final and, at times, openly misogynistic novels from the 1940s.

25 See the Introduction for discussion of Marx's theoretical elaboration of this historical 'shortcut'.

Chernyshevsky's retooling of the bildungsroman occupies a space outside the stark binary opposition between formal experimentation and mimetic realism that has dominated so much academic discussion of *Weltliteratur*. In combining experimental ('modernist') and mimetic ('realist') commitments, *What Is to Be Done?* forces us to 'reconsider the lively fate of realism in the peripheries of the . . . literary world-system – and with it the possible transcendence of the realism/modernism antinomy'.[26] As the literary scholar Joe Cleary has pointed out, the Cold War – during which the Soviet Union 'took "ownership" of realism' and 'modernism was taken into custodianship by New York (with generous backing from Washington)' – produced a situation in which realism and experimentalism were seen as irreconcilable opposites, 'as reified categories and as the obvious termini of modern "world literature"'.[27] This reductive opposition between realism and formal experimentation still tends to be taken as axiomatic in many academic debates about world literature.[28] By contrast, the radical bildungsroman cannot be slotted neatly into either of these categories, as the genre tends to combine more familiarly mimetic (Nexø) and more artistically experimental (Chernyshevsky) impulses. The intertwining of both impulses in the

26 The phrase here is Jed Esty and Colleen Lye's. Esty and Lye find echoes of this particular stylistic blending in the politically non-aligned fictions of twentieth-century 'Third World writers' such as Ngũgĩ, whose position 'entailed an agnostic stance, with both modernist and realist forms usable for anticolonial expression'. See Esty/Lye, 'Peripheral Realisms Now', *Modern Language Quarterly* 73.3 (2012): 269–87 (269).

27 Joe Cleary, 'Realism after Modernism and the Literary World System,' *Modern Language Quarterly* 73.3 (2012): 255–68 (262–3).

28 Extending Cleary's perspective, we can now see that the view that pits a formally innovative but largely inward-looking modernism against an artistically retrograde but socially active realism is also implicitly affirmed in publications such as *Aesthetics and Politics* (ed. Fredric Jameson [London: New Left Books, 1977], the landmark anthology that brought together key contributions to the realism-modernism debate of the 1930s. *Aesthetics and Politics* has been the go-to book on the topic for several generations of literary scholars, but it has narrowed our understanding of the formal richness of what counts as *realism* in these interwar debates. The book's running heads imply that interwar conversations about aesthetics were characterized by antagonistic theoretical positions: 'Bloch against Lukács' is followed by 'Lukács against Bloch', before Bertolt Brecht's essay (the third piece in the collection) happily sublates the realist's social ambition into a formally innovative experimentalism. The volume introduces Brecht's essay to move a stalled theoretical debate forward: in contrast to Bloch's and Lukács's contributions, Brecht's text is followed by a series of sympathetic elaborations (Benjamin's 'Conversations with Brecht', Adorno's 'Letters to Walter Benjamin', Benjamin's 'Reply to Adorno' and so on). A form of Western modernist experimentalism thus wins out over (Soviet-style) realism, enshrining a theoretical position that dramatically underestimates the aesthetic complexities of the literary map I recover in this book.

radical bildungsroman constitutes its essential aesthetic structure, its artistic double helix.

To the extent that *What Is to Be Done?* is still read outside the field of Slavic studies, this is due to the outsized influence the novel exerted on the history of Russian political radicalism (the title of Lenin's famous 1902 pamphlet 'What Is to Be Done?' is a direct allusion to Chernyshevsky's novel). Chernyshevsky had written *What Is to Be Done?* while imprisoned by the tsarist authorities, and the book became instrumental in shaping the materialist outlook and radical praxis of several generations of revolutionaries, including Peter Kropotkin as well as Lenin, Alexandra Kollontai and other Bolsheviks. There is a real sense that, in terms of its sheer cultural and political reach, *What Is to Be Done?* acted as a model for many subsequent radical bildungsromane – even though later writers would discover that it was nearly impossible to replicate the success of Chernyshevsky's novel as an exemplar of activist and didactic writing. Central to the book's political agenda is the figure of Rakhmetov – one of the prototypes for the ubiquitous literary figure of the Great New Man of the Soviet revolutionary era.[29] As Chernyshevsky's narrator notes admiringly at one point, Rakhmetov belongs to a new race of 'good, strong, capable people [that] have just begun to appear among us'.[30] Puzzlingly, however, Rakhmetov only makes brief appearances throughout the text and his interactions with other characters are so perfunctory as to intensify the mystery around him. While many accounts of *What Is to Be Done?* single out Rakhmetov as the novel's most important contribution to literary and political history, reading the book as a radical bildungsroman requires us to centre another character, Vera Pavlovna. In contrast to the essentially static figure of Rakhmetov, Vera undergoes a process of bildung that leads her to break out of the stultifying encrustations of her first bourgeois socialization.

When Chernyshevsky's novel is read in this way, the oddly marginalized figure of Rakhmetov can be seen as a fossilized relic of the novel's artistic genesis. *What Is to Be Done?* was conceived partly as a response to *Fathers and Sons*, Ivan Turgenev's celebrated novelistic chronicle of the divisions that were opening up between older Russians and the new generation of young radicals. Chernyshevsky felt that, in the figure of the nihilist medical student Yevgeny Bazarov, Turgenev had offered 'a

29 Clark, *The Soviet Novel*, p. 49.

30 Nikolay Chernyshevsky, *What Is to Be Done?* (Ithaca, NY: Cornell University Press, 1989), p. 49. Subsequent references are given parenthetically.

dastardly caricature' of the revolutionary movement as it existed in Russia at the time.[31] In response, Chernyshevsky borrowed and reframed key aspects of Turgenev's novel, using names from *Fathers and Sons* and making several of his key protagonists medical doctors.[32] Most importantly, Chernyshevsky decided to draw a revolutionary figure (Rakhmetov) whose radicalism would match Bazarov's. Chernyshevksy recognized that Bazarov embodied a new intellectual type – materialist, utilitarian and atheistic, with an arresting knack for acerbic one-liners ('A good chemist's twenty times more useful than a poet'[33]). However, Turgenev had presented this figure with a good deal of irony, and Bazarov's death from blood poisoning (he accidentally cuts himself during an autopsy) has often been read as Turgenev's rejection of Bazarov's materialist worldview.

Chernyshevsky reinvents Turgenev's Bazarov as a prophetic revolutionary – an artistic decision that testifies to Chernyshevsky's dissatisfaction with political liberals such as Turgenev, who advocated slow and piecemeal reform as a way of addressing some of Russia's persistent societal ills, including the socio-economic institution of serfdom. In the early 1860s, Chernyshevsky and other members of the intelligentsia concluded that the social reforms proposed by Tsar Alexander's autocratic regime had failed to bring about substantial change in this sphere. In this context, Chernyshevsky's New Man allegorizes the idea of an absolute revolutionary break that Russian radicals increasingly held to be unavoidable. Crucially, however, the radical newness of Rakhmetov – his status as a proto-revolutionary icon – also means that he is incapable of experiencing socialist bildung as a process that unfolds in fits and starts across time. It is precisely because Rakhmetov embodies an achieved revolutionary bildung that he occupies a more marginal position in the narrative compared to Turgenev's Bazarov. By the same token, it is other characters in the novel – including some of Rakhmetov's acquaintances – who undergo a transformational process that guides them away from their first bourgeois bildung and towards what we might call a *second* or *reparative* bildung.[34] The figure of Vera is key to this politico-narrative project. Even

31 Michael R. Katz and William G. Wagner, 'Chernyshevsky, *What Is to Be Done?*, and the Russian Intelligentsia', in *What Is to Be Done?*, pp. 1–36 (26–7).

32 Katz/Wagner, 'Chernyshevsky', p. 27.

33 Ivan Turgenev, *Fathers and Sons* (Oxford: Oxford World's Classics, 2008), p. 26.

34 In a related vein, the bildung of several characters in Turgenev's *Fathers and Sons* is kickstarted when they encounter Bazarov: Nikolay, Turgenev writes, met Bazarov 'every day, as he put it, to "learn something"' (143).

more programmatically than *Pelle the Conqueror*, her story prefigures key aspects of the tradition of the socialist bildungsroman that I will explore in the rest of this book: first, the process of Vera's political formation entails a profoundly disorientating reparative bildung; second, her narrative reframes bildung as a collaborative and collective rather than a narrowly individual process; and finally, the resistance of Vera's narrative to preformulated teleological narratives – Vera's hesitation and confusion as she learns to struggle against the combined hegemonic forces of patriarchy and tsarist autocracy – is encoded in a set of formally experimental narrative procedures.

The course of Vera's formation involves the remaking of her self – it is a self-determined bildung that differs from the more familiar patriarchal 'deformation' or 'unbecoming' (in Susan Fraiman's useful terminology) suffered by heroines in many nineteenth-century novels.[35] When we first meet Vera, she is already chafing at the tyrannical regime of her parents, who intend to marry her off to a young and self-important military officer. Her scheming parents assert that it is a daughter's absolute duty 'to obey her mother' (57), and they cynically present their desire to control their daughter as a response to the moral corruption of the world around her. Speaking of the radical philosophical and ethical tracts that her daughter has been reading, Vera's mother asserts:

> Your books say that we're not supposed to live like this. Don't you think I know that, Verochka? But in those books of yours it says that in order not to live like this, everything has to be organized differently. [D]o you think I don't know anything about those new systems described in your books? I know they're good ones. Only you and I won't live to see them! People are really stupid – how can you set up a new system with the likes of them. (59)

In treating Vera's case simultaneously as unique (her life is presented in much realistic detail) and as typical (her life mirrors the more general patterns of the socialist struggle that are 'described in [her] books'), Chernyshevsky sets up Vera's story as a microcosm of the larger social changes that the novel explores. Vera herself begins to be convinced of

35 Susan Fraiman, *Unbecoming Women: British Women Writers and the Novel of Development* (New York: Columbia University Press, 1993), pp. x–xi. For a related argument about the gendering of the political bildungsroman, see John Kucich's 'Genre Fusion and the Origins of the Female Political Bildungsroman', *Novel* 54.2 (2021): 163–88.

the imminence of revolutionary change when she meets the medical student Dmitry Lopukhov, who is her brother's tutor. Vera and Dmitry soon begin to meet in private to discuss socialism and gender equality, and they also conspire to save her from the arranged marriage plotted by her parents. Finally, Vera and Dmitry decide to elope in order to live together in accordance with their political convictions – they draw up an elaborate system of rules that is designed to afford both independence and the greatest possible privacy. Dmitry articulates the couple's emancipatory aspirations in terms of a determined and practically minded orientation towards a set of higher ideals: 'Now, Verochka, these ideas are apparent in life . . . these ideas are now part of the air we breathe . . . What's strange in your wanting to be a free and happy person? That desire is neither a very puzzling discovery of science nor a great feat of heroism' (104).

The new and radical ideas that Verochka and Dmitry desire to put into practice include the economic emancipation of women as well as a more broadly conceived 'new system' of production and distribution. Crucially, these ideas are depicted not as a form of 'abstract idealism' – that is, as the obsession of self-centred dreamers like Pontoppidan's Per – but as politically attainable to those who know how to deliberate and strategize with others. Partly under the influence of Rakhmetov, who makes sporadic appearances in these sections of the narrative, Vera and Dmitry hatch ambitious plans to set up cooperative workshops for seamstresses: 'Many good, clever people have written books on the subject of how one should live on this earth so that all people may be happy. According to them, the most important thing is to organize workshops according to the new system' (191). Putting into action plans advanced by utopian socialists such as Louis Blanc and Charles Fourier, Dmitry and Vera envision a new organization of work that will be fully cooperative. This new management of work, they believe, will no longer be subject to the whims of factory owners: it will be able to 'function without them . . . even without supervision from someone outside the seamstresses' ranks, but entirely as a result of the ideas and skills of the seamstresses themselves. That was Vera Pavlovna's fondest dream' (199). The autonomous workshops that are planned and finally set in motion by Vera (with assistance from Dmitry) are intended to liberate workers from the tyrannical control of the capitalists. And, as Vera's own story helps us see, these workshops also serve to protect the female workers from (familial and extra-familial) patriarchal domination. In contrast to the entirely self-willed political 'rebirth' (282) performed by Rakhmetov, the purposeful interweaving of the languages of private and public emancipation in the story of Vera indicates Chernyshevsky's deeper commitment to a type of transformation that links personal bildung and collective change.

Chernyshevsky literalizes the reference to Vera's visionary 'fondest dream[s]' that appears in the passage just cited: at central moments in her political and personal development, a goddess appears to Vera as she lies asleep. This creature identifies herself as the allegorical figure of 'Love for Humanity' but is also referred to by other names, such as 'Sister of Her Sisters'. Embodying the ideals of sisterly solidarity as well as of socialist internationalism ('First she's English, then French; now she's German, then Polish; she becomes Russian, English again, then German, again Russian', 130), the goddess, at times, appears to possess Vera's own face and form: 'Even though her face keeps changing, she still has the same face' (130). As an allegorical figuration of the ethos of comradeship that sustains the workshops' material praxis of communal redistribution, 'Love of Humanity' comes to represent socialism as a fully actualized form of life.

Chernyshevsky's language marks out this dreamlike vision as both political *and* libidinal, as the embodiment of political hope as much as of an intensely psychic need: 'People still don't know what genuine merriment really is because neither the kind of life nor the sort of people necessary for it exists yet. Only people such as these can enjoy themselves completely and know the full ecstasy of pleasure' (378). What Chernyshevsky anticipates through the female figure of Love of Humanity is a liberatory breakdown of the borders of the self – an ecstatic moment of unmaking and remaking. Bildung here culminates in an overpoweringly orgasmic 'ecstasy of pleasure' rather than in the subdued calm and resigned closure attained by the (male) protagonists of the nineteenth-century bourgeois bildungsroman.[36] Central to this disruptive and disorientating process of radical bildung is what Maxim Gorky, in an essay from 1908, called the necessary 'disintegration of personality'.[37] We can adapt Gorky's formulations to make sense of these moments of reparative bildung in the radical novel of formation: from Chernyshevsky's novel onwards, authors of radical bildungsromane celebrate moments at which

36 In Chapter 4, I discuss an analogous movement in Doris Lessing's *The Golden Notebook*, where the possibility of a new socialist praxis of living is signalled by Anna's psychological breakdown.

37 Maxim Gorky, 'The Disintegration of Personality', in *Collected Works in Ten Volumes*, vol. 10: *On Literature* (Moscow: Progress Publishers, 1982), pp. 89–150.

'the steady process of man's spiritual impoverishment, the inexorable shrinking of the "I"', is undone.[38] To the extent that 'capitalist organizations must of necessity constrict personality [and] foster a passive mentality', the radical 'disintegration' of the old self 'breathe[s] new life and freshness into the "I"'.[39]

As in the case of Pelle's dreamlike 'fantasies', the realization of Vera's visions is threatened by the social inertia and political intransigence of the world around her. In the Introduction, I discussed Chernyshevsky's metaphorical rendering of the work of revolution as a progressive cultivation ('drainage') of the 'soil'. As I pointed out, Chernyshevsky's use of this agricultural metaphor in Vera's second dream suggested that a complete remaking of society is necessary before a new socialist self can emerge: 'Society itself must be re-educated' (254) before a genuinely new subjectivity can materialize. Agricultural labour figures repeatedly as the novel's key metaphor for revolutionary action, but towards the end of Vera's second dream, Chernyshevsky adds an important qualification: 'a proviso needs to be added to that discussion of the properties of soil . . . in Vera Pavlovna's second dream,' the narrator informs us: 'The proviso is that whatever the quality of the soil, one can still come across tiny plots capable of producing healthy ears of grain' (274). In contrast to the idea that social change must precede the emergence of a new kind of subjectivity, the narrator's 'proviso' suggests that the work of revolution commences, against all odds, with the 'tiny plot' of the individual self or a small assembly of selves. Only later will this dialectic of disintegration and remaking – the process of radical bildung – be translated into a larger social dynamic. *What Is to Be Done?* offers no clear-cut answer to the question of whether revolutionary change begins with the remaking of the self or with the reordering of the society that shapes that self. In resisting such one-sided answers, Chernyshevsky offers his own riff on the question Marx had raised in the third Thesis on Feuerbach: 'How shall the educator be educated?'[40] How, Marx and Chernyshevsky ask, is revolution possible if socialist bildung becomes attainable only after the revolution has been actualized?

38 Ibid., p. 105.

39 Ibid., p. 115.

40 Marx's third Thesis is of immense conceptual importance for the history of the radical bildungsroman. Chapter 2 will explore this connection in more detail.

'Work a Bit on Your Own Development': Chernyshevsky's Readers

Many of the radical bildungsromane I explore in this book home in on the profound sense of crisis that accompanies what Gorky calls the 'disintegration' of the protagonist's self. For example, the opening scene of Peter Weiss's *Leavetaking*, a key exponent of the genre, shows the protagonist standing by the coffin of his recently deceased father. As Weiss's narrator notes, the life of his family was a 'wholly failed attempt at living together'.[41] The father's death marks the 'final disintegration of the family' (12), and it also triggers a sense of existential disorientation: 'There was no home any longer. The journey into the unknown had begun . . . That "I" that I carried around with me was used up, destroyed, worthless, it had to perish' (58, 85). In a later chapter, I will have more to say about this sense of disorientation – about the precipitous and liberatory dissolution of the subject – as a constitutive feature of Weiss's novels and the left bildungsroman more generally. At this point in the discussion, it will suffice to say that Chernyshevsky's novel attempts to contain the purely negative movement of disintegration by imagining political bildung as a distributed and collaborative process in which individual and collective formation sustain one another. As in the case of Pelle, Vera's bildung is supported by a large cast of minor and major characters. These figures range from the radiant New Man Rakhmetov to Vera's love interest Dmitry. They also include the prostitute Julie, whose desire for economic independence acts both as an inspiration and as a warning to Vera. Like Vera, Julie was 'a dreamer' who desired to 'live on [her] own', albeit one tempted by and 'too accustomed to . . . luxury': 'Therefore I tried to please, and had to do things I didn't want to do' (75). Vera heeds Julie's advice to 'run away, my child, run away' (75) and to build a new life among like-minded radicals and activists. Indeed, as Vera soon discovers, 'nowadays such options are becoming more and more available: decent people have begun to meet one another' (88).

In the case of Vera, emancipatory schemes of mutual support include marriage, which is reimagined by Vera and Dmitry as an institutional space capable of enabling collective and individual flourishing. Dmitry proposes to Vera that '[e]ach of us will guard his own independence as much as he can from the other, no matter how much he loves the other, no matter how much he trusts the other' (144). The sewing workshops

41 Peter Weiss, Leavetaking *and* Vanishing Point (London: Calder and Boyars, 1966), p. 9.

that Vera and Dmitry set up are presented as an expansion of this same principle of collective freedom and collaboration: '[The] goal was the greatest possible equality in distribution of the fruits of labor for participants in the enterprise . . . The nature of the workshop, its spirit, and its order consisted in the unanimity of all . . . each participant was equally important' (193). The expansion of solidarity and cooperative achievement promises to create new and more egalitarian opportunities for future-directed socialist bildung: 'Vera Pavlovna really enjoys this free, open, and active life . . . But years pass, and as they do, life gets continually better if it goes on as it should and as it does now among a very few. Someday it will be like that for everyone' (202, 212).[42] This orientation towards an unrealized horizon of future possibility – a 'future [in which] all things are possible' (304) because bildung will be a democratically attainable good – is indicative of the left bildungsroman's teleological structure and fundamentally aspirational political impulse.

As I have noted, the experimental features of *What Is to Be Done?* set it apart from the more conventional form of *Pelle the Conqueror*, with its authorial narrator and linear narrative structure. These features include Chernyshevsky's use of multiple interwoven voices and storylines as well as his audacious mixing of stylistic registers that blend fantastic, visionary and realist elements. Whereas the sheer generic hybridity of Chernyshevsky's novel seems atypical when the book is held up against Goethe's *Lehrjahre* and certain other eighteenth- and nineteenth-century bildungsromane, it resonates more closely with the formal openness of the *Wanderjahre*.[43] Among the key features that break open the self-enclosed narrative world of *What Is to Be Done?* are Chernyshevsky's repeated and probing addresses to the reader. In an early passage from the Preface to his novel, Chernyshevsky challenges his readers in the following terms:

> Yes, the first pages of my story reveal that I have a very poor opinion of my public . . . You, the public, are kind, very kind indeed, and therefore undiscriminating and slow-witted. You can't be relied upon to know from the first few pages whether or not a book is worth reading. You have poor instincts that are in indeed of assistance . . . So I was obliged

42 In the novel, Vera is sometimes presented as a highly individualized bildungsheld, while at other points she strategically figures as an allegorical type capable of representing 'the dissatisfactions of thousands and millions of people' (337).

43 See the Introduction for discussion of Goethe's *Wanderjahre* as an experimental novel of formation.

> to bait my hook with striking scenes. Don't condemn me for it: you deserve all the blame. It's your own simpleminded naiveté that compelled me to stoop to such vulgarity. But now that you've fallen into my hands, I can continue the story as I see fit without further tricks . . . You're nasty out of intellectual impotence. Therefore, even though I am blaming you, I am also obliged to help you. (47–8)

Chernyshevsky's handling of narrative voice in *What Is to Be Done?* is significant for the light it sheds on the radical bildungsroman as a genre of left world literature. In an argument that bears directly on the present context, Franco Moretti has observed that the translation of (metropolitan) genres into new (peripheral) geographical contexts often involves the triangulation of several constituent elements: 'foreign *plot*; local *characters*; and then, local *narrative voice*'. As Moretti explains, it is 'precisely in this third dimension [of narrative voice] that these novels seem to be most unstable . . . Which makes sense: the narrator is the pole of comment, of explanation, of evaluation, and when foreign "formal patterns" . . . make characters behave in strange ways . . . then of course comment becomes uneasy.'[44] The case of *What Is to Be Done?* indicates that the situation is different in the case of the left bildungsroman. The flexible narrative voice that characterizes the genre as a whole – and that frequently oscillates within a single text from the ironic, cajoling and exhortative to the analytic, allegorical and hagiographic – is not merely symptomatic of problems that arise in the genre's geographical transmission from some primary 'metropolitan' context to a more 'peripheral' one. Instead, these modulations of narrative voice help to ground the political commitments of the genre itself: they are integral to the radical bildungsroman's persistent concern to find the right rhetorical register through which to intervene in the reader's world beyond the text.[45]

The arsenal of rhetorical 'baits' and ruses referred to by Chernyshevsky

44 Franco Moretti, 'Conjectures on World Literature', *New Left Review*, January/February 2000: 54–68 (65).

45 By the same token, the central difference between Goethe's *Lehrjahre* (the novel whose teleological form is echoed by Nexø's *Pelle the Conqueror*) and the *Wanderjahre* (the novel more evocative of the experimental qualities of *What Is to Be Done?*) resides not only in the latter work's formal openness but also in the remarkable shifts in narrative voice that Goethe's last novel performs. Goethe's *Wanderjahre* replaces the authorial narrator of the *Lehrjahre* with a fictive editor (*Redakteur*) who keeps intervening in the narrative, assembling it from a range of archives that comprise narratives, reports, diaries, letters, speeches and aphorisms.

prominently includes the literary pyrotechnics of the sensation novel. *What Is to Be Done?* begins, incongruously, with an unresolved suicide, as though this book were a suspense novel rather than a call to revolutionary action. While this opportunistic foray into the low- or middle-brow seems to confirm the narrator's flaunted condescension towards the novel's readership, it also serves another purpose – to initiate the reader's own radical bildung. This bildung, which proceeds in lockstep with Vera's, takes as its point of departure the reader's underdeveloped revolutionary consciousness: 'even though I am blaming you,' the narrator observes in the passage just cited, 'I am also obliged to help you' (48). Indeed, the authorial voice intervenes most conspicuously in the narrative whenever the novel threatens to veer from generic predictability, as though to ensure that the reader will grasp the text's revolutionary implications. When Rakhmetov is introduced, we are told:

> Yes, he was an extraordinary man, a specimen of a very rare breed. I haven't described a specimen of this breed in such detail merely in order to instruct you, O perspicacious reader, in the appropriate way (unknown to you) to treat such people . . . Your eyes, O perspicacious reader, aren't constituted so that you can perceive such types. They're invisible to you. (292)

The spectacular abuse that the narrator heaps on the novel's readers should not distract from the fact that Chernyshevsky intends to nurture his readers' radical bildung. Readers are progressively brought to question their social conformism. As in the case of Vera, it is this slow process of unlearning on the part of the reader – the slow growth of a second (socialist) bildung, rather than the attainment of a fully realized revolutionary consciousness – that forms the novel's principal political objective:

> 'Well,' thinks the perspicacious reader, 'from now on the main character of this novel will be Rakhmetov. He'll outshine all the others . . .'
>
> Nothing of the kind will happen, my perspicacious reader! . . . He'll play neither a principal role nor a secondary one, nor any role at all in the rest of the novel. But why then was he introduced and described in such detail? Well, my perspicacious reader, wouldn't you like to guess the reason? (293)

The narrator taunts the reader for another twenty-odd pages ('You can have as much time as you need . . . pause over it and reflect as to whether you will or won't be able to guess the answer', 294) while Vera and Rakhmetov engage in a conversation about the paramount importance of individual freedom and socialist solidarity. Finally, however, the reader is 'spoon-fed' (310) the answer. The 'idealized figure' of Rakhmetov, we are told, has been introduced as a courtesy to the novel's readers. It is meant to render legible the novel's utopian anticipations because the reader's ability to 'perceive such types' is too constrained by the imperfections of the present ('it's not they who stand too high, but you who stand too low', 313). To put this another way: Rakhmetov matters to the novel because his ideal perfection introduces a utopian strain that is unassimilable into the novel's broadly realist narrative, thereby helping to initiate a process of counter-hegemonic (socialist) bildung on the part of the 'perspicacious reader' him- or herself. 'You can become an equal to the people described here,' we are instructed, 'if only you wish to work a bit on your own development . . . It's not so difficult. Come out into the light of day, where life is good . . . Try it: development, development' (313). The Russian term Chernyshevsky deploys here (*развитие*) suggests a spontaneous and sometimes unregulated development of the self that encompasses false starts and dead ends. By contrast, the term that is now often used to refer to bildung in Russian, *воспитание*, is closer to upbringing or *Erziehung*, that is, the type of education a parent might provide to their child – a set of habits, behaviours, manners instilled from without.[46] This terminological distinction is intended as a reminder that Chernyshevsky's novel presents bildung as an uneven and halting diachronic *process* rather than as the stable and ostensibly 'finished' *result* of that process.

The narrator's interventions indicate that Chernyshevsky imagines the reader's bildung as a collaborative process that does not follow a fixed or preordained pattern. In these respects, the allegorical figure 'Love of Humanity' is the presiding spirit not just of Vera's bildung but also of the reader's. After all, 'Love' – in Chernyshevsky's strategically broad understanding – simply 'consists of promoting someone else's development and of developing oneself' (357).[47] In Chernyshevsky's view, the growth of his

46 *Воспитание* had become the accepted term for bildung by the time Bakhtin wrote 'The Bildungsroman and Its Significance in the History of Realism' – the book fragment that famously commented on the genre's structural alignment of individual bildung and national development.

47 Anne Eakin Moss notes in a related vein that 'the development of the narrator's trust in the reader . . . is modelled earlier in the novel by the female characters' implicit

readers' world-making 'active powers' (357) is at the heart of the political mission of *What Is to Be Done*?: 'Observe, reflect, read those books that tell you about the pure enjoyment of life, and about the fact that man can be kind and happy' (313). In the next three chapters, I develop the idea that the radical bildungsroman – a genre that is included in Chernyshevsky's generically expansive category of activist literature ('those books') – is defined by the same kind of aspiration to be politically active, even after the space for large-scale revolutionary change began to diminish over the course of the twentieth century. In exploring the left bildungsroman's rich artistic mediations of political commitment, the following chapters will also flesh out further the genre's complex handling of narrative voice – the rhetorical coexistence of painstaking analysis and trenchant ideological critique; of coaxing solicitation and strategic impartiality; of insurrectionary spontaneity and probing (self-)consciousness. The different styles and formal repertoires deployed in *Pelle the Conqueror* and *What Is to Be Done?* have begun to indicate the breadth and capaciousness of the genre. The next chapter will place even more emphasis on the artistic richness and historical variability of the radical bildungsroman. We should not be surprised if this richness occasionally resists the structural unity and diachronic continuity implied by the term *genre*: the radical bildungsroman, I suggest, names not so much a transhistorically cohesive set of artistic forms (that is, a fixed 'genre') but an aesthetic mode of thinking about (and of correlating) individual formation, the collective nature of the political struggle and the vision of a juster world.

mutual understanding [and] the inspiration that comes from Vera's dream-goddess'. See Anne Eakin Moss, *Only Among Women: Philosophies of Community in the Russian and Soviet Imagination, 1860–1940* (Evanston, IL: Northwestern University Press, 2020), p. 31.

2

Educating the Educator: The Radical Bildungsroman and the Problem of Second Bildung

The preceding chapter homed in on two novels – Nexø's *Pelle the Conqueror* and Chernyshevsky's *What Is to Be Done?* – that illustrate the socialist reinvention of the bildungsroman at modernity's geographical periphery. In their distinct ways, these two novels indicate that left authors undertook a repurposing of the bildungsroman that was intended to render the genre hospitable to various forms of socialist commitment. The present chapter shifts attention from the more narrowly literary-historical question of generic remaking to an exploration of the particular techniques and processes of unlearning that support the bildung of the radical bildungsroman's protagonists. I have already begun to suggest that the term *second bildung* usefully captures the double movement comprised by this process: on the one hand, second (or revisionary) bildung involves a trenchant critique of the hardened hegemonic structures of life that characterize capitalist society; on the other, it entails the precariously emerging vision of a new postcapitalist order. This process of second bildung is hardly ever linear or continuous. Instead of drawing political reassurance from a set of pre-existing ideological convictions, many novels in the genre foreground the confusions, hesitations and uncertain hopes that characterize the socialist struggle for a new world order.

To think of the socialist struggle as involving a form of bildung is to think of it in broadly anthropological terms as a fight for the satisfaction of human needs and the realization of human potentialities. This view of the struggle is expressed in the novels I have discussed so far. It also finds articulation in the third of Karl Marx's 'Theses on Feuerbach' (1845):

> The materialist doctrine concerning the changing of circumstances and upbringing forgets that circumstances are changed by men and that it is essential to educate [*erziehen*] the educator [*Erzieher*] himself. This doctrine must, therefore, divide society into two parts, one of which is superior to society.
>
> The coincidence of the changing of circumstances and of human activity or self-changing can be conceived and rationally understood only as *revolutionary practice.*[1]

This passage strikingly suggests that the question of 'education' is intimately linked to that of '*revolutionary practice*' itself.[2] What connects the two, Marx notes, is their ability to effect the simultaneous remaking of self and world – a short-circuiting that momentarily reconciles the two extremes of vulgar materialism (with its belief that changing material circumstances will also automatically 'change men') and what could be called 'vulgar idealism' (with its view of revolution as the spontaneous self-expression of essentially autonomous individuals). But Marx's passage also raises the related question of revolutionary leadership that would continue to remain central to many prominent revolutionary (Marxist, Blanquist, Leninist) traditions: the educator's own political *Erziehung*, Marx points out, cannot be purely spontaneous but requires some model capable of providing it with political guidance. We can think of this foundational dilemma as Marxism's equivalent of the chicken-and-egg problem: what comes first, *Erzieher* or *Erziehung*? Chernyshevsky had hoped to resolve this dilemma by presenting his readers with the figure of Rakhmetov – a character whose bildung seems to have magically materialized *ex nihilo* in the absence of any role models. In a related vein, Nexø's depiction of Pelle's formation was intended to defuse the problem raised by Marx's third Thesis by presenting bildung as a collaborative and shared project. In this context, Marx's passage is best read as an early attempt to keep open the very question that socialist bildungsromane work so hard to resolve: instead of settling the question of radical bildung, Marx's phrasing – How does radical

1 Karl Marx, 'Theses on Feuerbach', marxists.org, accessed 18 November 2022 (emphasis in original).

2 Marx's own thinking on the topic of revolutionary subjectivity is famously fragmentary and (many critics have argued) beset by inconsistencies. For two useful synoptic accounts, see Guido Starosta, *Marx's* Capital, *Method, and Revolutionary Subjectivity* (Leiden: Brill, 2015); Paul Elias, *Revolutionary Subjectivity in the Thought of Karl Marx: Exploring the Psychosocial Dynamic of Emancipation* (Leiden: Brill, 2025).

bildung proceed in the absence of a fixed or authoritative model? What would it mean to 'educate the educator'? – creates a vertigo of anti-foundational bildung that cannot fall back on either historically established patterns of individual formation or on the imputed authority of a fully constituted collective historical subject (the revolutionary proletariat). To the extent that the literary works explored in this chapter remain committed to a universalist political project, they imagine it not through the fetishized figure of the (heroic, male, white, proletarian) bildungsheld but as the outcome of a series of complex and often fraught coalitions. As Judith Butler, Ernesto Laclau and Slavoj Žižek remind us, this type of 'universality . . . is not a static presumption' but rather 'a process or condition' irreducible to any single fixed identity.[3]

The problematic formulated in Marx's third Thesis is essential to the history of the radical bildungsroman. The novels I consider in this chapter are more willing than either *What Is to Be Done?* or *Pelle the Conqueror* to reckon with the force of Marx's injunction: they confront the perplexing whirl of political identifications and interrupted teleologies that take the place of the achieved and static bildung embodied in characters such as Rakhmetov. In doing so, these novels offer unsparing depictions of the difficulties that accompany the project of revolutionary (self-)emancipation.[4] The Argentine sociologist Guido Starosta explains that the process of building a revolutionary self cannot be 'a matter of recovering a pure subjectivity [currently] oppressed by private property'. Instead, this process must reckon with the lingering presence and force of the elements that made up the subject's first bildung: 'the alienated existence of human subjectivity,' Starosta observes, 'must play a determinate role in its development'.[5] In the texts I explore in this chapter, the project of radical bildung often comes to resemble a type of autodidactic learning, or unauthorized self-making, that must proceed in the absence of external teleological certainties. As the British historian E. P. Thompson

3 Judith Butler, Ernesto Laclau and Slavoj Žižek, *Contingency, Hegemony, Universality: Contemporary Dialogues on the Left* (London: Verso, 2000), p. 3.

4 Taking his cue from Marx's third Thesis, Michael Löwy observes that this problematic remained central to Marx's thinking, as it did to the radical bildungsroman: 'The theory of revolutionary self-emancipation by the proletariat was not a "youthful episode", a transitory moment, abandoned by the "mature" Marx. It remained, for the entire period between 1848 and his death, one of the fundamental assumptions of his political activity.' See Löwy, *The Theory of Revolution in the Young Marx* (Leiden: Brill, 2002), p. 149.

5 Guido Starosta, *Marx's* Capital, *Method, and Revolutionary Subjectivity*, pp. 34–5.

noted in a now-famous articulation of this idea: 'The working class did not rise like the sun at an appointed time. It was present at its own making.'[6] Because the radical bildungsroman presents the socialist struggle '*from the inside*', or phenomenologically, the genre is particularly well suited to capture this key aspect of the formation of revolutionary consciousness.[7] 'You have to learn from your own experiences', discovers the first-person narrator of Maxim Gorky's three-volume *Autobiography* (*My Childhood*, *My Apprenticeship*, *My Universities*, 1913–23): 'Nobody's taught us anything, we've had to learn it all ourselves.'[8] Gorky's comment echoes a key insight of Nexø's socialist epic *Pelle the Conqueror*: in the absence of fixed role models, all revolutionary knowledge must be 'learned by experience', through what Marx's third Thesis had dubbed '*revolutionary practice*'.[9]

The radical bildungsroman's attention to the halting process of second-order bildung – to the corrective revision of an earlier mis-bildung – makes it possible to identify a sizable subset of texts that would otherwise be hard to define as paradigmatic bildungsromane. Characters that call for our attention (and that will be discussed in this chapter) range from Maxim Gorky's ageing female protagonist in *Mother*, Fyodor Gladkov's Soviet citizen Gleb in *Cement* and Jean-Paul Sartre's dissatisfied bourgeois anti-hero Mathieu in *The Roads to Freedom*, to the autobiographical narrators of Richard Wright's *Black Boy*, Peter Weiss's *Leavetaking*, Nâzım Hikmet's *Life's Good, Brother* (1963) and Karin Struck's *Klassenliebe*. With the sole exception of *Mother*, all these texts hail from the decades after the October Revolution, and they respond to a keen sense of historical disappointment as further revolutions failed to materialize in Western Europe. In a gesture that is characteristic of the twentieth-century radical bildungsroman more generally, these later works prioritize the task of retrospective sense-making over that of political intervention: bracketing action in favour of the painstaking work of historical understanding, they do not neatly fit into the category of overtly activist or didactic art, what Gregory Sholette has dubbed the 'fragmented and boisterous reservoir of past

6 E. P. Thompson, *The Making of the English Working Class* (New York: Vintage, 1966), p. 9.

7 Georg Lukács, 'Critical Realism and Socialist Realism', in *The Meaning of Contemporary Realism* (London: Mellon, 1963), pp. 93–135 (93).

8 Maxim Gorky, *My Childhood* (Harmondsworth: Penguin Books, 1966), p. 204.

9 Martin Nexø, *Pelle the Conqueror* (New York: Mondial, 2006), p. 40. For a suggestive reading of Gorky's memoirs and Pelle's fictions as developmental narratives, see Sergei Treyakov, 'Comrade Martin', *International Literature* 6 (1934): 117–22.

interventions'.[10] It should come as no surprise that most of the texts I have selected for discussion in this chapter (again with the possible exception of Gorky's *Mother*) present the attainment of bildung not as a singular moment of revolutionary epiphany or political conversion but, instead, as a drawn-out process that involves the unmaking and remaking of the protagonist's self.

'Truth is Complex': Gorky's *Mother*, Gladkov's *Cement* and Post-Revolutionary Bildung

Gorky was the towering literary figure of the fledgling revolutionary movement in Russia in the early twentieth century. His novel *Mother* gives expression to his long-standing support for the working-class movement as well as his growing (though not entirely untroubled) political sympathies for Bolshevism. The book tells the story of Pelageya Nilovna Vlasova, a working-class woman whose twenty-something son becomes involved – at first without her knowledge – in subversive revolutionary activities. In front of her eyes, Pavel begins to transform himself into a Rakhmetovian New Man by leaving behind the alcoholism he had inherited from his father and embracing a new and proto-revolutionary vitality and vigour.[11] The deeply religious Nilovna, who is illiterate and has never learned to take an interest in political matters, is at first wary of Pavel's new circle of friends. However, when Pavel is arrested by the police, she takes over from her son the responsibility of distributing revolutionary propaganda. And, what is more, after learning about the movement's aims, Nilovna becomes convinced of socialism's fundamental political and social correctness: thoughts and prayers alone, she discovers, will not change the world. Nilovna soon overcomes her old belief in theocratic authority, and when her son is arrested for the second time, she is ready to lead a socialist demonstration by carrying the red flag.[12]

10 Gregory Sholette, *The Art of Activism and the Activism of Art* (London: Lund Humphries, 2022), p. 18.

11 Gorky's *Autobiography* records the influence which his early exposure to Chernyshevsky's *What Is to Be Done?* had on him: see Gorky, *My Universities* (Harmondsworth: Penguin, 1979), p. 104. Pavel's new political articulacy (he becomes an accomplished orator) is also symbolically linked to his ability to cure himself of a speech impediment which he seems to have picked up from his father.

12 Vsevolod Pudovkin's 1926 film adaptation of *Mother* ends with this rousing scene. By contrast, Gorky's novel closes more ambivalently and pessimistically with Nilovna's arrest at the hands of the tsarist regime.

Written partly in response to the failure of the 1905 revolution in Russia, *Mother* was Gorky's literary attempt to lift the spirits of his fellow revolutionaries after their harrowing defeat. And, in some ways, the novel offers the clearest articulation of the basic structure of the radical bildungsroman one could hope for: Gorky's book begins by showing that the attainability of first bildung is entirely dependent on class and economic status (Pavel's parents cannot afford to send him to school and, like his father, he very nearly succumbs to alcoholism); and the novel then proceeds to attribute supreme importance and political urgency to the attainment of a second (socialist) bildung. In presenting the ageing Nilovna as the protagonist of this second bildung, Gorky highlights for his readers the generic anomalousness of his novel, which refuses to limit the prerogative of (emotional, social, political) bildung to youth: 'She is probably the first mother who has followed in the footsteps of her son – the first.'[13] Pavel himself flags for us the importance of second bildung: 'When a person's grown to the age of forty and has fought so long with the bears in his heart, it's hard to make him over,' one character claims, to which Pavel retorts with a rhetorical question: 'Do you think it's impossible for enlightenment to destroy all the rubbish that's been crammed into a man's brains?' (132). Nilovna's story proves Pavel right. Her second bildung proceeds apace and it culminates with her recognition of the internationalist dimension of the revolutionary struggle: Pavel and his comrades, Nilovna concludes, embody 'the endless war for freedom and equality, [which] became more vivid and assumed a greater holiness . . . they became united with the world' (237).

Gorky's handling of the form of the bildungsroman is remarkable in several respects. Most importantly, Nilovna's second bildung proceeds so swiftly that the narrative comes to resemble a conversion story. This is a strategic artistic choice that enables Gorky to direct the reader's attention away from the hesitations and self-doubts that accompany the laborious process of socialist bildung in many other exponents of the genre.[14] By the same token, the novel privileges a language of abrupt revolutionary change that pits socialism – 'the victory of [its] truth' – against the demeaning conditions of life in tsarist Russia: 'We shall be victorious, because we are with the working people,' proclaims Pavel's friend Sofya: 'Our power to work, our faith in the victory of truth we

13 Maxim Gorky, *Mother* (Secaucus, NJ: Citadel Press, 1975), p. 231. Subsequent references will be given parenthetically.

14 These texts include Gorky's own voluminous memoirs which narrate his circuitous and painful path towards political 'regeneration'. See *My Childhood*, p. 217.

obtain from you, from the people' (221). When Pavel's revolutionary cell is crushed by the authorities and he is hustled into a police wagon, his friend Rybin calls out to the bystanders: 'Search for the truth. Guard it! . . . Don't spare yourself in the name of truth!' (298). *Mother* registers the disappointment of the failed revolution of 1905, but the novel also deploys – with remarkable success – the radiant iconography of the New Man (and New Woman) as a means of containing and transcending this sense of historical crisis. Gorky's novel forms an instructive contrast with the other texts explored in this chapter as it avoids the altogether more precarious trajectories of political becoming that are mapped out in later socialist bildungsromane. In *Mother*, the realization of radical bildung is presented as an event rather than a process – it is a matter of acceding to an absolute and transhistorical 'truth'.

For a clearer novelistic statement of the stops and starts that threaten to defer or sidetrack the process of socialist bildung, we can turn to Gladkov's *Cement*. Following his participation in the revolution of 1905, Gladkov had been exiled from Tbilisi to the remote Irkutsk Oblast. He returned in 1918 with the aim of contributing to the building of postrevolutionary Russia. The problem of revolutionary *Erziehung* was very much on Gladkov's mind in this period: he became involved in the work of reorganizing schools in the port city of Novorossiysk before being appointed the city's head of education in the early 1920s. Gladkov wrote *Cement* a few years after the revolution of 1917, but the novel hardly presents the October Revolution as an unqualified success or as an absolute historical turning point. Instead, *Cement* keenly registers that the events of 1917 failed either to set off a tidal wave of global revolutions or to freeze socialist bildung into a fixed or replicable pattern. Set shortly after the Russian Civil War (1917–22), Gladkov's novel describes the difficulties that are encountered by the revolutionary hero Gleb Chumalov as he returns to his hometown and tries to settle back into ordinary life. Gleb discovers that the revolution has brought about fundamental changes at the level of everyday life: eager to see his family after many years of absence, he is coolly received as 'Comrade' by his wife Dasha, who rushes off to a two-day meeting of the party's Women's Section shortly after informing Gleb that he must report to the Factory Committee to register for his food ration. Adjusting to this new postrevolutionary environment is painful for Gleb, but he finds new purpose when he begins to join in the difficult task of rebuilding the town's dilapidated cement factory. In the process, Gleb experiences what the novel presents as a form of second bildung: revising his earlier view of revolution as a sequence of violent upheavals, he arrives at a more adequate understanding of revolution as the laborious transformation of an entire way of life.[15]

Gleb's development from revolutionary romantic to conscious Soviet citizen shifts attention from the insurrectionary temporality that had governed the narrative of *Mother* – a temporality centred around singular events – to the painful psychological struggles of individuals who are caught up in the slow transition to a communist society. In performing this crucial shift, Gladkov's narrative helped to establish what Katerina Clark has called the 'master plot of the Soviet novel': offering a (Lukácsian) view of the socialist struggle '*from the inside*', this master plot shows that 'historical progress occurs not by resolving class conflict but through the working-out of the so-called spontaneity/consciousness dialectic'.[16] Revolutionary 'spontaneity', Clark explains, signifies 'actions that are not guided' but 'sporadic [and] uncoordinated', whereas conscious actions are 'controlled, disciplined, and guided by politically aware bodies'.[17] The tension between these two modes of social transformation – one evental, the other unfolding slowly – helps to explain why Gleb so keenly feels the conflict between his romantic belief in insurrectionary action and the careful, cautious and deliberate changes in everyday life that must be accomplished in the wake of the inaugural revolutionary event. As Clark notes, Soviet novels of the post-revolutionary era narrate '[t]he great historical drama of struggle between the forces of spontaneity and the forces of consciousness' by focusing on 'the way one individual mastered his wilful self, became disciplined, and attained to an extrapersonal identity'. In this way, they give rise to plots that 'might in effect be seen as a politicized variant of the bildungsroman, in which the hero achieves greater harmony both within himself and in relation to society'.[18]

There are good reasons to read *Cement* as a quintessential socialist realist novel in this sense. Following Gladkov's temporary falling out with the notoriously doctrinaire Russian Association of Proletarian Writers (RAPP) in the early 1920s, the novel successfully managed to

15 Dasha variously confronts Gleb about his outdated belief in revolutionary upheavals: 'How foolish you are, Gleb . . . so strong, but so foolish' (32; also 128, 157).

16 Katerina Clark, *The Soviet Novel: History as Ritual* (Bloomington: Indiana University Press, 2000), p. 15.

17 Ibid., p. 15.

18 Ibid., pp. 16–17.

ingratiate Gladkov with the new regime. Crucially, however, in *Cement* the historical revolution that has brought about this new society – the total sublation of individual interests in a collective revolutionary elan – is relegated to the book's backstory rather than presented directly. Gladkov implies that the revolution, owing to its unprecedented break with history, resists narrativization under hegemonic narrative protocols. The novel, instead, focuses on the immediate post-revolutionary period to show an individual's slow adjustment to the newly emerging social order – a plot that recalls the bildungsroman's 'narrative of individual socialization' insofar as it brings about 'strengthen[ing of] one's *sense of belonging* to a wider community'.[19] This formal choice on Gladkov's part is significant because it highlights the difficulty of imposing a static, non-developmental pattern on the narrative: Gleb's identity as a hero of the October Revolution fails to translate into the new conditions of post-revolutionary Russia. The non-congruence of Gleb's two identities – as revolutionary hero and Soviet citizen – begins to create disturbances at the level of the narrative. Gleb's recognition of the historical challenges of the post-revolutionary decade initiates a dynamic process of bildung that subjects his earlier developmental 'spontaneity' to a slow process of maturation. By maintaining the bildungsroman's narrative form in working order, *Cement* thus reclaims the idea of personal maturation for the socialist novel – as if to suggest that, in the wake of the revolution, the ideal of individual bildung can be resumed at a point higher up in the historical spiral.

As Gleb learns to 'discipline' himself, becoming a fully 'conscious' citizen in the process, he discovers that he will need to let Dasha go her separate way: the old Dasha 'was dead. This was another woman, with a sunburnt weathered face and stubborn, opinionated chin.'[20] Even more importantly, Gleb begins to recognize the wisdom of the government's New Economic Policy (NEP): having at first opposed the policy because it seemed to 'betray the revolution' by advocating 'the restoration of capitalism' (188), Gleb and some of the novel's minor characters recognize that the restoration of the nation's economic health will in the long run be essential to the durability of socialism. Similarly, Gleb teaches himself to see wisdom in the Communist Party's decision to expel some

19 Franco Moretti, *The Way of the World: The Bildungsroman in European Culture* (London: Verso, 2000), p. 19 (emphasis in original).

20 Fyodor Vasilievich Gladkov, *Cement* (Evanston, IL: Northwestern University Press, 1998), p. 27. Subsequent references are given parenthetically.

of his closest friends from the party's ranks for subversive activities, while other members, whom Gleb initially considered enemies of the communist cause, are exonerated. Among these potential enemies are Badin and Shramm, chairmen of two local Soviet committees. Gleb has difficulty understanding the need for new bureaucratic structures in postrevolutionary Russia, complaining to Badin that '[f]or a working man to get to see you, Comrade Chairman, is more difficult than to capture a trench' (94). And, while the novel highlights the potential dangers of bureaucracy, Gleb eventually recognizes the need for a new administrative apparatus. The complaint by some factory workers ('We've chased the masters away . . . And now look how it is: everything's disappearing' [22]), though legitimate, shows that they lack awareness of the Soviet Union's post-revolutionary conjuncture. Revolutionary action ultimately needs to be transformed into political institutions and discrete patterns of social behaviour – the growth of bureaucracy is not a betrayal of the revolutionary cause but its continuation by other means.

While few contemporary readers will be sympathetic to *Cement*'s more dogmatic endorsements of Soviet policy, the problem of translating revolutionary action into enduring institutions and behavioural norms offers an acknowledgement of the recognition that the 'truth' of the socialist struggle 'is *complex*'.[21] Instead of putting an end to history by realizing the absolute, event-like 'truth' of socialism, the October Revolution initiated a historical process that successively unfolds the meaning of that cataclysmic event. Central to the novel's formal design is the alternation between passages that focus on Gleb's actions and others that feature extended dialogues between Gleb and both revolutionaries and counterrevolutionaries about matters of communist theory and practice. By moving attention away from the bildungsroman's traditional focus on an individual protagonist, these long discursive passages emphasize the collective effort involved in building a post-revolutionary social world. The revolutionary's 'inside' view does not produce some kind of esoteric revolutionary knowledge: instead, these lengthy disquisitions illustrate that such knowledge is constituted collectively and that it is embedded in hermeneutic processes that are inescapably historical. True to Lenin's injunction that it is necessary to 'learn' even 'from the enemy', Gleb's knowledge about the nature of the

21 Clark, *Soviet Novel*, p. 220.

struggle is always subject to revision in light of the practical demands of the moment.[22]

Literary critics have not always done justice to the ambivalences that characterize even the most ideologically robust of political novels. In her landmark study of 'authoritarian fictions', Susan Rubin Suleiman claims that 'the unambiguous valorizations effected by the *roman à thèse* [the category to which Suleiman consigns socialist 'apprenticeship novels'] can be effected in two ways': either through the '*authority*' of the narrator who functions as 'the authoritative interpreter of [the story's] *meaning*', or 'through the story itself, the lived *experience* (or transformation) of a subject over time'.[23] Contrary to Suleiman's claim that the latter is a 'means of persuasion no less powerful than the voice of the omniscient narrator' (73), the radical bildungsroman forcefully illustrates that the socialist struggle does not rest on a set of 'absolute truths, absolute values' (10) that are somehow extraneous to the text. While socialist bildungshelden occasionally desire the guidance of 'a harder, more cruel voice, a voice that would [pull] the veil from my eyes and shake me up', that voice remains elusive in the medium of fiction.[24] By presenting the socialist struggle from the inside, socialist bildungsromane magnify the confusions and doubts that result from these historical contradictions. They suggest that the hesitations experienced during the course of the struggle prove the sincerity of the protagonist's commitment to the political cause, as they bring about a more mature view of the complex relationship between socialist theory and revolutionary practice.

The twentieth-century tradition of the radical bildungsroman – including novels by Sartre, Louis Aragon, Doris Lessing, Weiss and Uwe Tellkamp – features anti-heroes whose self-doubts offer an antidote to more doctrinaire kinds of revolutionary hero worship. When Gleb finally leaves behind the romantic heroism of the revolutionary period, he observes to Dasha: 'Our children will imagine us great heroes . . . raised to a higher power . . . The past is always generalized and exaggerated. They won't remember our mistakes, cruelties,

22 Lenin, 'Learn from the Enemy' [1905], in *Collected Works*, vol. 10 (Moscow: Progress, 1965), pp. 60–1.

23 Susan Rubin Suleiman, *Authoritarian Fictions: The Ideological Novel as a Genre* (New York: Columbia University Press, 1983), pp. 72–3 (emphasis in original). For Suleiman's discussion of 'apprenticeship novels', see pp. 63–100.

24 Peter Weiss, Leavetaking *and* Vanishing Point (London: Calder and Boyars, 1966), p. 85.

failures, weaknesses, our simple human sufferings and our damnable problems' (192). As the October Revolution begins to recede into the past and the possibility of a world revolution appears increasingly remote, the self-conscious protagonists of Gladkov's socialist bildungsroman are left marooned in an uncertain present that is described in national terms: 'the whole of Russia, we ourselves. All this immensity – the mountains, the factory, the distances – all were singing in their depths the song of our mighty labour' (34). Whereas Leon Trotsky's concept of the 'permanent revolution' attempted to salvage socialism's internationalist hopes, Stalin's 'socialism in one country' policy – publicly advocated for the first time in 1924, one year prior to *Cement*'s publication – sounded a retreat of socialism behind Russian borders.[25] Gladkov's novel develops a strategy that compensates for the elusiveness of a global socialist community in the present, and it does so by turning to the past, to key events in the history of the socialist movement that lend support to the hope that an international socialist community will be realized at some point in the future. The invocation of such events – from the October Revolution in Gladkov's and Weiss's novels to the Popular Front period of the 1930s in Sartre's literary works – is a central animating force in the history of the radical bildungsroman. *Cement* calls on the now-mythical moment of the October Revolution to suggest that the increasingly complex 'contradictions' besetting post-revolutionary Russia can be read as the dialectical unfolding of an underlying truth. When the factory finally reopens, Gleb admonishes his comrades that it is necessary to remember 'how our struggle began' (309). His bildung appears consummated only once he recognizes that the historical necessity of socialism must constantly be rearticulated at the level of political practice, and that its truth will, in this sense, always be incomplete.

25 Trotsky had first formulated his theory of permanent revolution in the early 1900s in response to the failed 1905 uprisings. He developed the concept further in the 1928 essay 'The Permanent Revolution'. In the case of Gladkov's novel, the pessimism about socialism's national boundedness is checked by the expectation – promulgated between 1919 and 1943 by the Third International (the Comintern) – that the triumph of the Russian Revolution would, in due course, lead to the overthrow of the international bourgeoisie and to the withering away of the nation-state as a historical formation.

Against Perfection: Slow Growth in Sartre's *Roads to Freedom*

The authors discussed in this chapter work hard to resolve the radical bildungsroman's constitutive friction between revolutionary spontaneity and political consciousness. They sometimes attribute an autonomous value to youth, but they also fear that an unqualified celebration of youthful radicalness will produce an insufficiently dialectical view of the political struggle. In maintaining this dual awareness, these writers reflect on the different speeds at which socialist bildung proceeds, as well as on the possibility that this movement of bildung might stagnate prematurely. For example, Gorky's *Autobiography* can be read as a performative attempt to exorcise – by way of intense self-scrutiny – the revolutionary impatience that had marked his earlier works, such as 'The Song of the Stormy Petrel' (Песня о Буревестнике, 1901) and 'Song of the Falcon' (Песня о Соколе, 1902). This biographically motivated labour of self-criticism allows Gorky to reimagine his own earlier political immaturity as part of a longer developmental arc that takes us up to (and beyond) the revolutionary year of 1917. In Gorky's memoir, autobiography is thus warped into new shapes by a powerful narrative impulse to correct and rearticulate earlier subjective experiences. Under the pressure of this retrospective narrative impetus, youthful radicalism is reframed as a form of political precociousness: 'I now felt that I had aged terribly . . . My friends were older than I was, but it struck me that I was really older, more mature and more experienced than all of them.'[26] The twinned narrative perspectives of Gorky's *Autobiography*, which combine experiential immersion and critical retrospection, work to fuse a quasi-documentary attention to the past with the teleological forward thrust of the political bildungsroman. The narrators in other novels are less successful in creating such syntheses: for example, the first-person narrator of Richard Wright's autobiographical fiction *Black Boy* discovers that his espousal of communism has provided him with no stable political point of view from which his own life narrative could be given a future-oriented shape. Instead, he learns that his desire for political maturity as a Black communist subject – what the book calls his 'yearning for a consciousness' – will remain unfulfilled.[27]

---

26 Maxim Gorky, *My Apprenticeship* (Harmondsworth: Penguin, 1974), pp. 110, 294.

27 Richard Wright, *Black Boy: A Record of Childhood and Youth* (New York: Perennial, 1998), p. 169.

As the examples of Gorky and Wright indicate, socialist bildung is often imagined as arriving either too early or too late: it can take the form of an aloof precocity, an impetuous youthful elan or a retrospective lament for missed opportunities. Other authors try to resolve these conflicting impulses by demarcating a clean break between the first and second bildung of their protagonists. Sartre's work offers a good example of this tendency. His satiric short story 'L'Enfance d'un chef' ('Childhood of a Leader', 1939) details the childhood of a future capitalist entrepreneur, and it focuses on the first cycle of hegemonic (bourgeois) bildung. This story was published in the same year that Sartre began work on *The Roads to Freedom* (*Les Chemins de la liberté*), the tetralogy that focuses on the formation of a genuinely socialist self. Sartre's decision to divide first and second bildung into two distinct narrative projects possesses an autobiographical dimension, as Sartre's largely apolitical stance during the years before the Second World War gave way to his role as a leading Marxist activist after 1945. The division between the two narrative projects seems intended to draw a *cordon sanitaire* around the process of socialist formation, guarding it against the political inertia of a bourgeois identity that has solidified into second nature.[28]

The protagonist of Sartre's *The Roads to Freedom* is Mathieu, a thirty-four-year-old intellectual who teaches at a boys' school in Paris. The three completed volumes of Sartre's cycle and the fragmentary draft versions of volume 4 describe Mathieu's slow maturation up to the point at which he is finally able to commit to socialism and the anti-Nazi Résistance. Unlike Gleb, Mathieu is not a revolutionary war hero, and the opening chapters of volume 1 repeatedly foreground Mathieu's disappointment at his failure to fight in the Spanish Civil War that is just drawing to an ignominious close.[29] Mathieu's inability to take sides in the Spanish conflict is all the more striking because he has previously felt drawn to other kinds of spontaneous, anti-authoritarian revolt: 'It had been his only desire to be available for the Spanish War. For a single action. A free and deliberate action that would call for the investment of

28 Sartre's decision, in turn, seems indebted to his communist friend Paul Nizan, who had opted for a similar division of labour in his novels *Antoine Bloyé* (1933) and *La Conspiration* (1938), and who features in *The Roads to Freedom* as Mathieu-Sartre's orthodox Marxist-Leninist mentor Brunet. I will discuss Nizan's work in more depth in the next chapter because it instructively exposes the weaknesses of this artistic (merely formal) solution.

29 Sartre, *Oeuvres romanesques* (Paris: Gallimard / Bibliothèque de la Pléiade, 1981), p. 395. Subsequent references are given parenthetically.

his whole personality and that would lead to a new life . . . He waited. And while he was waiting, the years had slowly crept up on him' (446). In a scene that signals the real starting point of the novel cycle and of Mathieu's second (socialist) formation, his friend Brunet blames the inability to take sides on the political liberalism of Mathieu's first (bourgeois) bildung: 'You are a son of the bourgeoisie. For this reason, you couldn't simply join us. You had to liberate yourself first. Now you're ready, you are free. But what's the use of freedom, if not to commit yourself?' (521).

Brunet's pronouncement carries great authority in the novel, partly because it reflects Sartre's own thinking about the question of militant engagement. Echoing Sartre's existentialist philosophy, Brunet insists that acts of political commitment can be measured according to their volitional 'purity' – that they can somehow remain unsullied by the confusions, hesitations and dead ends that make up the process of radical bildung itself.[30] *The Roads to Freedom* holds up Brunet's purist view of commitment as the gold standard by which other forms of political engagement can be measured, and the novel's first volume even closes with a passage that hints at Mathieu's achieved bildung. In this passage Sartre suggests that Mathieu's 'lived experience' (to recall Suleiman's phrase) is now essentially congruent with the authoritative 'voice of the omniscient narrator': '[H]is youth had passed . . . "It's true, it's true after all: I have grown up"' (729). And yet, in a marked departure from this privileging of the purity of commitment, the three completed volumes of Sartre's tetralogy – *The Age of Reason*, *The Reprieve* and *Iron in the Soul* – emphasize the tortuousness of the path that leads Mathieu towards a more mature understanding of the socialist struggle. Despite the emphasis that Sartre's philosophy places on engagement as an autonomous and unconditioned act, *The Roads to Freedom* shows that the real test of the protagonists' political commitment resides in their willingness to work though the painful contradictions that are immanent to the socialist struggle.

In Sartre's tetralogy, the idea of free and unconditioned agency is sometimes associated with the liberal-bourgeois belief in individual autonomy, but it is also linked to Sartre's broader inquiry – in turn informed by Sartre's philosophical existentialism – into different

30 For Sartre's comments on 'the commitment of immediate spontaneity', see 'What Is Literature?', in *'What Is Literature?' and Other Essays* (Cambridge, MA: Harvard University Press, 1988), pp. 21–246 (p. 77).

modalities of freedom. On the one hand, *The Roads to Freedom* posits a type of radical existential freedom (mirrored in Mathieu's attempt to find a meaningful life outside the Communist Party [CP]); on the other, it presents us with a form of social freedom that is articulated through schemes of progress and collective revolutionary action. The conflict between these two types of freedom often threatens to put individuality at odds with the concerted efforts of the collective. These deep structural strains are mirrored at a formal level in the syncopated developmental rhythm of Sartre's novel cycle, which contrasts phases of revolutionary activity with periods of solitary reflection that signal the moments of Mathieu's real intellectual and emotional growth. Sartre attempts to resolve these tensions by placing them in the context of an opposition between national community and socialist internationalism: as he points out, while one is born into a nation and takes it to be one's naturally given community and biographical destiny, socialist internationalism requires the voluntary union of solidary individuals.

Tracing the trajectory of socialist bildung, Sartre's novel cycle moves from the unreflective state of national belonging towards a realm of historical consciousness and maturity, but it also registers in painstaking detail the self-doubts that accompany Mathieu's second bildung, in particular his longing for the safe haven of his childhood and adolescence ('"Ah!" he sighed despondently. "Why can't I continue being a child?"', 919). Associating such safety with national belonging, the third book in Sartre's cycle contrasts Mathieu's melancholic yearning for an ethno-national community with his communist friend Brunet's anticipation of a collective socialist future. More than anything else, it is Brunet's internationalist aspirations that help to unsettle Mathieu's nostalgic vision:

> 'I am French,' and for the first time in his life he finds this comical. *It is comical.* France, we have never seen it: we were inside it, it was in the air pressure, in the earth under our feet, in the space around us, in the comforting knowledge that the world has been created for humans; it had seemed so natural to be French . . . Now France had been thrown on its back . . . We are still French, but it no longer seems natural. (1178)

Critics have often remarked that the end of the third volume shifts attention away from Mathieu's emotional and intellectual maturation towards the completed bildung of his more committed alter ego and fellow

Résistance fighter Brunet.[31] This reading of *The Roads to Freedom* suggests that Brunet figures in the novel as a latter-day Rakhmetovian New Man, as the embodiment of a fully realized socialist bildung. However, Sartre's subsequent work on the novel indicates that he came to doubt the possibility of an achieved second bildung – a view that is forcefully brought home by Sartre's drafts for the unfinished fourth volume of the novel cycle, *The Last Chance*.

The Last Chance shares in the enthusiasm that many leftists felt at the Comintern's espousal of the Popular Front policy at the Seventh World Congress in 1935. Advocating a broad political alliance against fascism, the Popular Front moved beyond the dogmatic excesses of the 'class against class' period of the early 1930s, during which reformers had been condemned as 'social fascists'. Yet, despite the striking shift from Mathieu's bildung-in-progress to Brunet's state of achieved ideological maturity, Sartre does not present Brunet as the novel's unambiguous hero. Instead, *Iron in the Soul* – and Sartre's incomplete drafts for the fourth volume – show that Brunet's internationalism is itself increasingly riddled with historical contradictions. Sartre introduces a further communist alter ego, Schneider, to dramatize the antagonisms that exist within the CP itself. While Brunet continues to appeal to the 'foundations of [the Popular Front period of] '36' (1420–1), Schneider points out that the Soviet-German Nonaggression Pact from August 1939 constitutes a flagrant betrayal of socialism's internationalist aspirations (1422) – and, indeed, the pact figures significantly in many other socialist bildungsromane, including Lessing's *The Golden Notebook*, Edward Upward's *The Spiral Ascent* (1962–77) and Weiss's *The Aesthetics of Resistance*, all of which ask whether the telos of the protagonists' socialist bildung can be located at the scale of the nation after all. Likewise, in the context of Sartre's novel, the military pressures of the Second World War are shown to cause a fragmentation of socialism in which the interests of the global proletariat are trumped by a dramatic resurgence of national(ist) concerns. But Sartre's decision to introduce several focalizer figures (Mathieu, Brunet, Schneider) who vie for the reader's attention also illustrates another important formal aspect of his novel: *The Roads to Freedom* often expands its central bildung narrative into a sweeping panorama of historical events, as if to embed the plot of individual formation in the more capacious narrative frame of a historical

31 Michel Contat, 'Drôle d'amitié: Notice', in Sartre, *Oeuvres romanesques*, p. 2014.

novel. Sartre's tetralogy shares this feature with the novels of Lessing, Upward and Weiss, but it also highlights the radical bildungsroman's inbuilt tendency to offer a narrative counterweight to the intensely individualistic focus of the nineteenth-century bildungsroman.

In the immediate postwar years, Sartre had flirted with communism, and he had helped to found the Rassemblement Démocratique Révolutionnaire, a socialist movement that urged the CP's return to a more fully internationalist policy.[32] Such a policy, Sartre argued under the impression of the Molotov–Ribbentrop Pact, was possible only if communists managed to emancipate themselves from the Soviet-style belief in 'socialism in one country'. Sartre's drafts for volume 4 of *The Roads to Freedom* reflect these tensions between internationalism and national retrenchment, and his political anguish finds expression in two strikingly different endings he drafted for *The Last Chance*. Revisiting the conflict between two forms of (individual and social) freedom, these endings indicate that the nature of the socialist struggle, as it presented itself in the 1930s and 1940s, was too 'complex' to allow for a unilinear, or predictably even, process of bildung: while the first version culminates with Brunet's decision to leave the CP and espouse an individualist form of commitment (he tells Schneider, 'Screw the Party: you are my only friend', 1534), in the second draft, it is Mathieu who takes on the role of Brunet's ideological mentor as he encourages Brunet to remain in the CP. Mathieu's second bildung turns out to involve an impossible imperative: 'Outside and inside at the same time. Completely committed and completely apart, desiring the impossible and knowing that you want it; desiring it as though it were possible: that's what it means to be human' (1654). Committed to socialism while also keenly aware of its historical failures, and believing in socialism's truth even as that 'truth' becomes increasingly hard to discern, Mathieu presents socialist bildung – the full actualization of the 'human' after the end of capitalism – not as an attainable goal but as a continued process of deferral.

Doppelsehen: Second Bildung and Narrative Voice

The radical bildungsroman's ingrained resistance to the idea of closure – its commitment to bildung as an open-ended movement – is centrally reflected at the level of narrative voice. Johannes R. Becher, the

32 Annie Cohen-Solal, *Sartre* (Paris: Gallimard, 1985), pp. 391–407.

communist writer and GDR cultural commissar, once observed that left bildungsromane are defined by the presence of 'two languages' – by a characteristic 'double-voicedness' or 'double vision' (*Doppelsehen*).[33] There is a sense in which Becher's observation restates a familiar general point about autobiographical writing as such – namely, that this type of writing is marked by the coexistence of a position of experiential involvement (associated with the past, narrated self) and an essentially retrospective narrative mode (rooted in the later reflections of the narrating self). Yet, as Becher points out, in the case of the autobiographical radical bildungsroman this doubleness assumes a distinctive form: on the one hand, '*Doppelsehen*' is grounded in a genuine desire to represent artistically the constitutive openness of the socialist struggle as it was experienced by the narrator's former self; on the other, it is animated by an attempt to discover in history the kind of order and teleological orientation that only becomes discernible with the knowledge of hindsight. Becher's prose captures the ways in which recollection and judgement, past and present, combine into a complex tectonic arrangement of temporal layers: 'My present and my past are positioned one on top of the other like tectonic plates, each one hazily visible through the other.'[34] Writing of the 'new age' that was so eagerly anticipated by his former self, Becher notes: 'Has it arrived already? Or is it about to arrive? Will it ever arrive? Why should it commence at the time set by us? Perhaps this century does not care, perhaps it is we who are at the mercy of time.'[35]

Many radical bildung narratives, some of them explicitly autobiographical, translate the genre's *Doppelsehen* into a dialectic of immersion (expressed through the use of the first-person singular pronoun) and analytic detachment (articulated through a third-person narrative voice). This bifocality had an important precursor in the bourgeois bildungsroman tradition with Gottfried Keller's semi-autobiographical *Der grüne Heinrich* (*Green Henry*). While the first version (1855) of Keller's novel had been narrated mostly in the third person, the second version (1879) adopted a first-person narrator. This shift in narrative voice allowed Keller to excise many of his more programmatically political authorial comments. As a result, the second version of *Green Henry* evinces a much stronger sense of experiential involvement, thereby

33 Johannes R. Becher, *Abschied / Wiederanders* (Berlin: Aufbau,1975), pp. 331, 87.

34 Ibid., pp. 178–9.

35 Ibid., p. 26.

performing the bourgeois bildungsroman's work of 'accustoming us to looking at normality *from within*' and making 'normality [appear] interesting and meaningful *as* normality'.[36] By contrast, a sizable number of radical bildung narratives attempt to transcend the stark choice between immersion and abstraction by staging a complex dialectical interplay of first- and third-person voices. Early examples of this tendency include Trotsky's *History of the Russian Revolution* (1930) and Gorky's autobiographical trilogy, both of which feature textual passages of intermittent involvement and detachment. As the intellectual historian Enzo Traverso explains, Trotsky 'admits that his participation in [the October Revolution] as an outstanding actor makes easier his understanding . . . of the inner connection of events' but then 'immediately adds that such a position can become an epistemological advantage only if he does not write as a witness, that is, providing a "testimony of his own memory"'.[37] In a similar vein, Gorky refers to his first-person narrator as 'Maxim' at certain moments of heightened existential crisis, as though to signal the sudden intrusion of a more authoritative knowledge, or higher-order bildung, into a narrative situation that is otherwise restricted to the first person. These shifts are even more striking because Gorky's autobiography – unlike, say, Alexander Herzen's socialist memoirs *My Past and Thoughts* (1870) – so insistently inhabits the narrowly circumscribed perspective of the child and adolescent. Indeed, in Gorky's autobiography, the omniscient narrator's detached point of view enters into conflict with Gorky's foundational insight that such authoritative external knowledge is by necessity unavailable to individual historical actors: 'Almost every man harboured, in the same awkward, chaotic way, a host of contradictions, not only in word and deed, but in feeling as well'.[38]

Another fictionalized memoir, *Life's Good, Brother* by the Turkish writer Nâzım Hikmet, written while Hikmet was living in exile in Moscow in the 1960s, recounts the author's poeticized memories of the communist struggle in interwar Turkey and Russia. The narrative oscillates between the first-person and third-person voice, and it includes flashforwards to historical events that serve to test the boundaries between private and public, inwardness and omniscience, memoir and fiction. The insertion of Hikmet's later knowledge of Soviet-style

36 For Moretti's now-classical description of the bourgeois bildungsroman's political work, see *Way of the World*, p. 11.

37 See Enzo Traverso, *Left-Wing Melancholia: Marxism, History, and Memory* (New York: Columbia University Press, 2016), pp. 54–5.

38 Gorky, *My Universities*, p. 91.

communism into an experiential first-person narrative serves to anticipate the horrendous outcomes of state socialism in the 1930s. At the same time, however, *Life's Good, Brother* asks readers to weigh the sobering recognition of socialism's historical failures against Hikmet's earlier willingness to sacrifice his life to a political cause that he knew to be fundamentally just: 'I knew that the Bolsheviks were enemies of the rich and friends of the poor.'[39] The fluidity of Hikmet's narrative voice produces tonal ambiguities that raise important political questions: on what historical or biographical grounds can Hikmet's youthful ('Bolshevik') radicalism be distinguished from the revolution's later ossification into state-sanctioned ('Stalinist') terror? The knowledge that is generated over the course of the protagonist's socialist bildung – what Gorky, Gladkov and Sartre had called the 'truth' of the struggle – turns out to be significantly more complex and ambiguous than ideological orthodoxy is prepared to grant.

The group of candidates for inclusion in this list of 'double-voiced' texts could easily be expanded. Lessing's *Golden Notebook*, for example, strategically blurs the boundary between diaristic (first-person) and authorial (third-person) narrative voices.[40] Or we could think of the British communist writer Edward Upward, who withholds the first-person pronoun until the third volume (*No Home But the Struggle*) of his *The Spiral Ascent* trilogy, which describes the climactic final stage in the narrator's 'struggle for a struggleless world'.[41] In the remainder of this chapter, I will explore texts by three authors – Richard Wright, Peter Weiss and Karin Struck – which spell out the confusions to which the process of (second) bildung gives rise. These texts turn away from large-scale historical teleologies to focus on the reconstitution and rebuilding of subjectivity itself. In doing so, they explore what Jacques Rancière, one of France's central post-1968 radical thinkers, has described as the emancipatory reinvention of the subject, 'the relearning of the sense of the most elementary actions: . . . seeing, listening, speaking, reading'.[42] Becher, whose own political formation had taken place during the

39 Nâzım Hikmet, *Life's Good, Brother* (New York: Norton, 2013), p. 58.

40 I turn to *The Golden Notebook* in some detail in Chapter 4. The novel pushes the register of critical self-examination to a formal breaking point, and in doing so it sheds light on the more recent and contemporary history of the socialist bildungsroman.

41 Edward Upward, *The Spiral Ascent: A Trilogy* (London: Heinemann, 1977), p. 282.

42 Jacques Rancière, 'The Red of *La Chinoise*: Godard's Politics', in *Film Fables* (Oxford: Berg, 2006), pp. 143–55 (144).

interwar years, hoped that his books would 'accelerate the intellectual development of the younger generation . . . Unlike the young women and men in 1914, this new generation must not remain underequipped to tackle the historical problems they are facing.'[43] By contrast, the works I turn to now reflect a different, and generationally distinctive, set of concerns. These books do not evince a longing for precocious ideological maturity. Instead, they explore what it would mean to attribute an autonomous value to the disorientating condition sometimes associated with youth itself. Sartre's close friend, the communist author Paul Nizan, engaged eloquently with this theme: 'To know what you're going to be', declares one of the characters in Nizan's *La Conspiration* (1939), 'is to live like the dead.'[44] Nizan's novels will be the subject of a later chapter, but Sartre's assessment of his friend's politics can help to frame the discussion of Wright, Weiss and Struck that will take up the rest of the present chapter. Sartre once described Nizan as the prototype of the '*negative man*', as an anti-type to the Soviet New Men of the 1920s: writers like Nizan, Sartre noted, were more concerned with phenomenologies of *un*learning – with the 'exposure' and eradication of hegemonic modes of subjectivity – than with the confident projection of new socialist ones.[45]

Phenomenologies of the Struggle and the Work of Unlearning

In what follows, my focus is on texts that present the unfastening of the protagonist's hegemonic first bildung as an existential crisis so profound that it threatens the very project of a second (socialist) formation. There are biographical and political reasons why these texts choose to home in on such moments of crisis-like unravelling. Wright, Weiss and Struck were all positioned at a slant to the main currents of early twentieth-century proletarian literature, and they felt alienated, for various reasons, from communist orthodoxy: Wright was the son of a Black sharecropper from Mississippi; Weiss hailed from a stolidly middle-class background (his father was a Czech textile merchant); and Struck – born to parents who had fled the GDR – became one of West Germany's most prominent feminist writers in the 1970s. The

43 Becher, *Abschied*, p. 612.

44 Paul Nizan, *The Conspiracy* (London: Verso, 2011), pp. 4–5.

45 Sartre, 'Foreword', in Nizan, *Aden, Arabie* (New York: MR Press, 1968), pp. 7–56 (46) (emphasis in original).

works of these writers respond to the crisis of state communism in the long 1960s, as well as to the New Left's reconstitution of socialism as a more capacious social movement. Gone, for these authors, is the possibility of tapping into the live political current of the Comintern – what Steven S. Lee calls the Comintern's 'lost genealogy', which 'demonstrat[ed] ways of connecting the local and the global, the personal-as-political and world revolution'.[46] In responding to these historical developments, the three authors I turn to here indicate the difficulty of anchoring a new sense of self outside the party form and outside familiar historical teleologies of the socialist struggle: Wright found himself increasingly ostracized by his white comrades in the CP, an experience that contributed to his decision to leave the party in the early 1940s; Weiss came to regard his experiences of rootlessness and exile after 1935 (rather than the ideological home provided by the CP) as key enabling conditions of a non-doctrinaire internationalism; and Struck, a second-wave feminist, felt profoundly alienated by the masculinist culture of existing socialist organizations.

Wright's memoir *Black Boy* consists of two parts. While the first ('Southern Night') concerns Wright's childhood in the segregated South, the shorter second section ('The Horror and the Glory') narrates his arrival in Chicago and his involvement in (and subsequent disenchantment with) the organized politics of the communist left. Written at a time when Wright had become hostile to state socialism (he later contributed to the infamous 1949 volume *The God That Failed*, alongside anti-communists such as Ignazio Silone, André Gide and Arthur Koestler), the book is nonetheless informed by the radical bildungsroman's attempt to divide radical formation into two distinct cycles, with the first relating the protagonist's early mis-bildung and the second isolating the course of his socialist (re)formation. Crucially, however, Wright torques this structure to reflect on his precarious position as a Black man vis-à-vis both the racialized politics of the American state and the hardline dogmatism of the Communist Party.

'Southern Night' poignantly shows that forms of hegemonic bildung are unavailable to racialized subjects in the segregated South. Growing up in conditions of extreme hardship, the young Wright gets involved in fighting and begins to drink before the age of six. As an adolescent in

46 Steven S. Lee, 'Introduction: Comintern Aesthetics – Space, Form, History', in *Comintern Aesthetics*, ed. Amelia M. Glaser and Steven Lee (Toronto: University of Toronto Press, 2020), pp. 3–29 (14).

the 1920s, he increasingly feels out of place as he experiences the brutal injustice of Jim Crow racism, which denies his elementary humanity: 'I was a non-man, something that knew vaguely that it was human but felt that it was not.'[47] As a Black man in the South, Wright thus inhabits what Frantz Fanon (a major influence on Wright in the 1950s) called the 'zone of nonbeing' – 'an extraordinarily sterile and arid region, an utterly naked declivity', where the possibility of growth is stymied.[48] In this 'zone', individual formation appears as 'a lumpish, loose, dissolved state' (194) – a mis-bildung whose apparent flaws and imperfections cast into sharp relief the social and economic inequalities on which the (white, middle-class, bourgeois) concept of bildung had always been premised. In contrast to the naturalized first bildung that is pictured in the novels of formation I have discussed so far, Wright's intellectual development in the South is laboriously autodidactic. Lacking a home, Wright must learn to raise himself: 'The substance of my hope was formless and devoid of any real sense of direction.'[49] This formation makes a mockery of the Eurocentric concepts of 'culture' that had supported the bildungsroman's nineteenth-century rise. 'This was the culture from which I sprang,' Wright's narrator observes in the closing sentence of 'Southern Night': 'This was the terror from which I fled' (257).

'The Horror and the Glory' comprises the second half of Wright's bildung narrative, and as such, it seems structurally predestined to relate the eventual fulfilment of Wright's 'yearning for consciousness' (169). Indeed, shortly after moving to Chicago, Wright joins the Communist Party and the local chapter of the John Reed Club. These two organizations initially seem capable of providing him with a 'sense of [political] direction': 'I was slowly beginning to comprehend my environment; a sense of direction was beginning to emerge from the conditions of my life' (301). Even though Wright soon feels alienated by the party's rigid leadership structures and its attempts to silence dissent, communism

47 Wright, *Black Boy*, p. 194. Subsequent references are given parenthetically.

48 Frantz Fanon, *Black Faces, White Masks* (London: Pluto Press, 2008), p. 2. In his brief discussion of *Native Son* – Wright's 1940 novel about Bigger Thomas, the Black man who accidentally kills his boss's daughter and later also murders a girlfriend – Fanon presents the refusal of white bildung as a necessary feature of Black radicalism. For Fanon's comments on *Native Son*, see *Black Faces, White Masks*, pp. 106–7.

49 This phrase appears in the single-volume edition of 'Southern Night' from 1945. 'The Horror and the Glory' was first published as part of *Black Boy* in the 1977 Library of America edition. See Richard Wright, *Black Boy: A Record of Childhood and Youth* (London: Vintage, 2000), p. 260.

continues to provide the narrator with a consciousness of himself as a social and political being:

> My ability to endure tension had now grown amazingly. From the accidental pain of southern years, from anxiety that I had sought to avoid, from fear that had been too painful to bear, I had learned to like my intermittent burden of feeling, had become habituated to acting with all of my being, had learned to seek those areas of life, those situations, where I knew that events would complement my own inner mood. I was conscious of what was happening to me. (282)

Central to this budding 'consciousness' is Wright's realization that his own life doubles as an allegory of the mis-bildung of the nation as a whole: 'Am I damning my native land? No; for I, too, share these faults of character' (273).[50] The sufferings and frustrations he endures are both product and symptom of US history. As Karen E. Fields and Barbara J. Fields remind us, the United States constituted itself as a nation by effectively barring large portions of its (Black, Indigenous, Asian) population from participating in the country's social life: non-white persons may hold 'the nominal status of citizens', but they have historically found that their lives are governed 'undemocratically' and without 'their participation and assent'.[51] Wright frames this internal contradiction in terms of the US's own malformed 'culture': 'Culturally the Negro represents a paradox. Though he is an organic part of the nation, he is excluded by the entire tide and direction of American culture' (272). What finds articulation in Wright's text is not a revolutionary consciousness capable of transcending such historical constraints through some new insurrectionary and emancipatory praxis. Instead, Wright becomes ever more keenly aware of the ways in which his own growth is inhibited by external factors outside his control. The bildung of Wright's protagonist consists precisely in this recognition. 'The days of my past, of my youth, were receding from me like a rolling tide,' Wright records towards the end of 'The Horror and the Glory', 'leaving me alone upon high, dry ground, leaving me with a quieter and deeper consciousness' (382).

---

50 'If the Negro solved his problem,' Wright notes elsewhere, 'he would be solving infinitely more than his problem alone' (298).

51 Karen E. Fields and Barbara J. Fields, *Racecraft: The Soul of Inequality in American Life* (London: Verso, 2012), p. 153. In the chapter from which I cite here, the two authors discuss the case of the New South in the post–Civil War era.

Notwithstanding the narrator's critique of 'my native land', it is true that, in *Black Boy*, the idea of the nation – the principal telos of the nineteenth-century bildungsroman – remains the object of significant affective investments. These sometimes take the form of a deep, albeit profoundly conflicted attachment to the American nation; but they also extend to the thinking of Marcus Garvey, who celebrated Africa as the revitalizing homeland of an African people currently living in global dispersion ('The Garveyites had embraced a totally racialistic outlook which endowed them with a dignity that I had never seen before in Negroes', 286). At the same time, Wright's bildung narrative produces important insights into the racialized dimension of the nation form. For example, Wright wryly ventriloquizes the anxieties harboured by a white member of the American middle class who dimly recognizes the exclusions on which the power of his class rests: 'The millions that I would fear are those who do not dream of the prizes the nation holds forth, for it is in them, though they may not know it, that a revolution has taken place and is biding its time to translate itself into a new and strange way of life' (302).

Wright's critique of the nation as a site of unreflective belonging is echoed in his searching engagement with the communist party form. At one point in the novel, the narrator is harangued in the street by a group of former comrades who are Stalinist hardliners. He defends himself by condemning the party's inability to offer an equal home to non-white subjects. While white party members are able to rise to the party leadership, the narrator points out that Black communists remain relegated to the CP's rank and file. This situation, Wright explains, has its roots in the party's nineteenth-century prehistory:

> There had existed in Old Russia millions of poor, ignorant people who were exploited by a few, educated, arrogant noblemen, and it became natural for the Russian Communists to associate betrayal with intellectualism. But there existed in the Western world an element that baffled and frightened the Communist party: the prevalence of self-achieved literacy. Even a Negro, entrapped by ignorance and exploitation – as I had been – could, if he had the will and the love for it, learn to read and understand the world in which he lived. (369–70)

Wright's passage calls up the spectre of the self-educated educator – the figure that had made its momentous appearance in Marx's third Thesis on Feuerbach. 'Self-achieved' (political, social, cultural) 'literacy' is here pitted against the vertical organization of a party that has no place for the unauthorized education of such autodidacts. Like the nation, the party threatens to stunt the growth of the individuals assembled under its name: 'Communism, instead of making [individuals] leap forward with fire in their hearts to become masters of ideas and life, had frozen them at an even lower level of ignorance than had been theirs before they met Communism' (296). And yet, despite his critique of the party, the popular image of Wright as a Cold War anti-communist is in some ways reductive. Notwithstanding the 'fanatical intolerance of minds sealed against new ideas, new facts, new feelings, new attitudes, new hints at ways to live' that he finds in the party (295), Wright's narrator believes that communism provides a shared political orientation for the globally dispersed collective of 'proletarians, slum-dwellers, and oppressed'.[52] Indeed, Wright's work is perhaps best understood as a strenuous attempt to account for, and work through, the artistic possibilities that are opened up by political commitment.[53] From this perspective, the party can continue to operate as an imperfect mediator of political bildung, as it does in the case of Wright's autofictional narrator. When it is framed in this way, radical bildung signifies not a progressive movement towards a final telos but a process beset at every step with failures and frustrations. It is a halfway house on the way towards a future internationalism: 'Few people understood the essence of Communism, its passional dynamic; but a few knew that Communism was more important than any of its individual parties, than the sum of all its tactics, strategies, theories, mistakes, and tragedies. I knew that once this system became entrenched on earth, for good or bad, it could not fail' (372).

Weiss's *Leavetaking* and *Vanishing Point* could be said to echo the narrative structure of *Black Boy*. Weiss's two books constitute the two halves of a single semi-autobiographical project that traces his early artistic and political development across the 1920s and 1930s.[54] Born in

52 I once more borrow this phrase ('Proletarier, Verwahrloste und Unterdrückte') from Karl August Varnhagen von Ense, whose influential socialist reading of Goethe's *Wanderjahre* I discussed in the Introduction. See 'Im Sinne der Wanderer' ['In the Spirit of the Wanderers'], *Über Kunst und Alterthum* 6 (1832): 533–51 (542, 540).

53 On the broader cultural resonance of this structure of feeling, see Nick Hubble, 'Looking Back on the 1930s without Being Anti-Communist: Cornford, Orwell, Spender, Sommerfield', in *Literature & History* 42.2 (2015): 57–72.

54 In this sense, the two volumes are important precursors of the monumental semi-autobiographical fiction *The Aesthetics of Resistance*, which resumes Weiss's story in the 1930s. I discuss *The Aesthetics of Resistance* in Chapter 4.

1916 to a Jewish father and a Christian mother, Weiss fled the Nazi threat with his family in 1935. Always inclined to left causes, he became increasingly radicalized during the 1960s, writing in support of revolutionary Cuba and against the US war in Vietnam. As with Wright and Sartre, the titles of *Leavetaking* and *Vanishing Point* suggest Weiss's attempt to divide his bildung narrative into two distinct cycles, with the first part representing the crisis of the narrator's early bourgeois misbildung and the second illustrating the future-directed reconstitution of the protagonist as a political radical. However, Weiss's novels brilliantly subvert this bifurcation by showing how the profound disorientation that is triggered by the decommissioning of an older self threatens to disrupt the process of socialist bildung itself.

Leavetaking begins with the death of the narrator's parents, as we are shown the nameless protagonist standing by his father's coffin. This scene alludes – either deliberately or by involuntary recall – to the opening sentences of *My Childhood* (the first volume of Gorky's memoirs): 'Father lay on the floor, by the window of a small, darkened room, dressed in white, and looking terribly long.'[55] Gorky's and Weiss's scenes fulfil similar functions by ushering in the possibility of a radical remaking of the narrator's self. But while Gorky casts the death of his father as the starting point for a new and self-determined way of life, it provides Weiss with the occasion for an extended and unsparing project of retrospective self-criticism: whereas Gorky's narrative points ahead to the emergence of a new ('socialist') identity, *Leavetaking* and *Vanishing Point* zero in on the fragmentation and negation of the protagonist's self. Weiss's narrator observes of his father:

> In this man's life there had been a ceaseless struggle [*unablässiges Mühen*] to maintain his home and family, through sorrow and sickness he had, together with his wife, clung to the possession of this home, without ever experiencing happiness in this possession. This man, who now lay lost before me, had never ceased to believe in the idealisation of the existent home.[56]

55 Gorky, *My Childhood*, p. 13. In Paul Nizan's *Antoine Bloyé* (1933), the death of the working-class father similarly figures as the key moment of disorientating liberation: 'A traitor to the proletariat, Monsieur Nizan had made his son into a traitor to the bourgeoisie: the-bourgeois-in-spite-of-himself would cross the line in the other direction. But that is not so easy. When communist intellectuals feel like joking, they call themselves proletarians.' See Sartre, 'Foreword', p. 48.

56 Weiss, Leavetaking *and* Vanishing Point, p. 11. Subsequent page numbers are given in the text.

In retrospect, the father's conformist hankering after the ideal of the bourgeois 'home' seems to have been doomed all along: with his death, 'the final disintegration of the family was completed' (12). The bourgeois fetishization of the 'home', which had also proved so alluring to Nexø's Pelle, is here exposed as veiling a 'wholly failed attempt at living together, in which the members of a family had persevered for the course of a few decades' (9). As Weiss observed in an early draft of the novel, the parents' ideal of domesticity also profoundly shaped the outlook of their children, with young Peter telling himself 'how blessed' he is 'to have such a wonderful life, such a wonderful life – echoing the words of his parents, what a wonderful life you have, all snug and comfortable amidst your pillows"'.[57] The parents' death abruptly shatters this self-image, leaving the narrator without a clearly articulated sense of self. Accordingly, the recollections that make up *Leavetaking* and *Vanishing Point* do not cast the protagonist's life as the linear story of an individual who is in charge of the shape his life will take. Instead, the two novels dramatize a halting and uncertain process of becoming, a 'time in which I was still without form' (16).

The story of *Leavetaking* and *Vanishing Point* comes to resemble a sequence of missed opportunities. We are informed that the narrator's 'situation' in the 1930s was that of a 'bourgeois who wants to become a revolutionary but is crippled by the weight of established conventions' (85). The narrator's failure to respond sympathetically to his friend Jacques, who considers joining the International Brigades in the Spanish Civil War, is symptomatic of this defective political formation. Weiss also renders the problematic of unachieved political bildung through the inflections of narrative voice: the 'voice' (*Stimme*) of the protagonist's politically radical friend Haller, we are told, is 'too remote for me in its mature wisdom [*Reife*]. It spoke of patient work [*geduldigen Arbeiten*], of slow, thorough studying and of the dangers of isolation' (86). Haller's view of the political struggle as a form of patient work – as an 'infinitely slow' growth (85) – is fundamentally at odds with the narrator's burning desire to grasp at some 'new freedom' (87) through 'blind self-abandonment to the extremes of the unruly and the instinctive' (86). It is only when he leaves home for the first time as a young man to enter the Academy of Fine Arts in Prague that the narrator

57 Weiss, *Abschied von den Eltern* (Frankfurt: Suhrkamp, 2007), p. 162. The German passage, which is reprinted in the appendix to the Suhrkamp edition, does not appear in the English translation of Weiss's novel.

begins to outgrow his anarchist leanings: 'Relieved of my parents and my teachers, I took over the tyranny [*Gewaltherrschaft*] over myself' (90). Weiss's phrase *Gewaltherrschaft* signals the sheer intensity of the narrator's desire to tear himself away from the familial structures that have conditioned his upbringing – it marks a foundational act of rupture and initiates a process of autodidactic self-making. As Weiss observes, this process must by necessity take place outside the safe domestic haven of the bourgeois family.[58] Rejecting the idea of bildung as a beatific state of (political, social, cultural) belonging, *Leavetaking* and *Vanishing Point* begin to reimagine it as an open-ended operation of unmaking and remaking. In Weiss's novels, exile becomes the central trope for this unconcluded process of bildung:

> The frustrated struggle for my vocation [*Berufung*] had put me in a state of derangement. My defeat was not the defeat of the emigrant in face of the difficulties of living in exile, but the defeat of one who does not dare to free himself from his dependence. Emigration had taught [*gelehrt*] me nothing. (101)

Weiss had fled Germany in the 1930s, moving to London and Czechoslovakia before taking up residence in Sweden, where he would spend his subsequent life. As he points out in *Leavetaking* and *Vanishing Point*, the narrator's politico-artistic formation (*Berufung*, *Lehre*) involves the ability to inhabit the condition of exile rather than dream of a return to some fictitiously pure home. What results from this endeavour is a geographically ungrounded and resolutely anti-foundational praxis of bildung: 'I had never possessed a native soil' (101), the narrator discovers in the climactic closing pages of *Leavetaking*. Weiss's two novels repeatedly seem to recall Varnhagen von Ense's remarks about Goethe's unhoused 'wanderers' as harbingers of an emerging radical internationalism: 'I belonged to a group of wanderers . . . The coddled and conciliatory revolted me, I felt oppressed when I read of good children, of benevolent parents, of rewards' (47–8). Socialist bildung consists in learning to inhabit the 'world of a fugitive' (130): it is the task of the bildungsheld to embrace 'my lostness, my uprootedness', to make 'my not belonging the source of power for a new independence' (55).

58 Georg Lukács, *The Theory of the Novel: A Historico-Philosophical Essay on the Forms of Great Epic Literature* (Cambridge, MA: MIT Press, 1999), p. 132.

The 'world of a fugitive' comprises multiple uncoordinated vectors of movement rather than a single line of travel directed towards a stable 'vanishing point' (*Fluchtpunkt*) or Lukácsian earthly home. Weiss's novel accordingly imagines the protagonist's bildung as the dismantling of a self and of that self's connection to the idea of home: 'I did not believe in a return to the land of my origin' (155). *Vanishing Point* presents exile not just as an existential loss but also as an active embrace of a less (geographically, organizationally, ethno-nationally) circumscribed concept of *home*. Exile, so understood, is the precondition for an incipient internationalism. The same belief infuses the radical vision of poetic language with which *Vanishing Point* closes: 'the natural language that was my tool, that now belonged to me alone[,] had nothing more to do with the land where I had grown up' (275). It also helps to explain Weiss's fascinating reactivation and retooling of the genre of the bildungsroman. While Weiss claims to dispense with 'the cumbersomeness of the novel form' (*die Bremsklötze eines Romans*),[59] he still opts to cast his protagonist's development in the recognizable form of a bildung narrative: after opening with a moment of liberation or departure, his novels proceed to chronicle the protagonist's growing involvement in socialist political projects. As I have indicated, Weiss's texts are radical not in the sense of being aligned with some pre-existing (revolutionary) political project or teleological vision of history; instead, bildung, in these novels, takes the form of an open-ended and crucially unfinished work of transformational unmaking and recomposition that cuts to the 'root' (*radix* in Latin) of the protagonist's sense of self and his place in the world.[60]

Such keen artistic attention to the work of negation and unmaking is also central to the writing of Karin Struck, the last novelist I turn to in this chapter. Struck's *Klassenliebe*, though little known to anglophone audiences, is one of the central literary texts of German second-wave feminism. A dizzyingly poetic mix of autobiography and fiction, the book takes the form of a diary written between May and August 1972. In the pages of her diary, Struck's protagonist Karin reflects on her

59 Weiss, *Fluchtpunkt* (Frankfurt: Suhrkamp, 1965), p. 167. The term *Bremsklötze des Romans* is once again taken from an earlier manuscript version of Weiss's novel that is reprinted in the Suhrkamp edition but has not been translated into English.

60 Weiss's distance from socialist bildungsromane that are grounded in historical teleology can be measured by recalling Gorky's critical dismissal of the futility and aimlessness of exiled 'wandering': 'They all seemed lost and homeless, and everywhere they went appeared strange to them. And they were all terrible cowards' (Gorky, *My Apprenticeship*, p. 117).

proletarian upbringing, her experience working shifts in a factory, her struggles as a first-generation university student, her troubled relationship with the middle-class poet 'Z' and her unsuccessful attempts to find artistic inspiration in an organization that promotes writing by workers. In an influential study that touches on Struck's novel (among many other texts), the literary theorist Rita Felski has suggested that the bildungsroman is one of the privileged genre templates of second-wave feminist writing:

> The first kind of text, which can be designated as a feminist bildungsroman, is characterized by a historical and linear structure; female self-discovery and emancipation is depicted as a process of moving outward into the public realm . . . The second depicts self-discovery as a process of awakening to an already given mythic identity or inner self and frequently occurs in nature or in a generalized symbolic realm.[61]

Klassenliebe does not fit neatly into either of these paradigms. Struck recognizes that the bildungsroman genre has traditionally framed self-actualization as a male prerogative, and she concludes that Karin's emotional and political formation must, therefore, proceed independently of such established bildung trajectories. Instead of offering a predictable narrative structure that either leads towards emancipation and self-actualization or takes recourse to a biologically rooted 'mythic identity', *Klassenliebe* offers a distinctive inflection of the radical bildungsroman's anti-foundational narrative momentum.[62] When we first meet Karin, she is teaching a weekend class at the local branch of a workers' union. Owing to the union's hierarchical and male-dominated structure, this type of work has long ceased to provide Karin with a sense of political belonging: 'I felt like a shrunk [*geschrumpfter*] human: shrunk into myself from fear. Constrained: I dare not leave my shell, without someone else holding my hand.'[63] Struck's language here suggests that her sense of fulfilment is inhibited by the same organizational

61 Rita Felski, *Beyond Feminist Aesthetics: Feminist Literature and Social Change* (Cambridge, MA: Harvard University Press, 1989), pp. 126–7.

62 Christoph Schaub offers a diverging account of Struck's novel as an anti-bildungsroman. See Schaub, 'An Autofictional Intervention into Working-Class Literature', in *The Political Uses of Literature: Global Perspectives and Theoretical Approaches*, ed. Benjamin Kohlmann and Ivana Perica (London: Bloomsbury, 2024), pp. 181–98 (187–8).

63 Karin Struck, *Klassenliebe* (Frankfurt: Suhrkamp, 1973), p. 8. Further references will be given in the text.

structures that once enabled her (political and artistic) self-expression. The opening pages of *Klassenliebe* poignantly show that the humiliations Karin suffers in the union have been prefigured by similar experiences in high school (where her teachers' and fellow students' class bias gave her 'an inferiority complex that produced crippling depressions', 13). This debilitating sense of (cultural, social, economic) inferiority culminates in Karin's pathological response to her love affair with Z. ('I felt drained after years of disappointment, by childhood, by my depression, by anxieties. I drove myself crazy imagining that you were sleeping with another woman', 43). At the root of her 'stunted' (*geschrumpft*) development is an acute inability to belong:

> I realize that all this suffering, all this overpowering sadness, is the result of my feeling of disconnection: cut off from the working class. Cut off from both sides. As soon as I turn into an 'intellectual', the workers reject me, anti-intellectual from a feeling of inferiority; the others also push me away, because I am no 'proper' intellectual and never will be. (49)

Struck reminds us that Karin's sense of uprootedness from the proletarian milieus of her youth is symptomatic of the larger socio-economic conjuncture of the 1960s and 1970s. The dissipation of revolutionary energies after 1968, Karin observes, is personified in the self-defeating figure of a 'proletariat . . . that liquidates its dreams at the very moment that it organizes its power and its industry' (55). The old organizational structures of class solidarity – unions, workers clubs, mutual trusts and so on – begin to wither once they cease to be animated by collective 'dreams' [*Träume*] of a different, postcapitalist future.

Like the bildungsheld of *Leavetaking*, Karin is brought to an unsparing re-evaluation of her own past. This process of self-examination involves the retrospective erasure of her former sense of self. '*I* never had an I' (180), she now understands: on the one hand, her working-class upbringing discouraged attention to the self as too 'intellectual' and 'solipsistic' ('Whenever I tried to say "I", they told me: "Pull yourself together"', 180); on the other, her attempts to integrate herself with a middle-class lifestyle have invariably served to destroy whatever sense of (proletarian) selfhood Karin may have once possessed. Faced with this double dilemma, Karin happens to pick up a copy of Weiss's novel *Leavetaking*. The book's rendering of the experience of exile speaks directly to her own feeling of intellectual, affective and cultural displacement: 'What language can I speak? I speak a no-man's-language [*Niemandssprache*] in no-man's land. In an in-between realm [*Zwischenreich*]. Neither Bavarian nor Pommeranian, neither Bourgeois nor Proletarian. I have lived nowhere. In no place. I have only ever lived in a state of suspension' (82). In contrast to Weiss's novel, however, *Klassenliebe* does not offer up the consolatory vision of a future internationalism. Instead, Struck presents Weiss's 'world of a fugitive' as a near-inescapable and irremediably personal condition: 'They took me from my place of birth when I was seven. Ever since then, I have been on the run. Without language, without home, without class. Where will I be able to live?' (245).

And, yet, Struck's biographically rooted scepticism of collectivist politics does not lead her to renounce the aspirational vision of second bildung altogether. It is more accurate to say that, for Struck's narrator Karin, the crisis of actually existing socialism renders the question of a future political bildung all the more acute: 'Yes, yes, the need to write a necessary book. One will be enough for this life . . . What is work? Must study Marx. Work and activity [*Arbeit und Tätigkeit*]? What does it mean "to develop, to grow" [*sich entwickeln*]? A yearning for something positive . . . To drain away all the dirt from one's life. All the melancholy' (80). Struck's passage looks back to the problematic that Marx had formulated so pointedly in his 'Theses on Feuerbach': how shall 'the educator' herself be 'educat[ed]'? What knowledge will be available to Karin in writing her 'necessary book'? *Klassenliebe* indicates that her political 'education' will have to be autodidactic to an important extent, because it can no longer fall back on the external guidance or *Erziehung* afforded by the Communist Party or some other collective organizational structure. But what form can this unauthorized and self-generated growth take? Karin recognizes the existential force of this question, which continues to haunt her: 'How shall we organise our autodidactic studies?' (117). And again: 'Where can I learn and grow [*in die Lehre gehen*]?' (270).[64] Karin's *Lehrjahre* involves a close study of Marx, even as she chafes at his 'difficult terminology' (144) and at the forbidding conceptual abstractions of historical materialism. For her, the question 'Was ist Dialektik?' ('What is the dialectic?') takes on sensory immediacy and intense personal urgency: 'The

64 The celebration of child-like spontaneity offered by her friend Herbert ('Prior to indoctrination through the family, every child is a visionary and revolutionary', 13) is roundly rejected by Karin.

dialectic is a form of yearning: for air, for woods, for land, for fields, for proper food, for real love' (123).

The title of Struck's novel is pointedly ambiguous. In German, the compound noun 'Klassenliebe' can signal a deeply held attachment to one's own class, but it can also signify a love that extends *across* classes (such as Karin's love for the middle-class writer Z). *Klassenliebe* holds up the contradictions of Karin's bildung for scrutiny both by herself and by the novel's readers. The book closes with a remarkable passage that offers one final nod to the long history of the radical bildungsroman. This passage invokes the possibility of a future rebirth and the promise of an achieved second bildung: 'This is my situation: a life before birth' (275). The difficulties that Karin encounters in her attempts to complete her second bildung mirror the existential dilemmas that are faced by the other bildungshelden discussed in this chapter. This group of novelistic protagonists extends as far back as Chernyshevsky's Vera Pavlovna, whose visionary dreams had merely offered brief glimpses (rather than a fully formulated utopian vision) of an achieved future bildung. As a committed feminist, Struck cautions us not to take her closing metaphor of bildung as a type of self-birthing too uncritically. After all, the act of giving birth is itself deeply politicized through its association with patriarchally organized structures of reproduction and creativity. 'Neither a man nor a child', Karin discovers, 'is a replacement for creative activity [*Tätigkeit*]' (275). In *Klassenliebe*, the question of what it might mean to 'give birth' to a new self – a question that is analogous to the problem of autodidactic self-education raised by Marx, Gorky, Gladkov, Wright and Weiss – remains generatively open and unanswered.

3

'Knowledge in Struggle': Collective Formation and Revolutionary Pedagogy

Readers of this book will by now be familiar with one of its central claims – that radical bildungsromane decentre attention to the autonomous growth of the (bourgeois, male, white) bildungsheld by emphasizing the collaborative character of bildung. The literary texts and films I explore in this chapter foreground this particular feature of the left novel of formation. They altogether displace the conception of individual formation as an achieved *state* in favour of a vision of radical becoming as an essentially unfinished and collaborative *process*. This body of artistic work ranges from Paul Nizan's writings of the 1930s to Nanni Balestrini's Autonomia novels, and from a set of Maoist-influenced texts and films (Ding Ling, Li Wenhua, Jean-Luc Godard) to African bildungsromane by Ngũgĩ wa Thiong'o. While these works hail from different radical traditions, they innovate the bildungsroman genre in closely related ways by presenting collectivity as the necessary and enabling precondition of individual formation rather than merely as an ancillary or contributing factor. The account I offer here starts in France and Italy, but this chapter also indicates that the need to imagine bildung as a fully collective endeavour became particularly acute for writers in the so-called Third World. It was in these seemingly peripheral regions of the International – including Africa and China – that such alternative articulations of the bildungsroman's generic parameters acquired intense political urgency as activists sought to break with models of individuation that they regarded as unduly Eurocentric or as complicit with authoritarian (Stalinist) forms of communism.

The revisionary model of anti-individualist bildung that I outline here was first given cogent and programmatic articulation in an important body of pedagogical writings from the mid-century. Some of these writings emerged from Maoist traditions, others sprang from Latin American and European schools of critical pedagogy. This body of work can help us clarify the larger political stakes of the texts and films under discussion, and I will repeatedly touch on it in the pages that follow. In the words of Paulo Freire, the important Brazilian educator and philosopher, it was the aim of critical pedagogy to tear down the hierarchies between educator and educated by asserting the essential equality of teacher and student:

> Through dialogue, the teacher-of-the-students and the students-of-the-teacher cease to exist and a new term emerges: teacher-student with students-teachers. The teacher is no longer merely the-one-who-teaches, but one who is himself taught in dialogue with the students, who in turn while being taught also teach. They become jointly responsible in a process in which all grow. In this process, arguments based on 'authority' are no longer valid; in order to function, authority must be on the side of freedom, not against it. Here, no one teaches another, nor is any one self-taught. People teach each other.[1]

Freire's key work, *Pedagogy of the Oppressed* (1968), from which this passage is drawn, recasts pedagogy as a distributed and fundamentally democratic enterprise. Freire points out that this kind of pedagogy is anti-authoritarian because it rejects established models of self-actualization. He notes that 'those who recognize, or begin to recognize, themselves as oppressed must be among the developers of this pedagogy . . . The oppressed must be their own example in the struggle for their redemption.'[2] As I describe it here, Freire's brand of critical pedagogy is in dialogue with certain forms of Maoist thought that crystallized around the mid-twentieth century. One of the European thinkers whose understanding of anti-hegemonic pedagogical praxis was energized by this line of Maoist thought is the French philosopher Jacques Rancière. In a series of writings dating from the 1970s and 1980s, Rancière theorizes a praxis of 'universal teaching' that experimentally suspends social hierarchies by insisting that intelligence is a shared property belonging

1 Paulo Freire, *Pedagogy of the Oppressed* (London: Penguin, 2017), p. 53.

2 Ibid., pp. 27–8.

in equal parts to teacher and pupil. This radically democratic mode of pedagogy, which Rancière developed in partial dialogue with the ideas of the nineteenth-century educational reformer Joseph Jacotot, 'was not a method for instructing the people; it was a benefit to be announced to the poor: they could do everything any man could'.[3] While Freire's concept of the student-teacher will help me articulate the broader stakes of my discussion in this chapter, Rancière's related thinking resonates more specifically with the Maoist pedagogy that underpins the works of Ding Ling, Li Wenhua and Jean-Luc Godard.

Freire's liberationist Third World pedagogy, much like Rancière's universal teaching, can be understood along the lines of Marx's third Thesis on Feuerbach, which I explored in the previous chapter. Marx had asked how the socialist 'educator himself' was to be educated in the absence of a fully realized postcapitalist society. Like Marx, Freire and Rancière attempt to imagine forms of individual becoming that proceed without recourse to existing models of self-formation. They develop this Marxian line of thought in two complementary directions. First, they radicalize the democratic implications of Marx's argument by repudiating the assumption that 'society' will need to be 'divided into two parts, one of which is superior'.[4] By renouncing the polarization of pedagogy into 'teachers' (leaders) and 'students' (led), they dispense with the vision of a revolutionary leadership whose consummate socialist bildung serves as a normative model by which any successful radical bildung is to be measured. As Freire warns, this hierarchization of bildung – whether it is encoded in the figure of the teacher, the (Chernyshevskyan) New Man or the (Leninist) revolutionary vanguard – quickly 'hardens into a dominating "bureaucracy"' so that 'the humanist dimension of the struggle is lost and it is no longer possible to speak of liberation'.[5] Second, Freire's and Rancière's rearticulation of radical bildung as a collective endeavour works to contain the unsettling possibility of a completely anti-foundational bildung that was opened up by Marx's third Thesis. Far from rejecting the idea of bildung as such, for Freire,

3 Jacques Rancière, *The Ignorant Schoolmaster: Five Lessons in Intellectual Emancipation* (Stanford, CA: Stanford University Press, 1991), p. 18. Rancière attempts to salvage these elements of democratic thought from the historical wreckage of Maoism. For a more sceptical account of Maoism as an authoritarian form of rulership and of the Little Red Book as 'a pedagogy for the Red Guard', see Eduardo Cadava and Sara Nadal-Melsió, *Politically Red* (Cambridge, MA: MIT Press, 2023), pp. 31–2.

4 Freire, *Pedagogy*, p. 31.

5 Ibid., p. 31.

the ultimate political horizon of critical pedagogy is the raising of revolutionary consciousness (*conscientizição*) – a process that is imagined as emerging dialectically from within the inherently plural subject of 'the masses' (*massas*).[6] The works I explore in this chapter respond sympathetically to the democratic and collective dimension of this counter-hegemonic pedagogical vision: they explore its utopian dimension, but they also test its limitations and investigate the continuing allure of vertically (rather than horizontally) organized forms of bildung.

Youth's Radical Spontaneity: Nizan and Balestrini

Paul Nizan was one of the pre-eminent socialist writers of 1930s France. He had been a member of the Communist Party since 1927 and acted as a regular contributor to its party organ, *Humanité*. Nizan's unfaltering commitment to the ideal of individual freedom and his resistance to authoritarian tendencies put him at odds with the hardening Stalinist orthodoxy within the Communist Party. As a consequence of these deep ideological differences, Nizan resigned his party membership in 1939, shortly after the signing of the Nazi–Soviet non-aggression pact. He subsequently suffered a CP-led smear campaign that culminated with Louis Aragon's high-profile defamation of his former comrade Nizan in his novel cycle *Les Communistes* (1949–51) – an attack that was all the more reprehensible because it was launched posthumously, a few years after Nizan (aged thirty-five) had tragically perished fighting the Nazis at the Battle of Dunkirk. Nizan's novels only found a larger and more sympathetic audience in the 1960s, when a new generation of young revolutionaries began to carve out a political space to the left of the CP by aligning its politics with the emerging struggles in the Third World. No one did more to boost Nizan's reputation than his old school friend Jean-Paul Sartre, who penned a long 'Foreword' to the 1960 reprint of Nizan's early autobiographical fiction *Aden, Arabie* (1931). In this Foreword, Sartre voiced his hope that the anarchist bent of Nizan's socialism would help to instil new life in 'the Left, that great, supine, worm-eaten corpse', following the Stalinist perversion of state socialism.[7]

6 Ibid., pp. 27–8.

7 Jean-Paul Sartre, 'Foreword', in Paul Nizan, *Aden, Arabie* (New York: MR Press, 1968), pp. 7–56 (p.15). Subsequent references to Nizan's novel refer to this edition and are given in the text.

The nameless first-person protagonist of *Aden, Arabie* is dissatisfied with his bourgeois existence and the novel begins just as he has made up his mind to leave France to travel to the Middle East. However, this attempt to find distraction through the encounter with Eastern 'exoticism' quickly unravels, and his dissatisfaction only intensifies over the course of his trip as he witnesses the effects of Western colonialism. Nizan's protagonist begins to acknowledge the full extent to which he is alienated from his own culture and from the heinous effects of Western modernity: 'All that nasty mess of abstract forces and ideas is the true cause of slavery and the confused fear it inspired in me' (103). Yet, while the targets of Nizan's anti-capitalist satire (colonialism, bureaucracy, commerce, technology) are clear enough, his protagonist continues to be beset by an overpowering sense of existential aimlessness. In the famous opening passage of *Aden, Arabie*, this directionlessness is associated with the condition of adolescence: 'I was twenty. I will let no one say it is the best time of life. Everything threatens a young man with ruin: love, ideas, the loss of his family, his entrance into the world of adults. It is hard to learn one's part in the world' (59). Unable to transition into the 'world of adults', Nizan's protagonist appears frozen in an anti-developmental in-between state. Youth, in *Aden, Arabie*, is identified with a position of resolute negativity: it resists assimilation to a stifling status quo, but it also fails to energize a more definite political programme for collective political action. Nizan's narrator explains:

> We were lost in a dimly lit museum of our fathers' works . . . On awakening in the morning, each man finds himself confronted with the great disorders of the time, reduced in scale to the petty dimensions of a personal anxiety. We have within us divisions, alienations, wars, debates. We were dissatisfied in advance with the professions for which we were being trained . . . And the things we feared were not illusions: we were threatened with real diminutions, with real constraints we could not begin to enumerate. In vain did you try to make us believe in the simple conflicts between freedom and determinism, predestination and grace, maturity and puberty. (65–6)

Aden, Arabie takes up several developmental motifs from the traditional bildungsroman: the protagonist's youthful dissatisfaction with life; the decision to escape on a journey; and finally, the return home. Yet, in sharp contrast to the nineteenth-century bildungsroman, the references to stunted youth in the passage just quoted ('real diminutions', 'real constraints') create a claustrophobic sense of anti-developmental stasis, instead of providing a point of departure for a future-directed process of bildung. Most importantly, the protagonist's various attempts at escape – his journey to the Middle East, his desire for exoticized distractions – all fail to generate a developmental forward momentum capable of propelling the protagonist towards maturity and preparing his reintegration into the (ethno-national) community. The literary scholar Jed Esty has observed that some twentieth-century bildungsromane, notably ones written in the colonial periphery, seek to 'create an autonomous value for youth' in order to imagine a place of freedom from the inexorable pressures of Western modernity: by 'separating adolescence from the dictates of bildung', Esty explains, the colonial bildungsroman managed to 'resist linear [developmental] plots'.[8] By contrast, in Nizan's text, this stalling of narrative momentum is registered not as a suspension of developmental pressures – or even as the sign of some imminent emancipation – but as the symptom of the protagonist's profound and growing alienation. The freedoms that are gained through his escape and Eastern 'wanderings' all turn out to be quite minimal or illusory. 'The freedom of the roads and of the sea is completely imaginary,' Nizan's narrator finally understands: 'At the beginning of a journey it resembles freedom because you are comparing it to the terrible slavery of the life that went before. But all it really means is that you have license to execute certain physical movements and are no longer constrained to make gestures demanded by others' (87–8).

With *Aden, Arabie* we approach the possibility of a fully collective bildung by way of its opposite – the novelistic dramatization of a purely individualist and instinctive revolt. Sartre's 'Foreword' points out that this tension is central to Nizan's book: the failure of Nizan's protagonist to progress beyond his feeling of alienation is reflected in his inability to embrace a richer form of *engagement* – the commitment to the communist cause. To Sartre's mind, the protagonist's political timidity mirrors Nizan's own complex relationship to party-centric communism. Describing Nizan's political position as that of a 'grave child . . . a *negative man*' (46, emphasis in original), Sartre argues that this stance seriously constrained the terms on which Nizan was able to commit himself to the communist movement:

8 Jed Esty, *Unseasonable Youth: Modernism, Colonialism, and the Fiction of Development* (New York: Oxford University Press, 2013), p. 25.

> Before joining the Party, he clung to his refusals . . . As a Communist he consolidated his resistances . . . The Party socialized him painlessly. Its collective being was none other than his individual person. He thought he was a monstrous freak. They hoisted him onto the stage and he displayed his deformities saying, 'This is what the bourgeois have done to their children.' (46)

For Nizan, as for other prodigal children of the bourgeoisie, the party's promise of 'collective being' remains unfulfilled, partly because the political stigma of being bourgeois proves insurmountable. As a former philosophy student at the École normale supérieure, Nizan believed that the French education system was partly to blame for fostering such conformism: 'All the philosophizing, with its protestation of spiritual purity,' notes Nizan in his contemporaneous remarks on liberal education in *The Watchdogs* (1932), is 'only an expression of their approval of this world'.[9] 'Till the very end,' Sartre concludes in his Foreword, Nizan 'was the friend of those who had never "succeeded", but he never managed to become their brother' (49).[10]

Nizan's difficulties in depicting forms of collective solidarity in his fiction are on full display in his 1938 novel *The Conspiracy*. This autobiographically inspired book focuses on a group of young bourgeois revolutionaries who are estranged from their social and familial backgrounds. Following their damp squib of an anti-establishment journal (aspirationally titled *La Guerre civile*), the group conspires to obtain the secret defence plans of the City of Paris. Initially, everything seems to go their way, but, when one of the group's members, the Jew Bernard Rosenthal, starts a liaison with his brother's wife, the cell begins to fall apart: the conspirator who is tasked with carrying out the operation to steal the plans gets arrested, and the group's only working-class member, Serge Pluvinage, becomes a double agent who betrays the cell to the police. *The Conspiracy* is divided into three sections, each of which narrates key events in the story from the point of view of one of the central characters. As in *Aden, Arabie*, Nizan is at pains to show that

9 Paul Nizan, *The Watchdogs: Philosophers of the Established Order* (London: Monthly Review Press, 1971), p. 57.

10 Sartre alludes to Goethe's *Wilhelm Meisters Lehrjahre* to explain Nizan's stalled socialist bildung. Nizan's communist formation, Sartre argues, remained stuck at the stage of what the *Lehrjahre* call the 'beautiful soul' – a self that seeks to maintain its purity from the viscosity of the world by adopting a purely negative attitude towards it. See Sartre, 'Foreword', p. 10.

these youthful characters are frozen at the stage of spontaneous revolt and unable to progress towards a condition of more meaningful collective action. There is a real sense that revolt comes too easily to these characters precisely because it remains limited to an instinctive individualist anarchism:

> When a young French bourgeois like Laforgue is seized by a desire to rebel against the condition his class imposes on him . . . the race and its mythologies, the complicities of church, clan and charity, do not long mask from him society's true contours. A deviation from the path is traced for him, like the reaction of a foal that takes fright and shies; the rift with paternal allegiances: these are enough to cast him back into the midst of a human space bereft of history, or which history scarcely trammels.[11]

Unable to ground their radical aspirations in the ('historical') realities of political struggle, Nizan's youthful radicals indulge in undirected and narcissistic dreams of revolt. *The Conspiracy* astutely renders the restlessness with which their minds flit from one idea to the next:

> Bernard took a bath, and went to bed . . . He then thought about the Revolution . . . He told himself things had to be settled one way or another, without really knowing whether it was a matter of covering Paris with barricades; catching a train next morning that would take him for a few weeks far away from his father and mother . . . or simply going down to the kitchen – he was really too sleepy, eventually he fell asleep. (11)

Bernard's revolutionary dreams are precisely that – a form of escapism from the drab bourgeois reality he inhabits. Nizan's novel does not celebrate the self-indulgent radical fantasies of its youthful protagonists; instead, it shows up their inability to overcome the social inertia of their first bourgeois mis-bildung. Like the groups of wannabe revolutionaries that populate so many left films of the 1960s – including Jacques Rivette's *Paris nous appartient* (1961) and Godard's *La Chinoise* (1967) – Nizan's protagonists are trapped in the thoroughly conventional and politically inefficacious role of 'youthful radicals'. They are frozen into the very stereotype that society projects upon them: 'In order to keep young

11 Paul Nizan, *The Conspiracy* (London: Verso, 2011), p. 8.

people quiet, men of forty tell them that youth is a time of surprises, discoveries, and great encounters' (13). Fixed in place by society's conventional ideas about youth, Nizan's young radicals are the precise opposite of the hyperconscious revolutionaries who featured in much early twentieth-century communist fiction: whereas the latter had 'grown up without ever having had the chance to be young',[12] the protagonists of *The Conspiracy* fatally fail to outgrow their youthful anarchism.

Written as the Popular Front of the 1930s began to fall apart, Nizan's novel can be read as a sobering and satirical retort to Engels and Marx's hope – famously articulated in the *Communist Manifesto* – that 'entire sections of the ruling class are, by the advance of industry, precipitated into the proletariat . . . They supply the proletariat with fresh elements of bildung [*Bildungselementen*].'[13] Whereas Marx and Engels envisioned a historical union of workers and bourgeois, the protagonists of *Aden, Arabie* fail to shed the last remaining traces of their earlier bourgeois formation. Indeed, despite the novel's sophisticated multiperspectival narrative structure, the vision of an integrated revolutionary collective proves elusive in *The Conspiracy*. In particular, the figure of Serge Pluvinage – the proletarian police agent – embodies Nizan's acute fear that the material reality of the proletarian struggle will remain unintelligible to those members of the bourgeoisie who 'can't see communism as anything other than one system of ideas among all the rest' (156). The cast of characters in *The Conspiracy* is made up of anarchist bourgeois radicals and proletarian turncoats – the total absence of proletarian revolutionaries from the text is an artistic symptom of what Walter Benjamin, in a discussion of Nizan's book, called the historical 'isolation of the proletariat' from the (political, social, aesthetic) structures of bourgeois culture.[14]

Nizan's exploration of anarchist revolutionary spontaneity is profoundly sceptical, but it nonetheless exerted an important influence on New Left authors of the 1960s and 1970s, because it spoke directly to the desire of younger authors who were trying to imagine modes of

12 I borrow this phrase from *Rummelplatz*, Werner Bräunig's brilliant novelistic insider's account of the early years of the GDR. See Werner Bräunig, *Rummelplatz* (Calcutta: Seagull, 2016), p. 7.

13 Friedrich Engels and Karl Marx, *Manifesto of the Communist Party*, marxists.org, accessed on 20 December 2022.

14 Walter Benjamin, Letter to Max Horkheimer, in Nizan, *Conspiracy*, pp. 231–47 (236).

collective action outside the ossified hierarchical structures of the Communist Party. For example, we can detect echoes of Nizan's interest in anarchist forms of political action in the Italian Autonomia novels of Nanni Balestrini, to which I now turn. These novels frequently deploy forms of narrative multivocality that resemble those in Nizan's *The Conspiracy*. Yet, while Nizan limits himself to critiques of a revolutionary bildung that remains purely theoretical and fails to translate into politically effective action, Balestrini's novels – including his two best-known books, *We Want Everything* (*Vogliamo tutto*, 1971) and *The Unseen* (*Gli invisibili*, 1987) – work towards a more positive vision of the new knowledge that will be gained through collective radical praxis. It is the great historical achievement of the Autonomia movement that it was able to generate a new understanding of the revolutionary struggle that emphasized the workers' collective ability to develop an autochthonous revolutionary praxis, theory and art. Reflecting these key aspirations of the Autonomia movement, Balestrini's novels seek out alternatives to the historically specific understanding of the revolutionary struggle enshrined in the party form – that is, the structural hierarchy between educator and educated, theory and praxis, leader and led. This search leads Balestrini to envision a fundamentally anti-individualist form of radical bildung. While not all autonomists agreed that existing organizational forms were irredeemably compromised, most argued that it was incumbent on radicals to imagine more democratic forms of collective organization. In this context, literary techniques of multiperspectival narration and collective voicing afforded writers promising avenues towards an autonomist aesthetic – the artistic rendering of what Balestrini calls 'a mass consciousness' that emerges from 'inside the movement' rather than being imposed on it by a party.[15]

In Balestrini's novels, revolutionary consciousness crystallizes in momentary flashes of collective political awareness rather than by way of a drawn-out process of sustained theoretical reflection. The novels' anti-work politics are similarly articulated through bursts of spontaneous insight that appear to belong to no one character in particular and that materialize whenever bodies assemble in shared spaces. For example, at one point in *We Want Everything*, the narrator recalls a conversation with his father. The father reflects on his decision to take the family from Italy's South to the industrialized regions of the North:

15 Nanni Balestrini, *The Unseen* (London: Verso, 2011), p. 179.

> I'm not telling you to go to school or to get a job. I'm only telling you one thing: work is bad, so try to avoid it. I send you to school because I think that's one way to avoid work. I felt this explanation, that work was a horrible thing . . . And I began to think that what my friends who'd gone to work in the building sites understood wasn't true, either: that money equals work, and that therefore work equals happiness. I began to have doubts about my discovery that happiness meant going to work on a building site.
>
> It was as if, with this perspective on work and on his life, my father had said: See this family, see me, see yourself? Is this a happy family? . . . And then I understood that work is a fraud and nothing more[.][16]

This is a remarkable passage. Omitting quotation marks and thereby refusing to distinguish between direct speech and inward reflection, the narrative voice shuttles seamlessly back and forth between different subject positions: at the beginning of the passage, the first-person pronoun is used to refer to the father, but it soon begins to indicate the growing consciousness of the narrator himself ('I felt this explanation'), while also opening out to the minds of others ('my friends . . . this family'). Awareness of the brutality of alienated work is here distributed across a cast of characters – it is attained collaboratively through a series of empathetic identifications, acts of ventriloquizing and snippets of (recollected) dialogue: 'I learned about these things by talking to the comrades,' as the narrator observes elsewhere (4). To put this another way: Balestrini does not suspend protocols of bildung, as some critics have argued;[17] instead, he recasts bildung as a democratic and distributed endeavour. In *We Want Everything*, this co-production of radical knowledge displaces the authority of institutionalized dispensers of Marxist theory such as the party or the union.[18] As Balestrini insists, knowledge that is rooted in first-hand experience and lived political praxis lends itself to situational reactivation in ways that the highly

16 Nanni Balestrini, *We Want Everything* (London: Verso, 2016), p. 26. Subsequent references are given parenthetically.

17 For example, Michael Hardt in *Deleuze: An Apprenticeship in Philosophy* (Minneapolis, MN: University of Minnesota Press, 1993), p. 45.

18 In the previous chapter, I discussed the shifting pronouns that mark key exponents of the autobiographical socialist bildungsroman. In a related vein, Balestrini's fictions deploy a rich web of overlapping pronominal identifiers – 'I', 'he', 'we', 'they' – that is intended to demonstrate the emergence of revolutionary consciousness as a transindividual process.

codified body of (communist) theorizing does not: 'When spring came,' the narrator notes of one such moment of spontaneous anti-work resistance, 'I started to be late every morning. I was pissed off with it, I wanted to get back down south and go to the beach' (42).

We Want Everything often analogizes the regime of factory work to the prison system and the army ('the chief engineer says: I am your colonel', 66). Balestrini's novel emphasizes that opposition to these disciplinary regimes is often spontaneous, and that it produces forms of knowledge that are grounded in specific moments of practical resistance: 'The struggle went on for more than two months, a brutally spontaneous struggle . . . You could feel the consciousness in the air' (128). In contrast to the more doctrinaire idiom of political 'consciousness' that we encountered in novels such as Gladkov's *Cement*, Balestrini imagines consciousness as something 'you can feel', as the embodied '*life-force* of that immediate destruction' (in the words of the autonomist theorist and activist Mario Tronti) – that is, as a quasi-somatic property inseparable from the sites and experiences of the struggle itself.[19] The spontaneous eruptions that characterize this collective politics of refusal place it outside the purview of the period's more orthodox left ideologies: 'We were shouting the strangest things, things that had fuck-all to do with anything, to create a moment of rupture: Mao Tsetung, Ho Chi Minh, Potere operaio. Things that had no connection to anything there but that we liked the sound of' (87). Because *We Want Everything* places such importance on the distributive, non-hierarchical and collective nature of revolutionary consciousness, the book's narrator is not individuated in the way that more conventional bildungshelden are. Balestrini's novel, as Rachel Kushner has noted, 'is not a story of one remarkable man. It's the story of [all] the nameless and unknown who went north.'[20]

We Want Everything shares Nizan's concern with revolutionary spontaneity, yet in contrast to Nizan, Balestrini wants to defend spontaneous action against the suspicion that it might be nothing but an (irredeemably

19 Mario Tronti, 'The Strategy of Refusal', in *Autonomia: Post-Political Politics* (Los Angeles, CA: Semiotext(e), 2007), pp. 28–35 (33) (emphasis in original).

20 Rachel Kushner, 'Introduction', in Balestrini, *We Want Everything*, pp. ix–xix (xv). The masculinist bias of Balestrini's novels – and of the workers' movement he depicts – is often painfully apparent. Feminist critiques of the movement's gender politics (and of Balestrini's novels) range from Luisa Passerini's remarkable collective-voice memoir *Autobiography of a Generation: Italy, 1968* (1988) to Kushner's novel *The Flamethrowers* (2013). Passerini's memoir even features a character who provided 'Balestrini's model for the protagonist of *Vogliamo Tutto*'. See *Autobiography of a Generation: Italy, 1968* (Middletown, CT: Wesleyan University Press, 1996), p. 126.

immature and self-indulgent) form of youthful rebellion. In Balestrini's novel, radical spontaneity is indexed to a postcommunist politics that prioritizes resistance to the discipline of work over the constructive task of building a unified proletarian movement. As such, it is positioned critically against the hierarchical 'transmission of theoretical production from the Party to the proletariat': whereas the institutionalized hierarchies of the CP 'make the Party the organon of a totalizing structural knowledge', revolutionary spontaneity contains the promise of more democratically organized ways of knowing and struggling.[21] These site-specific knowledges provide an arsenal of radical tactics and techniques, but they resist aggregation into a single and unified body of revolutionary doctrine. *We Want Everything* thus combines two complementary visions of the process of radical bildung: on the one hand, the novel suggests that revolutionary consciousness can accrue over time; on the other, Balestrini insists that such growth does not adhere to pre-established protocols of linear growth but, rather, remains dependent on singular moments of experiential involvement in the struggle.

Breaking with Old Ideas: Maoist Pedagogy and Collective Bildung from Ding Ling to Godard

In the penultimate chapter ('Assembly') of *We Want Everything*, the narrator informs us that the autonomist workers who have positioned themselves outside the organizational structures of the CP and trade unions are referred to by their enemies as 'revolutionary *cinesi*' (166). The Italian moniker *cinesi* ('Chinese') indicates that Autonomia's revisionary understanding of bildung was inspired in part by Maoist ideas about the nature of the socialist struggle and radical pedagogy. The following pages will backtrack a little from the historical moment of Autonomia in the 1970s to sketch in the artistic import of Maoist ideas about bildung and education in the three decades after 1945. As I suggest, the aesthetic mediation of collective theorizing and revolutionary praxis that I have identified in Balestrini's novels was prefigured in the work of authors such as Ding Ling and of filmmakers such as Li Wenhua and Jean-Luc Godard. These writers and directors re-envisioned bildung as a

21 I adapt this phrase from Nathan Brown's excellent discussion of communization theory in *Rationalist Empiricism: A Theory of Speculative Critique* (New York: Fordham University Press, 2021), p. 210.

process in which the hierarchies of educator and educated, self and other, are temporarily suspended, if not fully undone. 'The new man and the new woman,' Paulo Freire explains, 'will not be constructed in the heads of educators but in a new social practice, which will take the place of the old that has proven itself incapable of creating new persons.'[22] The novels and films I discuss here undertake the work of imagining what such a new collective social practice will look like.

Born in 1904, Ding Ling became an early member of the Chinese Communist Party, and she assumed leading government positions after the establishment of the People's Republic of China in 1949. Even though her relationship to the party leadership was often strained (leading to her temporary expulsion from the party in 1958), Ding was an important voice in the CP's literary circles throughout the 1940s and early 1950s. Her great novel *The Sun Shines Over the Sanggan River* was published in 1948, and it offers an exemplary artistic statement of early Maoist doctrine. If it is true, as the literary scholar Alex Woloch has observed, that '*minor characters are the proletariat of the novel*', then it could with some justification be said that there are *only* proletarians in *The Sun Shines Over the Sanggan River*.[23] Of course, because this is a novel about the Maoist land reform movement of the 1940s, most of the characters in the book are not technically members of an industrial proletariat but rather peasants, exiled intellectuals and minor party functionaries. But the point still stands: Ding's novel carefully avoids positioning any single character as the story's protagonist or bildungsheld. As a result, when it is compared to the other works I discuss in this chapter, *The Sun Shines Over the Sanggan River* is the novel that comes closest to rendering a fully collective (or indeed collectivist) narrative situation. Ding's novel successfully presents bildung as a cooperative process that undermines the bildungsroman's traditional claims for the relative ontological stability of the self and the possibility of autonomous self-actualization.

The sheer number of characters in Ding's novel goes well beyond anything achieved by Nizan's more cautious and limited modernist

22 Paulo Freire, *Pedagogy in Process: The Letters to Guinea-Bissau* (London: Bloomsbury, 2016), p. 127.

23 Alex Woloch, *The One vs. the Many: Minor Characters and the Space of the Novel* (Princeton, NJ: Princeton University Press, 2009), p. 26 (emphasis in original). All quotations from Ding's novel refer to *The Sun Shines Over the Sanggan River* (Beijing: Foreign Languages Press, 1984). Subsequent references will be given parenthetically in the main text.

experiments with multiple narrative perspectives. To list only a few characters from the novel's vast cast: there is Wen Cai, the smart-alecky party functionary; the sickly landlord Li Zijun; the female shaman Wu; Li Baotang, a former farmhand who finally receives his own share of the land; the unmarried teacher Ren Guozhong, an avid reader of romance novels; the superstitious union leader Old Dong, who 'must still work for the people' because 'as long as he lived he was a Communist, and he would die a Communist too' (137–8); Zhou Yueying, the shepherd's wife, who becomes head of the newly founded women's union; and the wise-cracking beggar Wang Xintian. Most of these characters – and there are many more – are fleshed out to an extraordinary degree.

It has been argued by some critics that the form of Ding's novel looks back to medieval Chinese epics: these epics often featured one biographical chapter per character, narrating their past and detailing their relationship to other figures in the narrative.[24] However, Ding's novel is best understood as a complex artistic response to its own historical and cultural moment. Much of the politically engaged writing that aligned itself with the nationalist, anti-colonial May the Fourth Movement of the 1920s and 1930s – including literary work by Lu Xun, Mao Dun and Zhou Zuoren, as well as journalism by Chen Duxiu and Hu Shih – had placed unprecedented emphasis on 'individualism, self-awareness, and personal freedom'.[25] The May the Fourth Movement also forms the centre of an influential essay on 'Third-World Literature in the Era of Multinational Capitalism' by the Marxist literary theorist Fredric Jameson. Jameson's wide-ranging piece homes in on a number of writers and filmmakers, but it singles out Lu Xun as a key exponent of the alleged tendency among Third World writers to produce literary works that double as 'national allegories'. Jameson contends that texts such as Lu Xun's 'Diary of a Madman' (1918) and *The Story of Ah Q* (1926) – as well as a number of other works from decolonizing territories, for example the Senegalese novels and films of Ousmane Sembène – 'always [present] the story of the private individual destiny' as 'an allegory of the

24 L. Posdneyeva, 'Nachwort des russischen Übersetzers' [Afterword by the Russian translator], in *Sonne über dem Sanggan* (Berlin: Dietz, 1952), pp. 455–65 (461); and Yi-tsi Mei Feuerwerker, *Ding Ling's Fiction: Ideology and Narrative in Modern Chinese Literature* (Cambridge, MA: Harvard University Press, 1982).

25 For an account of these developments, see Mingwei Song, *Young China: National Rejuvenation and the Bildungsroman, 1900–1959* (Cambridge, MA: Harvard University Press, 2015), esp. p. 115.

embattled situation of the public third-world culture and society'.[26] Jameson's argument has drawn much criticism, partly because it seems to suggest that the works of Third World writers were historically unable to attain the aesthetic complexity of the Western-style realist novel. More germane to my present discussion of early Maoist-inflected literature in China, however, is the fact that Jameson's argument focuses almost exclusively on the intensely nationalist years of the late 1910s and 1920s, which saw nationwide mobilization against the Japanese and European imperial powers. The formal affordances of the bildungsroman were particularly suited to this conjuncture: as I noted in the Introduction, the bildungsroman genre has long been regarded as hospitable to 'national allegories' that cast the individual bildungsheld as a stand-in for the destiny of the nation. By contrast, Jameson fails to explain how the genre's allegorical functions were warped over the course of the 1930s and 1940s by the subsequent resurgence of the communist movement in China. He also does not account for the fact that, by the time certain nineteenth-century Western literary forms became available to Chinese writers, they had already been transformed and retooled by authors committed to socialist causes in the Soviet Union and elsewhere. One problem with Jameson's argument, the Slavic scholar Rossen Djagalov rightly notes, is that it 'chooses to compare "Third-World" literature with "ours", the literature of the First World': in truth, however, the communist 'Second World' – including countless Soviet-aligned artists – 'provided the mediating term between the First and the Third'.[27]

The Sun Shines Over the Sanggan River indicates that some Chinese novelists responded to the early years of communist rule in China by freeing the genre of the bildungsroman from its narrow attention to the life of a *single* protagonist. In one of the first chapters of her novel, Ding Ling refers to the 'wishful thinking' (36) that animated the moment of the late 1940s, when land reforms were launched in the communist-controlled regions of China. Ding herself had joined one of the land reform teams travelling around the provinces with the aim of redistributing land from the big landowners to hitherto landless peasants. The land reforms promised to realize what one character in Ding's novel, the

26 Fredric Jameson, 'Third-World Literature in the Era of Multinational Capitalism', *Social Text* 15 (1986): 65–88 (69).

27 Rossen Djagalov, *From Internationalism to Postcolonialism: Literature and Cinema Between the Second and Third Worlds* (Montreal: McGill-Queen's University Press, 2020), p. 112.

party secretary Zhang Yumin, calls the desire 'to live a better life . . . to live more purposefully' (45). While this desire is shared by many of the characters in the novel, it is thwarted by several factors – not just by the resistance of the former landowners but also by a party bureaucracy that is out of touch with the urgent and popular need for more communally owned land.

The uneven realization of communism in rural China, which Ding's novel so powerfully depicts, recalls the recognition of the 'complex truth', or historical ambiguity, of the post-revolutionary conjuncture explored in Soviet novels such as Gladkov's *Cement*.[28] However, it is also important to recognize just how radically *The Sun Shines Over the Sanggan River* departs from these Soviet novels of formation, with their stronger generic commitment to a single bildungsheld. Contrary to many Soviet bildungsromane from the 1920s and 1930s, Ding's novel stresses the positionality of each character in relation to the masses rather than to party cadres or a single revolutionary leader-figure. This dimension of Ding's novel faithfully mirrors key aspects of Maoist thought.[29] In a speech delivered on 30 October 1944, Mao had demanded that party activists as well as educational and cultural workers

> must link themselves with the masses, not divorce themselves from the masses . . . All work done for the masses must start from their needs and not from the desire of any individual, however well-intentioned . . . There are two principles here: one is the actual needs of the masses rather than what we fancy they need, and the other is the wishes of the masses, who must make up their own minds instead of our making up their minds for them.[30]

The speech ('The United Front in Cultural Work') became a central reference point for the early development of Maoist doctrine, and it also sheds important light on the aesthetic ambitions of Ding's novel. Instead of pegging her narrative's allegorical functions on a single protagonist, Ding's

28 See Chapter 2 for my discussion of this aspect of Gladkov's book. On 'truth production' in Chinese novels about the land revolution (*tudi geming*), see Lauren Eidal Parker, 'Cadre Ethnographer: Chinese Land Reform Novels and the Making of Socialist History', *Critical Asian Studies* 53.4 (2021): 583–60.

29 A friend of Mao Zedong and a former classmate of his second wife, Yang Kaihui, Ding found herself at odds with other elements of Maoist doctrine at various points in her career, including the party's double standards concerning women.

30 Mao Zedong, 'The United Front in Cultural Work', marxists.org, accessed on 18 December 2024.

multifocal bildungsroman is best read as a dialogic exploration of the political significance of its own historical moment, the mid- and late 1940s. The novel presents us not with a single narrative arc centred around a solitary protagonist but with a host of developmental vectors that reflect the necessarily collective nature of the struggle. 'The distribution of land seemed to him no easy problem', we are told of Zhang Yumin; 'Only if they satisfied the whole village that justice had been done could they be considered to have succeeded. Otherwise there would be disagreement among their own people, and the work would be held up' (48).

In Ding's novel, the party functionary Wen most closely approximates the type of 'well-intentioned' individual identified in Mao's 1944 speech. Wen loves to pontificate to the peasants about party doctrine, including Mao's insistence on the importance of the masses ('He decided to call a meeting of all the village cadres, and explained that this would be taking the mass line', 53). Wen holds all the right opinions but, as the novel makes amply clear, he is too inexperienced to understand that party dogma must sometimes be adjusted in response to conjunctural pressures. In this respect, party activists who possess less formal education than Wen, such as the youthful Yang Liang, have a better first-hand grasp of the demands of the moment: 'Although Yang, too, lacked experience, he could look at things comparatively objectively. Because he had drawn close to some of the poor peasants he had an intimate understanding of the masses, and was thus better able to grasp their problems' (239). In her illuminating preface to the novel's Russian translation, Ding stressed the distance between the narrative procedures of her book and the characterological types to be found in much contemporaneous Soviet fiction: 'Wen is not yet the strong comrade . . . He does not find a way to approach the masses and is too beholden to ideological dogmatism.'[31] Distinguishing her novel's complex character system from the New Man trope of Soviet art and literature, Ding indicates that true revolutionary action cannot be brought about by isolated individuals: 'One man's strength is small, but the strength of the group is great' (259). As a result, in Ding's prose, collective entities ('the village', 'the masses', 'the peasants') take precedence over any single protagonist as subjects of bildung: '[T]he masses had risen . . . Without urging they wanted to

31 Ding Ling, 'Vorwort zur russischen Übersetzung', in *Sonne über dem Sanggan*, p. 6. As Mingwei Song has recently pointed out, the key Soviet precursor for mid-century Chinese rewritings of the bildungsroman genre was Nikolay Ostrovsky's socialist realist *How the Steel Was Tempered* (1934), with its New Man protagonist Pavel Korchagin. See Song, *Young China*, pp. 291–2.

settle accounts' (238). In a striking culmination of this technique, the novel's closing chapter (Chapter 58) features almost exclusively plural subjects: 'the village cadres'; 'the comrades'; 'the peasants'; 'the toilers'; and so on (360–1). Again and again, Ding drives home the need for her characters to remain receptive to critiques coming from others: only in this way is it possible 'to be human' (255).[32] For example, Wen Tsai's capacity for 'self-criticism' is severely tested in the book, and it is only when he abandons his 'self-importance and self-righteousness' (343) that he learns how 'to approach the masses' (318). Wen finds that the roles of teacher (party functionary) and student (peasant) are decisively reversed: 'As he sat in the land assessment committee listening to arguments he might speak on the matter of principle, but he could not settle specific problems' (343).

The view of revolutionary pedagogy that undergirds Ding's novel animates a large number of literary texts and films from Maoist China, the period when many of these ideas were given their sharpest doctrinal articulation. For example, Li Wenhua's film *Breaking with Old Ideas*, though shot decades later, is set in 1958 and is built around a related artistic dynamic. In contrast to *The Sun Shines Over the Sanggan River*, Li's film features a principal protagonist – Long Guozheng, a recent graduate of the Counter-Japanese Military and Political University, who is sent to supervise the newly established Jiangxi Communist Labour University. But, similar to Ding's novel, the underlying problematic of Li's film can be framed in terms of the demand for a radically new pedagogical practice.[33] Seeing that bourgeois elements are still in control of education at the Labour University, the dilemma presents itself as a large-scale version of the problem formulated in Marx's third Thesis ('How shall the educator himself be educated?'): 'If this problem isn't solved, then where will the successors to our proletarian revolutionary cause come from? . . . This is a fierce and complex struggle.'[34] Over the

32 In his now-classic account of Maoist land reform in the late 1940s, William H. Hinton comments that party cadres and peasants had to learn 'how to struggle and unite simultaneously, how to deepen unity through struggle'. Ding's novel, also set in Shanxi, relies on a similar dialectic of struggle and solidarity. See William Hinton, *Fanshen: A Documentary of Revolution in a Chinese Village* [1966] (Berkeley, CA: University of California Press, 1997), p. 679.

33 For discussion of these concerns and their cinematic repercussions, see Paul Clark, 'Film-Making in China: From the Cultural Revolution to 1981', *The China Quarterly* 94 (1983): 304–22.

34 *Breaking with Old Ideas*, dir. Li Wenhua, youtube.com, 01:17:24, accessed 22 December 2023.

course of the film, the school becomes the site for the production of what Paulo Freire called 'teacher-students' and 'student-teachers': the teachers are enriched through their encounter with the practical-minded labourers, as they learn (some more quickly than others) that their own university education has been one-sidedly theoretical; at the same time, the university environment teaches the peasant-students to formulate and embrace new political demands, including calls for women's emancipation. 'Students of our Labour College,' a beaming Long informs his students, 'must have both communist consciousness and knowledge as well as production skills. You should become both red and expert' (00:41:40). Li Wenhua's film captures the slow and painful process whereby the school reinvents itself and begins to provide a more worldly and practical-minded education. The film shows that this process of institutional remaking must by necessity entail the remaking of the roles of teachers and students alike. In this sense, *Breaking with Old Ideas* – despite its focus on a smaller cast of characters – aims to convey the mass character of radical bildung. Needless to say, in view of the brutality of the Maoist regime from the 1950s onwards (Wen's film is set on the cusp of the Great Leap Forward, the industrialization campaign that would famish and kill millions), *Breaking with Old Ideas* is a work of propaganda more than anything else.[35]

In Europe, the early Maoist inflection of the bildungsroman genre that I have begun to sketch out finds its most pointed articulation in Godard's *La Chinoise*. The film, which was shot during Godard's most intensely political period as a director, explores student activism in the immediate lead-up to the protests of May 1968. At the time of the film's making, Godard had begun to sympathize with Maoism, and this new-found political commitment would before long lead him to embrace entirely new forms of documentary filmmaking and to break with the French New Wave movement, of which he had been a key member. *La Chinoise* prefigures some of these developments, as several scenes

35 Joris Ivens's *The Football Incident* (1976), which forms part of Ivens's monumental documentary about the Cultural Revolution, *How Yukong Moved the Mountains*, offers an even clearer (and even more awkwardly stage-managed) filmic distillation of the radical pedagogical premises that underlie *Breaking with Old Ideas*. The film begins shortly after a student at a Peking high school has ignored an order by his teacher to stop playing football. Following this seemingly inconspicuous 'football incident', the entire class meet to discuss at length the political implications of this occurrence. Teachers and students are present as equals: one teacher moderates, but everyone in attendance is given equal voice, which includes the right to be listened to by everyone else.

explicitly position the revolutionary struggles in Western Europe in relation to longer radical traditions as well as to emerging socialist struggles in the Third World.

Set during the French summer holidays, Godard's film begins by showing how a group of students (all of them aspiring revolutionaries) installs itself in a spacious Parisian apartment that belongs to the factory-owning parents of one of the group members. Each student represents a distinctive ideological persuasion and personality type, ranging from the aspiring actor Guillaume Meister (named for Goethe's Wilhelm Meister) and his dominant girlfriend Véronique (the more politically committed of the pair), to the flat-cap wearing Soviet sympathizer Henri (who is finally expelled by the others for his ostensible 'revisionism') and his girlfriend Yvonne (a country girl who is unable to keep up with the highfalutin theoretical discussions among the middle-class members of the cell). Several other characters, such as the Black student Omar, appear briefly as they give lectures to the group and engage in discussions with them. In one of the first scenes, Guillaume and Véronique debate the name of the cell – they discuss two options, both inspired by Nizan's novels of the 1930s. Rejecting the initial suggestion of 'La Conspiration', they quickly settle on 'Aden Arabie': it seems safe to assume that Guillaume and Véronique, both of whom are from bourgeois families, are uncomfortable with the suggestion that they resemble the failed revolutionaries of Nizan's *La Conspiration* ('liberalism in militant groups based on collectivism is very harmful', a voiceover by Véronique informs us, as we are shown shots of the plushy bourgeois interior of the apartment that the group inhabits for the summer).

In the film's opening scene, we are shown Henri, who reads out some notes for an essay he is working on: 'The French working class won't politically unite nor go to the barricades . . . In the foreseeable future there will be no capitalist crisis great enough for the workers to fight for their vital interests.'[36] It is against this background of apparent revolutionary stagnation in Western Europe that each character's trajectory of socialist bildung unfolds: Véronique will finally engage in a (botched) terrorist attack on the Soviet minister of culture, who is in France on a diplomatic visit; Henri decides to leave France to take up work at a scientific lab in the GDR; and Yvonne, who has done most of the house-cleaning for the others and is patronized by her middle-class

36 *La Chinoise*, dir. Jean-Luc Godard, 1967, Blu-Ray, Arrow Academy, 00:00:25.

co-revolutionaries, noiselessly disappears from the film. Some of the film's central concerns are framed by the character of Guillaume: like his Goethean namesake Wilhelm Meister, Guillaume (played by Jean-Pierre Léaud) hopes to create a theatre that will be genuinely popular. Early in the film, he is asked by a voice off-screen – presumably Godard's – whether he has considered embracing Maoism because it might offer valuable lessons in mass politics: 'Yes, I have,' the characteristically hot-headed Guillaume self-confidently proclaims: 'such a theatre needs honesty – it needs violence' (00:07:56). As we approach the end of the film, however, it becomes clear that Guillaume's attempt to take the theatre to the masses has led him into an artistic and political dead end: he is finally reduced to selling fruit and vegetables from a makeshift stall only to have the cabbages and apples thrown back at him by an unappreciative audience.

Godard treats all his characters ironically, so we cannot be sure whether Guillaume's artistic and political failures are caused by his own personal inaptitude or whether Godard is more broadly satirizing the attempt to turn art into a political force in the world. On the one hand, Guillaume's left-populist ambitions, like Véronique's vacuous speechifying, are contrasted repeatedly with the revolutionary credentials of real-life figures such as Omar Blondin Diop or the older Francis Jeanson. Diop and Jeanson were activists who had fought in the anti-colonial struggles in Senegal and Algeria, and both appear in *La Chinoise* playing versions of themselves. On the other hand, some of Guillaume's grandiose pronouncements seem to capture the essence of Godard's own politicized aesthetic in the late 1960s. For example, Guillaume's observation – that 'especially in the realm of political actuality, we must examine different aspects [of a single problem], not just one' (00:33:30) – resonates with Godard's decision to stage a set of different perspectives on the socialist struggle, ranging from Soviet (Henri) to Maoist (Guillaume), and from bourgeois (Véronique) to agricultural worker (Yvonne). The decision to place these different perspectives side by side – thereby allowing them to act as ironical commentaries on one another – is central to *La Chinoise*'s open-ended, deliberative Maoist aesthetic.[37] To put this another way:

37 Peter G. Christensen observes that when *La Chinoise* is compared to Goethe's two *Meister* novels, it bears special 'similarity' to the *Wanderjahre* 'in its reliance on montage': 'We must intuit, grope, and deduce. [T]here are no characters who engage our sympathy totally, no characters to put the failure of the others into perspective.

instead of simply parodying the revolutionary commitments of these young revolutionaries – as other films of the period, such as Jacques Rivette's *Paris nous appartient* or Bernardo Bertolucci's *Prima della rivoluzione* (1964), often seem to do – Godard attempts to give artistic expression to processes of political formation that cannot be reduced to a matter of individual self-actualization. Several shots in *La Chinoise* emphasize the necessarily collective dimension of radical bildung. This includes the moment when Véronique comes to stand in front of a Chinese revolutionary propaganda poster that shows a group of schoolchildren imbibing Maoist ideas and modes of argumentation – her face seems to emerge from this background, stressing the ways in which the revolutionary aspirations of French radicals such as Véronique must rely on, and draw inspiration from, the political work of these young Chinese. These students, the striking composition of Godard's shot suggests, have acquired the art of thinking in other people's heads.

Still from *La Chinoise*

Consequently, critics were puzzled by Godard's feeling about the relative merits of the philosophies . . . expressed.' See Peter G. Christensen, 'Jean-Luc Godard's Use of Goethe's *Wilhelm Meister* Novels in *La Chinoise*', in *Goethe in the Twentieth Century*, ed. Alexey Ugrinsky (Santa Barbara, CA: Greenwood, 1987), pp. 13–21 (18).

The distributed nature of knowledge production in Godard's film has led some critics – including Jacques Rancière – to celebrate *La Chinoise* for embodying a mode of filmic mass thought and radical democracy.[38] In a crucial self-reflexive move that instantiates the film's tendency to erase hierarchies of authority (for example, between actor and director), the film lays open its own representational strategies to critical scrutiny: Godard brings this about by alternating between scenes in which the characters deliver lectures to the other Communards and a related set of scenes (announced by the intertitle: 'Dialogue') in which these same characters attempt to justify or explain their positions to the off-camera director. The film's peculiar cinematic dialectic creates surprising connections between seemingly distinct artistic and political positions. For example, it becomes clear that Véronique's embrace of terrorism mirrors her boyfriend Guillaume's desire to stage spectacular scenes on the theatre stage. By the same token, the film ends up giving more attention to supposedly reactionary positions such as Henri's: it is the closing 'Dialogue' with the level-headed Henri that immediately precedes the grotesque double failure of Véronique's terrorist plot (she shoots the wrong person before eventually managing to kill the culture minister) and of Guillaume's revolutionary theatre (he is booed off the stage by his audience).

Because Godard's film prizes irony and collective deliberation over individual self-actualization, it can be difficult to say precisely what constitutes the positive doctrinal content of *La Chinoise*. How can solidarity grow from a movement that is so riven and that has had such internally divisive effects? Godard's film stakes its political force on a paradox whereby artistic-cum-political estrangement effects – for example the use of non-diegetic speech to disrupt the illusion of a closed storyworld, as well as the artistic defamiliarization of 'naturalized' political assumptions – are intended to deepen the audience's commitment to the socialist struggle. What the film values over any specific or positive doctrinal content is precisely a set of formal procedures that are held to support a future-oriented process of critique and deliberation – a collective procedure that remains open to the practical demands of the moment and that can accommodate experiences of revolutionary deferral and failure. *La Chinoise*, much like *The Sun Shines Over the Sanggan River*, gives us the image of an unevenly emerging and precariously unified collective – of the socialist movement not as a safe haven or transcendent earthly home, but as an unconcluded and necessary struggle.

38 For Rancière's Maoist-inflected account of the film, see his 'The Red of *La Chinoise*: Godard's Politics', in *Film Fables* (Oxford: Berg, 2006), pp. 143–55.

It would not be wrong to say that, while *La Chinoise* attempts to channel Ding Ling's capacious Maoist vision of radical bildung as an essentially collective process, Godard's radical youngsters ultimately find themselves trapped in a self-defeating cycle of revolutionary failure and contradiction that looks like an updated version of Nizan's *La Conspiration*. The programmatic ironies of Godard's film are partly a response to its own political conjuncture, the lifting of the oppressively authoritarian atmosphere of Stalinism. As the Senegalese student Omar observes in his lecture on 'Perspectives of the European Left' (delivered in front of a portrait of Chairman Mao): 'Stalin's death meant freedom for research and a fever of people rushing to philosophise about their feelings on liberation and their taste for freedom.' Following the end of Stalinism, Omar argues, bildung will cease to be the prerogative of the Soviet New Man, or of a small coterie of revolutionary leaders. Instead, radical self-knowledge will become fully collaborative and dialogic: 'Stalin's death allowed us to get partially away from our provincial theories – to recognise and know the existence of others aside from us, and seeing this exterior, begin to see ourselves better' (00:18:29).

'An Unashamed Immersion in the Struggle': Bildung and Collectivity in Ngũgĩ's Anglophone Fiction

The main shortcoming of Guillaume and his fellow middle-class revolutionaries – as the cell's patronizing attitude towards the peasant girl Yvonne and their inability to learn from Omar Blondin Diop amply illustrate – is their failure to understand that the revolutionary 'lesson and apprenticeship must come . . . from the oppressed themselves and from those who are truly solidary with them'.[39] The situation is markedly different in the works of authors from decolonizing territories who were either engaged in anti-colonial struggles or actively involved in building new postcolonial nations. Many of these writers chose to cast their stories about uneven national emergence in the form of bildung narratives that present the development of their protagonists as halting or incomplete.[40] Authors whose works speak to the decolonial conjuncture in this way include the Kenyan Ngũgĩ wa Thiong'o, the Barbadian George

39 Freire, *Pedagogy*, p. 12.

40 Esty, 'The Colonial Bildungsroman: *The Story of an African Farm* and the Ghost of Goethe', *Victorian Studies* 49.3 (2007): 407–30.

Lamming, the Haitian Jacques Roumain, the Jamaican Claude McKay and the Senegalese Ousmane Sembène. Many of their novels reflect the recognition that (in Ngũgĩ's words) 'decolonization at the economic, political, cultural, and psychic levels has to involve both the colonizer and the colonized'; there is no development for one without the other.[41] In what follows, I will focus on the work of Ngũgĩ because it offers a particularly clear indication of the artistic ambitions and conjunctural pressures encountered by these writers. As I point out, Ngũgĩ inflects the established parameters of the European bildungsroman by focusing on the necessarily *collective* work of social reconstruction.

Ngũgĩ's novels have been celebrated for chronicling the course of Kenyan history from colonial subjugation to independence. However, Ngũgĩ is equally remembered for his spectacular mid-career renunciation of English as the chosen linguistic medium for his own fiction: 'This book,' he announced in his 1981 work *Decolonizing the Mind*, 'is my farewell to English as a vehicle for any of my writings. From now on it is Gikũyũ and Kiswahili all the way.'[42] Ngũgĩ's simultaneous decision to change his name from James Ngũgĩ to Ngũgĩ wa Thiong'o indicates that the process of 'decoloniz[ation]' flagged in the title of his influential book cuts to the heart of questions about selfhood, community and national belonging. We can begin to explore the artistic implications of these (cultural, social, political) shifts by turning to Ngũgĩ's early novels. His first published book, *Weep Not, Child*, and his third, *A Grain of Wheat*, raise fundamental questions regarding the adaptability of Western literary forms to the historical context of decolonization. Both novels were penned in the immediate wake of Kenya's independence, or *Uhuru*, in 1963, and they are Ngũgĩ's attempts to think through the problem of decolonization several years before his radical renunciation of English as the medium of his literary writing. While these early novels do not reject English in favour of African vernaculars, I will suggest that they offer programmatic variations on the Western genre of the novel of formation. Ngũgĩ's revisionary enterprise highlights the genre's limits in addressing the African context, but it also opens up radically new post-colonial futures for the genre. Finally, Ngũgĩ's fourth novel, *Petals of Blood* (1977) – the last book he wrote and published in English – demonstrates the internationalist and collectivist horizons that drove this

41 Ngũgĩ wa Thiong'o, 'Foreword', in Walter Rodney, *Decolonial Marxism: Views from the Pan-African Revolution* (London: Verso, 2022), p. viii.

42 Ngũgĩ wa Thiong'o, *Decolonising the Mind: The Politics of Language in African Literature* (Portsmouth: Heinemann, 2005), p. xiv.

process of revision as it splices several different narrative voices to project an image of bildung as a decentred and cooperative process. We can think of Ngũgĩ's programmatic revision of the bildungsroman genre in analogy to his thinking about the historical movement of decolonization itself. As Ngũgĩ noted in his 1972 essay collection *Homecoming*, with an eye to the process of decolonization in 1960s Kenya:

> There has been little attempt at breaking with our inherited colonial past – our inherited economic and other institutions, apart from blackanizing the personnel running them. There has been no basic land reform; the settler owning 600 acres of land is replaced by a single African owning the same 600 acres. There has been no change in the structure and nature of ownership of various companies, banks, and industries; the two or three European directors go away to be replaced by two or three indigenous directors – the companies remain foreign-owned.[43]

Similarly, for Ngũgĩ, the necessary undertaking of decolonizing the European novel must go beyond the tokenist politics of 'blackanizing the personnel' of individual novels – it must not remain limited to the act of inserting Black characters into novelistic plots previously reserved for white characters. Instead, what is required is a change in the genre ontology – in the 'structure and nature' – of those artistic forms themselves.

Weep Not, Child is centrally concerned with the Mau Mau rebellion of the 1950s, the anti-colonial rebellion against the British that was led by the Gĩkũyũ, Kenya's largest ethnic group. Ngũgĩ's novel explores the lives of several fictional characters who get caught up in the uprising, but it also begins to consider the nature of the Kenyan nation that will emerge in its wake. At the heart of the book is the character of Njoroge, an intellectually gifted boy who is given the opportunity to attend school. His family lives on land owned by Jacobo, an African who has become rich by sidling up to the colonialists. Njoroge is urged to pursue an education by his mother – she desires a better future for her children as well as emancipation from the whites, without quite realizing how compromised the idea of an education provided by the white colonizers really is. Njoroge's bildung, his formation inside and outside the school system, is at the heart of *Weep Not, Child*. In the first half of the novel,

43 Ngũgĩ wa Thiong'o, 'Author's Note', in *Homecoming: Essays on African and Caribbean Literature, Culture, and Politics* (London: Heinemann, 1972), p. xvi.

Njoroge – much like his mother – imagines that school education will contribute to the cause of national independence. Many other characters share this optimism, and when Njoroge passes his final examination, his father is exultant. Njoroge's bildung seems to tie him closer to his community, creating a moment of near-mystical union of self and nation: 'The news of his success passed from hill to hill. In spite of the troubled time, people still retained a genuine interest in education . . . At last his way seemed clear. The land needed him, and God had given him an opening so that he might come back and save his family and the whole country.'[44] Njoroge's overwhelming sense of historical vocation is presented as the 'fulfilment' of the expectations invested in him by his community: 'He knew that for him education would be the fulfilment of a wider and more significant vision – a vision that embraced the demand made upon him, not only by his father, but also by his mother, his brothers, and even the village' (41). Similar to the nineteenth-century bourgeois novel of formation, bildung here effects the integration of the individual into the social whole, inseparably linking the destiny of the individual to that of the community. Njoroge cannot at this point conceive that his smooth developmental trajectory could possibly be upset by his family's implication in the Mau Mau's revolutionary violence. As we learn, however, Njoroge's family is profoundly affected, and ultimately torn apart, by these larger historical forces. Following the assassination of a white man, the landowner Jacobo (ever eager to ingratiate himself with the white rulers) accuses Njoroge's father of being the leader of the Mau Mau and attempts to have the whole family imprisoned. Njoroge's self-image – along with his understanding of national emancipation as an even progress from colonialism to liberation and independence – is thrown into crisis when it is revealed that members of his family were indeed implicated in the assassination. Jacobo learns that one of his brothers is the leader of the Mau Mau and that his father has been protecting him. Before long, his brother dies in the revolt, and Njoroge (and his father) are thrown into prison, where they are tortured.

The nineteenth-century bildungsroman's orientation towards accomplished nationhood is rendered problematic in *Weep Not, Child*, as the uneven and interrupted process of Njoroge's education begins to mirror the profoundly fractured emergence of the Kenyan nation itself. But *Weep Not, Child* does not give in to historical defeatism. Instead, the

44 Ngũgĩ wa Thiong'o, *Weep Not, Child* (London: Penguin, 2012), pp. 115–16. Subsequent references will be given in the text.

bildungsroman genre's teleological orientation acts as a structural support that allows Ngũgĩ to present defeat as a necessary element of Kenya's future-oriented, emancipatory political struggles. In the novel, the intensity of this aspirational political vision is sometimes rendered through moments of collective voicing: 'We are no longer children,' Njoroge concludes in the novel's final pages, 'We have a duty. Our duty to other people is our biggest responsibility as grown men and women' (144). *Weep Not, Child* tries to resolve the problem of stunted or interrupted growth that so often marks postcolonial bildungsromane by holding out glimpses of a redemptive return to the native soil: the novel closes by remobilizing what the postcolonial scholar Simon Gikandi has called the 'romance of decolonization' – that is, the idea that the communal return to a shared homeland will be possible.[45]

As the 1960s progressed, Kenya's multiethnic composition, its deepening class stratification and the long shadow cast by the country's colonial past made such unifying national myths appear increasingly implausible.[46] At this time, Ngũgĩ also immersed himself in the theoretical writings of Frantz Fanon, the West Indian activist and theorist of decolonization, and it has been argued that the emerging contradictions of the new Kenyan nation led Ngũgĩ to share Fanon's scepticism regarding the possibility of a fully autonomous 'national consciousness' in decolonizing territories around the globe. In his 1961 book *The Wretched of the Earth*, Fanon had dismissed the flattering illusions of 'national consciousness' in no uncertain terms:

> Instead of being the coordinated crystallization of the people's innermost aspirations, instead of being the most tangible, immediate product of popular mobilization, national consciousness is nothing but a crude, empty, fragile shell. The cracks in it explain how easy it is for young independent countries to switch back from nation to ethnic group and from state to tribe – a regression which is so terribly detrimental and prejudicial to the development of the nation.[47]

45 According to Simon Gikandi, the 'nationalist romance of restoration' had to contend with increasing and 'unprecedented violence' from the 1950s onwards – a point I explore further in what follows. Gikandi points to 'the gap' which Ngũgĩ's fiction opens up 'between the romance of *retour* and its overwhelming realities'. See Gikandi, *Ngũgĩ wa Thiong'o* (Cambridge: Cambridge University Press, 2000), pp. 72, 103.

46 Gikandi, 'On Culture and the State: The Writings of Ngũgĩ wa Thiong'o', *Third World Quarterly* 11.1 (1989): 148–56 (152).

47 Frantz Fanon, *The Wretched of the Earth* (New York: Grove Press, 2004), p. 97.

Ngũgĩ's later fiction of the 1960s, including *A Grain of Wheat*, registers these disintegrating pressures, but it does not give in to Fanon's scepticism regarding postcolonial nationhood as such. In Ngũgĩ's fiction, as Nicole Rizzuto observes, 'the nation-state remains a form many still hope can be marshaled to resist the depredations of an expanding neoimperial world system'.[48] *A Grain of Wheat* begins to imagine the land of the emerging Kenyan nation in terms of local and circumscribed processes of work – a custodial and future-oriented attention to the material soil that is never allowed to harden into a master narrative of total national restoration. Like *Weep Not, Child*, *A Grain of Wheat* asks who the land has been expropriated from, who owns it now, and who will get to build a postcolonial future on it. But instead of presenting this soil as the materialization of a homogeneous, ethnically unified homeland, Ngũgĩ's novel reimagines the nation as an open-ended, unfinished and plural project, as a telos that is inseparable from the innumerable acts of work, attention and care that are expended in its name.

A Grain of Wheat presents us with two distinct plotlines. The first is set in the four days leading up to Kenya's independence in 1963; the other offers a backstory set during the State of Emergency, the regime of brutal military terror declared by the British in October 1952 in their attempt to quell the Mau Mau rebellion. The two plots are connected by the character of Mugo, who was once imprisoned and tortured by the British and who is now hailed as a hero by Kenyans looking to assemble a new pantheon of national heroes. Mugo is regarded by most other characters as a well-nigh mythical national figure. In defiance of the British colonizers, he is reported to have proclaimed during his imprisonment in the 1950s: 'What thing is greater than love for one's country? The love that I have for Kenya kept me alive and made me endure everything. Therefore it is true, Kenya is black people's country.'[49] Mugo is transformed into a key symbolic figure in the romance of decolonization: his individual formation is cast in the mould of a forward-looking developmental narrative, from rural youth to national icon, from social outsider to celebrated member of the national community. As we learn at the end of the novel, however, Mugo has deceived his community about his actions during the State of Emergency. Mugo, we discover,

48 Nicole Rizzuto, *Insurgent Testimonies: Witnessing Colonial Trauma in Modern and Anglophone Literature* (New York: Fordham University Press, 2015), p. 183.

49 Ngũgĩ wa Thiong'o, *A Grain of Wheat* (London: Penguin, 2002), p. 64. Subsequent references will be given in the text.

gave up the Mau Mau leader Kihika to the British, who then had him publicly tortured and executed. This revelation casts a completely new light on the events of Mugo's life. Ngũgĩ forcefully suggests that the foundational ethno-nationalist myths on which the Kenyan nation is being built are deeply compromised.

Much literary criticism about the postcolonial bildungsroman would argue that *A Grain of Wheat* – like other late colonial and postcolonial novels such as Lamming's *In the Castle of Our Skin* (1953) – gives us an image of failed nation-building, which is in turn reflected in the deeply troubled formation of a single individual.[50] This observation is correct insofar as the allegorical functions of Mugo's story are concerned, but it misses the ways in which Ngũgĩ's narrative manages to hold out an alternative understanding of the idea of formation. Ngũgĩ achieves this by rearticulating the underlying vision of a national homeland – by translating it into the relationship that individuals have to the material soil they inhabit and on which they work. Ngũgĩ's novel renders working on the soil as a future-directed activity that in turn contributes to the formation of the individual. 'He turned to the soil,' Ngũgĩ writes of Mugo:

> He would labour . . . There was, for him, then, solace in the very act of breaking the soil: to bury seeds and watch the green leaves heave and thrust themselves out of the ground, to tend the plants to ripeness and then harvest, these were all part of the world he had created for himself and which formed the background against which his dreams soared to the sky. (8)

Here and elsewhere in the book, the act of working on the soil is positioned against the large-scale industrialized projects of the white colonizers, symbolized by the modern Forestry Research Station that is set up as part of a new colonial development plan. Crucially, this agricultural work is presented not as a nationalist or nativist act of reclaiming a lost homeland but as a local, material act of labour that opens up the soil

50 Lamming's narrator comments on the self-alienating attempt to identify with a nation that is riven by settler colonialism: 'This was worse, *the thought of being a part of what you could not become*' (*In the Castle of My Skin* [London: Penguin, 1983], p. 335, emphasis in original). Ngũgĩ considered Lamming's 'picture of a peasant revolt in a white-dominated world . . . one of the great political novels in modern "colonial" literature' ('A Kind of Homecoming', in *Homecoming*, p. 81). For a broader discussion of the aporias of the postcolonial bildungsroman, see, for example, Ericka A. Hoagland, 'The Postcolonial Bildungsroman', in *A History of the Bildungsroman*, ed. Sarah Graham (Cambridge: Cambridge University Press, 2018), pp. 217–38.

for future work and habitation. The novel foregrounds the workers' custodial care for, and attention to, the land:

> He raised the jembe, let it fall into the soil, lifted it and again brought it down. The ground felt soft as if there were mole-tunnels immediately below the surface. He could hear the soil, dry and hollow, tumble down. Dust flew into the sky, enveloped him, then settled into his hair and clothes. Once a grain of dust went into his left eye. He quickly dropped the jembe in anger and rubbed his eye which smarted with pain as water tossed out from both eyes. He sat down: where was the fascination he used to find in the soil before the Emergency? (6)

Passages such as this abandon facile ethno-nationalist organicism and instead pay close attention to the back-breaking acts of work that are required to prepare the ground so that future collective endeavours can take hold in the first place. In *A Grain of Wheat*, the idea of a unified individual formation – of a process of bildung that moves in lockstep with the romantic master narrative of nation-making – is bracketed.

The effect of this bracketing is that nationhood becomes temporarily unfastened from the kinds of historical macro-teleologies that critics have long associated with the European bildungsroman tradition. But Ngũgĩ does not resign himself to the disenchanted vision of frozen growth that critics have sometimes found in postcolonial novels of formation. What Mugo learns by tilling the soil is that whatever the Kenyan nation might eventually become will depend on a multitude of such local, circumscribed acts of work.[51] And he also discovers that the growth of his own self is inseparable from the painstakingly described acts of work that connect him to the changeable conditions of the (collectively inhabited) soil – the grounding condition of what Ngũgĩ called, in a later novel, 'humanity – [the] fruit of the work of our hands and minds striving together'.[52] As the Guyanese historian and activist Walter Rodney noted, the revolutionary momentum that accumulates among the members of the peasantry is thus not merely 'spontaneously

51 In an important 1981 lecture that resonates with Lukács's Marxist-humanist explication of the world-building dimensions of work in *Ontology of Social Being*, Ngũgĩ remarks on the ontological primacy of work: 'In struggling with nature man enters into relations with other men . . . He must cooperate with others, through division of labour, to face hostile nature.' See Ngũgĩ wa Thiong'o, 'Education for a National Culture', in *Ufahamu: A Journal for African Studies* 12.2 (1983): 20–34 (21).

52 Ngũgĩ wa Thiong'o, *Devil on the Cross* (London: Penguin, 2017), p. 53.

revolutionary' but rather builds on a deep and rooted knowledge of the modes of collective world-building that are available to them.[53]

Ngũgĩ's early fiction returns us to a version of the problem I explored in the previous chapter. Similar to the educator in Marx's third Thesis on Feuerbach and the student-teachers of critical pedagogy, 'the oppressed' in Ngũgĩ's bildungsromane 'must be their own example in the struggle for their redemption'.[54] In *Petals of Blood*, the last novel he wrote in English, Ngũgĩ strikingly departs from the comparatively unified narrative form of his early bildungsromane in order to spell out his evolving vision of bildung as a collective rather than individual process. The novel traces the stories of four men and women – Abdulla, Munira, Wanja and Karega – whose lives are connected as a result of the Mau Mau rebellion. All four characters seek to leave behind the existential precariousness of city life by escaping to the little village of Ilmorog. However, like the characters in Ngũgĩ's earlier bildungsromane the protagonists of *Petals of Blood* must finally come to terms with the consequences of the Mau Mau rebellion for their own lives. Completed while he was a guest of the Union of Soviet Writers in Yalta on the Crimean Peninsula, *Petals of Blood* is, in many ways, Ngũgĩ's most overtly socialist novel, unsparing in its assault both on governmental corruption and on the capitalist rapaciousness that was creating social inequality in a rapidly Westernizing Kenya.

The titles of the novel's four main sections flag Ngũgĩ's interest in personal and collective development as a process that includes a sense of teleological directedness (Part 1: 'Walking . . .'; Part 2: 'Toward Bethlehem'); but they also begin to indicate the book's concern with the presiding motifs of the radical novel of formation (the theme of second bildung and rebirth in Part 3: 'To Be Born'; and the ongoingness of the struggle in Part 4: 'Again . . . La Luta Continua!'). The four central characters in *Petals of Blood* – the newly divorced teacher Munira; the attractive barmaid Wanja; the handicapped shopkeeper Abdulla; and the young communist revolutionary Karega – share a sense of displacement

53 Walter Rodney, 'A Brief Tribute to Amílcar Cabral', in *Decolonial Marxism*, pp. 3–6 (5). This conviction is also central to the radical thought of Julius Nyerere, the Tanzanian anti-colonial activist, theorist and prime minister. See in particular his 'Socialism and Rural Development' and '*Ujamaa* – The Basis of African Socialism', which build an African vision of socialism through recourse to the idea that 'in traditional African society everybody was a worker'. Both essays are reprinted in Julius Nyerere, *Freedom and Unity / Uhuru na Umoja: A Selection from Writings and Speeches* (Oxford: Oxford University Press, 1966).

54 Freire, *Pedagogy*, p. 28.

and exile. For some of these figures, the political desire for a home that will belong to all Kenyans has biographical roots. Karega, we are told, was 'born into a landless home' – 'but' (the narrator continues) 'even those with land, for how long could it continue to be subdivided into plots and sub-plots so that each son could own a piece? . . . Kenya, the soil, was the people's common *shamba* [cultivated ground].'[55] As Karega explains to Munira, the oppressive experience of homelessness is a question of national importance, but it also pertains more broadly to the diasporic experience of the African community, whose members are condemned to live the life of 'jobless wanderers' (177):

> 'The scattering of Africans into the four corners of the earth is a fact . . . That Africa is one of the richest continents with infinite possibilities for renewal and growth is a fact . . . Our children must look at the things that deformed us yesterday, that are deforming us today. They must also look at the things which formed us yesterday, that will creatively form us into a new breed of men and women who will not be afraid to link hands with children from other lands on the basis of an unashamed immersion in the struggle against those things that dwarf us.
>
> 'Liberation: no child is ever too young to think about this: it is the only way he can truly experience himself as he collects, breaks, collects, rejects, assimilates and tries to discover himself.' (293–4)

In contrast to the national closure achieved by certain canonical nineteenth-century bildungsromane, this internationalist vision – the prospect of a second bildung that will undo the 'deform[ations]' of an earlier colonial bildung – remains open-ended: it constitutes a future political telos rather than an already-existing home to which the protagonist is able to return at the end of their wanderings. Whereas many bourgeois bildungsromane aimed to naturalize the class-ridden world of capitalism by making it appear meaningful and ethically compelling, the course of socialist bildung reveals just how profoundly alien and alienating – 'driven by forces they could not always understand' (106) – the politico-social world of the novel's protagonists really is.

Karega's utopian vision of internationalist solidarity remains unrealized at the end of the novel, as *Petals of Blood* paints a sobering picture of the African diaspora and the overwhelming repercussions of

55 Ngũgĩ wa Thiong'o, *Petals of Blood* (London: Penguin, 2005), p. 359. Subsequent references will be given parenthetically.

colonialism and capitalist 'neocolonial imperialism' in Kenya.[56] The four interwoven storylines that make up *Petals of Blood* offer further variations on the theme of frustrated collectivity. For example, the conformist Munira, raised as a Christian, despairs because he is unable to pull the others into religious salvation; and Wanja becomes pregnant by Abdulla, but her pregnancy carries little of the hopeful promise conveyed by Karega in the previously quoted passage. Indeed, it is only Karega, the committed revolutionary, whose embrace of communism and trade unionism appears to offer a path beyond the constraints of the postcolonial present. This does not mean that the plural processes of bildung that are represented in *Petals of Blood* are all pressed into a fixed developmental grid or subordinated to a single authoritative narrative voice. Karega, full of self-doubt, is no Chernyshevskyan Rakhmetov, and it is testimony to the multi-voiced quality of Ngũgĩ's novel that all of his characters are capable of attaining insight into the fundamentally collective nature of political bildung. Recalling an episode from his previous life in the city, Munira confesses to Abdulla that he feels shame at his failure to commit to the anti-colonial cause: 'Ambition should be made of sterner stuff. Mine was of soft material. Withdrawal into self . . . depersoning myself before a crowd demanding passionate commitment to a cause became, thenceforth, my way of life' (36). In contrast to Munira's shameful moment of political hesitation and 'depersoning', Ngũgĩ's novel shows that individuation is possible only through the experience of being part of a collective. Indeed, the relationship between individual and collective formation is the foundational problem that the novel's narrative form – with its programmatic splicing of narrative voices and points of view – dramatizes for us.

In *Petals of Blood*, passages of individual voicing often culminate in affectively heightened moments in which a particular 'experience' comes to be shared across a group of characters rather than being contained in the mind of a single figure: 'She had somehow drawn Abdulla and Munira into her world,' the narrator remarks of Wanja's feeling of being adrift, 'and they seemed also to experience this wound or maybe it reminded them of their own wounds' (49). And again: 'Brooding not too far below their tranquil existence was their consciousness of the journey and the experiences which spoke of another less sure, more

56 I am borrowing the phrase from Ngũgĩ. 'To all Kenyans struggling against the neocolonial stage of imperialism' reads the dedication that prefaces *Devil on the Cross*, published in Gĩkũyũ three years after *Petals of Blood*.

troubled world' (235). This shared and almost physical sense of rootless unease expresses a collective historical condition:

> who could not feel the subterranean current of unrest in the country? Schoolboys and girls on strike and locking up their recalcitrant, authoritarian headmasters and headmistresses in office cupboards: workers downing their tools and refusing the temporary consolation of tripartite agreements; housewives holding processions and shouting obscene slogans in protest against the high food prices; armed robbers holding up banks in daylight with crowds cheering; women refusing to be relegated to the kitchen and the bedroom, demanding equal places in men's former citadel of power and privilege.(50)

This passage forcefully drives home the idea that Kenya's pervasive social ills require a collective (though not necessarily vertically orchestrated) response – a type of activism that exceeds the constricted orthodoxies of Soviet-style communism and instead takes the form of an anti-hegemonic struggle extending across all classes and spheres of social life. The breadth of the popular resistance Ngũgĩ envisions also leads him to take seriously certain culturally and ethnically rooted modes of collective response that might otherwise fall outside the purview of communist politics. For example, the novel invokes Mumbi, the mythical mother of the Gĩkũyũ people, as a figure around whom the anti-colonial struggle can rally: 'The true house of Mumbi, Mumbi the mother creator, is all the black toiling masses carrying a jembe in one hand and three bullets in the other, struggling against centuries of drifting, sole witnesses of their homecoming' (282). The deployment of agricultural work as a trope for collective emancipatory struggles ('all the black toiling masses') looks back to Ngũgĩ's earlier bildungsromane, *Weep Not, Child* and *A Grain of Wheat*, while the allusion to directionless 'centuries of drifting' poignantly recalls the historic conditions of Black diasporic dispersal.

In another passage that speaks to the historical importance of ethnically rooted types of community, a minor character, the female village elder Nyakinyua, is described as 'the spirit that guided and held them together' (149). Nyakinyua's larger-than-life presence awakens 'a feeling that the crisis was a community crisis needing a communal response': 'Nyakinyua, mother of men: there was sad gaiety in her voice, she was celebrating rainbow memories of gain and loss, triumph and failure, but above all of suffering and knowledge in struggle' (149). Nyakinyua, who brews a drink from the Thang'eta plant to celebrate the arrival of the rains, is presented as a quasi-mythical figure in her own right, and her association with communal ritual comes to signify an ethnically grounded, proto-political mode of collectivity. Here, as in Ngũgĩ's later Gĩkũyũ novels and in the work of writers such as Roumain, McKay and Sembène, the rootedness of local traditions provides a halfway house on the road towards a more expansively global socialist movement among Third World nations: 'In the past, before imperialism, we had a system of age-groups, of extended families, of sub-clans and clans. In those days we had many types of people's organization. We had *Ukamaa wa Mwafrika* . . . in English, *African socialism*.'[57]

Ngũgĩ, as I have suggested, uses a number of different narrative procedures to adumbrate the collective rather than individual process of radical bildung. Similar to Ding's *The Sun Shines Over the Sanggan River*, which achieves the impression of collective voicing partly by mobilizing the narrative patterns of ancient Chinese epics, Ngũgĩ's novel self-reflexively calls attention to time-honoured traditions of African literature: 'We wanted to be taught African literature, African history,' Karega explains, 'for we wanted to know ourselves better' (204). To the extent that the telos of African nationalism appears compromised by centuries of white colonialism, Ngũgĩ advises a selective return to the past against the depredations of capitalist neo-imperialism:

> Which past was one talking about? . . . The past of a broken civilization, retarded growth, black people scattered over the globe to feed the ever-demanding god of profit . . .? Or was it the past of L'Ouverture, Turner, Chaka, Abdulla, Koitalel, Ole Masai, Kimathi, Mathenge and others? . . . Africa, after all, did not have one but several pasts which were in perpetual

57 Ngũgĩ, *The Devil on the Cross*, pp. 70–1 (emphasis in original). Ngũgĩ's view of ritual as a motor of the counter-hegemonic struggle is echoed by other anti-colonial writers who picture the emergence of postcolonial collectivity in terms of communal ritualistic experience. For example, the protagonist of Jacques Roumain's *Masters of the Dew* (1947) returns to Haiti after several years abroad, but he only succeeds in reconnecting with his community once he joins in a local ritual: 'Manuel, conquered by the magic beat of the drums in the depths of his being, was dancing and singing with the rest.' His Western-style atheism notwithstanding, Manuel's ability to fulfil the role of organic intellectual and revolutionary leader is contingent on this experience of ethnic rootedness: 'He wanted to sing a greeting to the trees: "Growing things, my growing things! . . . You are my house, you're my country."' It is only after this moment of reintegration that Manuel is able to impart to his community the forms of political awareness and collective solidarity he acquired during his years in Cuba. See Jacques Roumain, *Masters of the Dew* (Oxford: Heinemann, 1978), pp. 67, 55–6.

> struggle. Images pressed on images. [Karega] tried to wrestle with each, fix it, study it, make it yield the secret that had thus far eluded him. (255)

The anti-imperialist struggle is here turned inwards, towards those cognitive processes and historical objects that might come to constitute a future emancipatory self-knowledge. In *Petals of Blood*, this self-reflexive turn is presented as an enabling condition of Africa's (political, social, cultural) liberation. The struggle for a 'new world' and 'new earth' that is anticipated in the novel's visionary closing pages resembles the multiple open-ended work-like activities described in *A Grain of Wheat*: 'The true lesson of history was this: that the so-called victims, the poor, the downtrodden, the masses, had always struggled with spears and arrows, with their hands and songs of courage and hope . . . that they would continue struggling until a human kingdom came' (360). The political struggle is here no longer limited to a particular historical moment of anti-colonial resistance: it comes to include a much more expansive groups of 'victims', the 'poor', and the 'downtrodden'. The universalist thrust of Ngũgĩ's fiction – much like Karega's recuperative attention to dispersed pan-African rituals and traditions – takes the place of the nineteenth-century bildungsroman's more geographically circumscribed orientation towards a narrowly national telos.

Petals of Blood, like the other novels and films I have examined in this chapter, attempts to shore up the possibility of radical bildung by shifting the site of its realization from the individual to the collective. In doing so, the works I have explored here take up a variety of influences ranging from Maoism and radical pedagogy to a reinvigorated interest in work and ritual. The next chapter will ask what happens when the very idea of an organizing telos – along with the aesthetic forms that are conventionally deployed to organize narrative teleology – comes under pressure. I will turn to a range of novels that responded to communism's crises after 1950 by interrogating the forms hitherto taken by the socialist struggle. Rather than simply abandoning the generic affordances of the bildungsroman, these novels – by authors as varied as Guido Morselli (Italy), Doris Lessing (Rhodesia/Britain), Maryse Condé (Guadeloupe/France) and Peter Weiss (Germany/Sweden) – use the motif of strenuously work-like bildung to articulate acute experiences of (organizational, political, historical) formlessness.

4

No Home but the Struggle: The Left Bildungsroman and the Formlessness of History

This chapter homes in on a distinctive variant of the radical bildungsroman that gained prominence from the 1950s onwards. The novels I discuss here were composed after 1956, the year in which Nikita Khrushchev's condemnation of the crimes of Stalinism plunged communism into its deepest crisis to date. The year 1956 occupies an outsized position in the history of twentieth-century communism, and its larger political fallout – the critique of actually existing socialism and of the CP's ossified ideological structures – reverberates through many left bildungsromane produced in this period. 'By the 1970s and '80s,' the political theorist Jodi Dean has recently noted, 'wide swathes of the Left had become convinced that the party form was no longer adequate to left aspirations.'[1] For much of the twentieth century, the party had served as the principal vehicle for radical social energies – as the organizational form most evidently capable of directing the revolutionary impulse towards its future fulfilment. The novels explored in this chapter treat the crisis of the party form after 1956 as the symptomatic index of a profound historical crisis within the socialist project itself. They do so in strikingly innovative artistic ways. In these texts, the subjectivity of the bildungsheld becomes uncoupled from the fulness of a macro-historical political telos – the kind of goal that Georg Lukács's *Theory of the Novel* had described as the protagonist's longed-for 'earthly home'.[2] While this

1 Jodi Dean, *Crowds and Party* (London: Verso, 2016), p. 22.

2 Georg Lukács, *The Theory of the Novel: A Historico-Philosophical Essay on the Forms of Great Epic Literature* (Cambridge, MA: MIT Press, 1999), p. 132. See the Introduction for discussion of Lukács's claims.

telos had helped to anchor the bildungsroman's allegorical functions by giving 'unified articulation' (Lukács) to the protagonist's biography, the left bildungsromane I examine here figure the socialist struggle in terms of a resistance to such quasi-transcendent historical teleologies.[3] The artistic sign of this resistance, I argue, is an aesthetic of formlessness. 'In discarding the party form', Dean tells us socialist movements run the risk of 'jettison[ing] the possibility of building collective power.'[4] *Formlessness*, as I use the term here, refers to this threat of directionlessness, but it also signifies the deliberate and experimental suspension of discredited organizational forms in an attempt to imagine the emergence of new political solidarities and coalitions.

I will begin by turning to *The Communist* (1976) by the Italian novelist Guido Morselli because this text gives exemplary expression to the broader historical problematic that structures the works explored in this chapter. I will then consider novels by Doris Lessing (*The Golden Notebook*, 1962) and Maryse Condé (*Hérémakhonon*, 1976) before concluding with a discussion of Peter Weiss's trilogy *The Aesthetics of Resistance*. Unlike Morselli's formally more conservative novel, Lessing's, Condé's and Weiss's texts deploy innovative aesthetic strategies that push narrative cohesion to its breaking point. These books articulate experiences of homelessness that beset the political struggle at the time of state socialism's profoundest crisis, but it is not my intention to suggest that the works considered in this chapter are simply artistic outliers. Instead, these novels foreground one of the radical bildungsroman's central insights by pushing to an extreme the tone of uncertainty and self-questioning that marks the genre's understanding of the socialist struggle. As the left-wing historian Hannah Proctor reminds us, to be involved in any political struggle is to render oneself vulnerable to experiences of defeat and despair. 'Against those who would characterise despair as a form of treason and a betrayal of the hopeful revolution', Proctor holds that such 'denial of despair' stems from 'an overly romanticised image of past hope' – it involves 'a refusal to speak frankly about hopeless or difficult conditions in the present'.[5] As my previous chapters have indicated, experiences of crisis – and the aesthetic conveyances by which these experiences are given expression in the left bildungsroman – are central to the genre's political vision and provide much of its

3 Ibid., p. 81.

4 Dean, *Crowds and Party*, p. 29.

5 Hannah Proctor, *Burnout: The Emotional Experience of Defeat* (London: Verso, 2024), p. 8.

narrative fuel. In contrast to the nineteenth-century bourgeois bildungsroman, which had held out a symbolic form capable of containing the revolutionary changes wrought by modernity, the socialist novel of formation insists on the essential ongoingness of the struggle. It forces us to confront the ways in which subjects are constantly made and unmade – formed and de-formed – by history. The protagonists of the radical bildungsroman, to borrow Proctor's words, 'are not newborn babies in an already transformed world; they are fucked-up people trying to transform their fucked-up realities and often getting even more fucked up in the process.'[6]

'The Weight of Things': Work and Struggle in Morselli's *The Communist*

Guido Morselli was born in 1912 into an affluent bourgeois family in Bologna. And, even though Morselli never joined a socialist party, *The Communist* offers a subtle and ultimately sympathetic account of the political disillusionment experienced by an Italian communist politician in the wake of Khrushchev's so-called Secret Speech of 1956. Khrushchev's speech had sent shockwaves through communist parties across the globe when it was leaked to the West by Israel's secret agency, Shin Bet – it denounced Stalinist atrocities in the 1930s and mounted a scathing indictment of the cult of personality surrounding Stalin. Many radical bildungsromane that were published around this date involve a determined attempt to come to terms with socialism's historical defeats, as well as to create new spaces for socialist commitment outside the CP.[7] *The Communist* shares this sense of crisis. It centres on the life of an Italian communist cadre, Walter Ferranini, in the late 1950s. The early portions of the novel offer a retrospective account of Walter's early embrace of communism – what I have called the second-order (socialist) bildung that works to undo the effects of an earlier bourgeois misbildung. By contrast, the central sections of Morselli's book focus on Walter's painful attempts to reformulate his socialist commitments in response to the events of 1956. *The Communist* is something of an anomaly in relation to the other works I discuss in this book, insofar as

6 Ibid., p. 28.

7 Lukács's reflections on the 'socialist bildungsroman' – published in that symbolically important year of 1956 – also reflect these tensions. See my discussion of Lukács's 'Critical and Socialist Realism' in the Introduction.

it was not penned by an (ex-)communist or fellow traveller. But it is partly for this reason that Morselli's novel – neither an unreconstructed defence of Soviet-style communism nor a savage attack on the communist God That Failed – offers a helpful entry point into the set of artistic and historical problems I explore in this chapter.

Walter is a veteran PCI (Partito Comunista Italiano) deputy representing the northern industrial region of Emilia-Romagna in the Italian parliament, with an even longer history as a communist labour organizer and bona fide revolutionary (including time spent fighting Franco's fascists in the Spanish Civil War). Walter recognizes that 'Communism was something he had earned. Temptations, large and small, had presented themselves, but he had resisted.'[8] For Walter, becoming a rank-and-file member of the party after the war initially served a threefold purpose: it acted as a cure for his loneliness; as a continuation of his revolutionary commitments of the 1930s; and finally, as atonement for the years he spent married to the daughter of an American capitalist following the socialists' disappointing defeat in the Spanish Civil War. *The Communist* tells the story of the twists and turns of Walter's life as well as of the unwavering commitment to the party that underpins them. We are shown that Walter's deeply held political convictions are increasingly at odds with the dogmatic rigidity of the party: when he is sent by his superiors to interrogate a young comrade accused of deviation from the official party line, Walter recognizes in the young and idealistic activist aspects of his own former self.

Walter's growing feelings of isolation and despair are aggravated by the revelations of 1956. In an attempt to make sense of the (political, ideological, historical) causes for this crisis, Walter decides to write an article for the party newspaper. Entitled 'Labour, the Physical World, and Alienation', the essay is dryly academic ('Nina read the article to him', we are told, 'her voice tense in an effort to liven up the text, which needed it', 225), but it can without much difficulty be decoded as a direct and deeply felt response to the political problems that beleaguered the communist movement. The article is partly an attempt to map out a way forward – to chart the future course of Walter's political bildung. The passages from Walter's article that we are given to read form the heart of Morselli's novel. What is required, Walter insists in these pages, is a critical revision of Marxism's foundational theoretical tenets. The essay

8 Guido Morselli, *The Communist* (New York: New York Review of Books, 2017), p. 176. Subsequent references will be given in the text.

traces these principles to the humanism of Marx's early *Economic and Philosophical Manuscripts* (1844), according to which 'the axis of reality is History, meaning, of course, our history. Man' (227). At the heart of Marx's early thought, Walter finds a set of intractable contradictions: while Marx ostensibly rejected the idealist belief in 'reason, consciousness, the idea, the subject or the self', he did remain 'a humanist in other lofty meanings of that term'. Marx's 'humanism' therefore

> makes him kin (despite the noted fundamental differences) to the family of Western speculative thought, a body of thought that is deeply anthropocentrist and inclined to measure every quality, every energy, every living existence in relation to man. Man as the end, if not the beginning of the universe. (227)

Walter takes aim at the anthropocentrism he finds enshrined in Marx's writings on alienation. Crucially, however, his article does not call for a total rejection of humanism but rather advocates humanism's intellectual recalibration and political repurposing. In contrast to the speculative thought of the early Marx, Walter appeals to the everyday (and, he claims, anthropologically universal) experience that the world resists our desires. These experiences remind us that we are fundamentally vulnerable to the world around us, as the individual is not free to reshape the material structure of 'physical nature' according to her (or his) wishes:

> Daily experience teaches us that the external, physical world does not depend on us but quite the contrary: we depend on it . . . If for a moment we deceive ourselves into thinking we are independent, reality and above all that reality we call physical nature will quickly make us understand we are part of it, mere elements of a natural system . . . Labour, production, is never a spontaneous act, an affirmation of our personality, it is simply a necessity that never ceases . . . Alienation presupposes that man and his activity preexist in an *expansive* state, and this seems to me optimistic, unrealistic. Mortification, I would call the condition of the worker. And in my view, we must recognize that his is merely one example of a more general human condition. (228–9, emphasis in original)

Walter's article rejects the delusion that we can ever attain full control over the conditions of our own existence. What we are given in this passage is a view of the 'human condition' that severely diminishes the space available for human thought and agency: our actions and thoughts, as Walter describes them, can never transcend – or 'expan[d]' beyond – the constraints of the material world but must remain fully and inextricably enmeshed in them.

As the title of Walter's article indicates, the central category of his text is *lavoro* (work), rendered into English as *labour* by Morselli's American translator. Walter acknowledges that the critique of the alienation of labour under capitalism has given the communist movement its distinctive political identity. However, in a signal departure from this critical tradition, Walter's essay calls for a return to a more foundational meaning of the term *lavoro* as physical *work*. The category of alienation, he insists, obscures the fact that human work is always already alienated because it confronts a mute material world that is fundamentally indifferent to human needs. The alienation of labour under capitalism is, in this sense, only a historically contingent version of the anthropologically universal alienation of work as such:

> In [work] (and not only in [work]) we feel the weight of things that we must *move aside* in order to live. Liberation is not (contrary to what the theory of alienation asserts) the recovery of that part of ourselves dispersed in things. Anything but. Liberation, if it were at all possible, and *it is not* possible, would mean distancing things from us, enlarging the space we need to breathe and to move about. (231, emphasis in original)

Walter views work as an ineradicable fact of human life. His comments echo the remarks by Hegel – apropos of the bondsman's work – that I discussed in the Introduction and that I have described as the conceptual heart of the radical bildungsroman's work-centred deep grammar. Walter's article causes a scandal when it is published, in no small part because the bourgeois press is able to seize on it as evidence of the doctrinal rifts that are tearing the CP apart in the wake of 1956. In due course, Walter is expelled from the party: 'Ferranini has not merely mounted a criticism of alienation,' the leadership declares; 'He has mounted a criticism of socialism! He has criticized the Marxist promise to give human beings a better life under socialism' (254).

In the context of our discussion, what matters most in these passages is how faithfully Walter's immanentist understanding of material work tracks with his experience of the socialist struggle. As Walter comes to see it, revolutionaries are guided by no transcendent historical goal that has the Communist Party as its privileged vessel. Responding to this situation, Walter's article proposes a revisionary ontology of work that has a good deal in common with Lukács's *Ontology of Social Being*. Like Lukács, Walter positions *work* as a central model for Marxist thought and he reframes the socialist struggle itself as a type of collectively undertaken work-like praxis; but, compared to Lukács, *The Communist* presents us with a much bleaker account of the emancipatory potential of work as a series of localized human-scale positings.[9] Walter finds himself embroiled in acrimonious party battles, and these internecine struggles turn out to be every bit as central to his slow and painful political formation as the party's doctrinally sanctioned fights against the proletariat's class enemies. 'Let me just say that so long as we live, we will be obliged to struggle,' Walter concludes: 'Struggle, and therefore be under constant stress. [Work] is only one aspect of that stress. The appearance may change, but the substance will always be this' (259).

Walter's growing estrangement from the party is echoed in a considerable number of left bildungsromane from the second half of the twentieth century. But there is a key difference: whereas Morselli's novel presents Walter's account of the work-like immanence of the struggle as evidence of his irremediable estrangement from left-wing politics, radical bildungsromane written by socialists such as Lessing and Weiss reframe this pessimistic ontology as part of the left bildungsroman's long-standing generic commitment to describe '*from the inside*' the frustrations of the socialist project.[10] To put this another way: while Morselli treats the ontology of work outlined in Walter's essay as a symptom of communism's historical defeat, authors who remained committed to socialism developed new aesthetic strategies that made it possible to reconcile this understanding of work with their broader artistic vision of the inevitable difficulty and laboriousness of socialist struggles.

The need to develop new artistic forms was given special urgency in the second half of the twentieth century, as the historical crisis of communist parties inspired artistic thinking about the alternative (organizational, historical, aesthetic) forms which the left struggle might take. We can get a handle on the specific artistic problems that were thrown up by 1956 if we think of this historical moment as a crisis in the structure of revolutionary subjectivity itself. The Brazilian

9 See my Introduction for discussion of Lukács's foundational text.

10 I discuss the implications of Georg Lukács's phrase ('describ[ing] the forces working toward socialism *from the inside*') in the Introduction. See Georg Lukács, 'Critical Realism and Socialist Realism,' in *The Meaning of Contemporary Realism* (London: Mellon, 1963), pp. 93–135 (95).

political theorist Rodrigo Nunes has explored this question by adapting the concept *transitivity* from the French communist intellectual Alain Badiou. Nunes glosses the term as follows: 'What I am calling "transitivity" here . . . refers to the idea that there is a deterministic connection between social structure and revolutionary subjectivity in the sense that some social groups, by virtue of their structural position, are both *endowed with a unique capacity to transform that structure* and *determined to become politically conscious and active*'.[11] The concept of transitivity captures an understanding of the political struggle that had found expression in key works of early twentieth-century Marxist theory such as Lukács's *History and Class Consciousness* (1923). According to this view, the revolutionary subject has its privileged home in the party, and it is the party's historical mission to foster, unify and direct revolutionary energies towards the movement's ultimate historical goal: the realization of communism. As Nunes points out, it is when this 'transitive' dimension of revolutionary selfhood disintegrates – that is, when its ties to the party form are severed and the vertical (party-centric) organization of the revolutionary movement is dispatched in favour of more dispersed and horizontal modes of organization – that the socialist struggle can temporarily appear formless.[12]

In the novels I discuss in the remainder of this chapter, the reluctance to index revolutionary subjectivity to some privileged organizational form or macro-historical narrative produces such moments of politico-artistic disorientation. Lessing, Condé and Weiss all describe this experience by invoking the category of *the formless* and by developing a corresponding aesthetic that is intended to lend it expression. Crucially, however, the crisis of transitivity does not lead these writers to renounce the radical bildungsroman's future-oriented view of the socialist struggle: following their release from the confines of the party form, the protagonists of Lessing's, Condé's and Weiss's novels experience the struggle as an ongoing process of coalition-building across

11 Rodrigo Nunes, *Neither Vertical nor Horizontal: A Theory of Political Organisation* (London: Verso, 2021), pp. 97–8 (emphasis in original). Bruno Bosteels provides some helpful further discussion of Badiou's theorization of 'the transitivity of political subjectivity' as 'the basic underlying principle of all Marxism-Leninism'. See Bruno Bosteels, *Badiou and Politics* (Durham, NC: Duke University Press, 2011), pp. 151–2. We'll return to Badiou's thinking at the end of this chapter.

12 On the categories of 'vertical' and 'horizontal' in this connection, see Nunes, *Neither Vertical nor Horizontal*, esp. pp. 81–121.

shifting divides of class, gender and race. In the absence of a clear historical goal or quasi-transcendent 'earthly home', these bildungsromane show us a process of self-making that is open-ended and ongoing and that involves the crystallization of new solidarities and new collective demands.

Radical bildungsromane from the second half of the twentieth century possess a particularly keen artistic sensorium for such moments of political-cum-existential disorientation. Before we move on to a few of these novels, however, it is worth remembering that the uneasy balancing of transitive and immanentist accounts of the socialist struggle had long been a feature of the radical bildungsroman genre. Many of the texts and films that I discussed in previous chapters give expression to a related dialectic of reflective distanciation and experiential immersion in the messy here and now of the struggle. As I pointed out in Chapter 2, we can trace such patterns in texts ranging from Gorky's autobiographical trilogy and Leon Trotsky's *History of the Russian Revolution* to Nâzım Hikmet's *Life's Good, Brother* and the fictionalized recollections of Johannes R. Becher, one of the GDR's most celebrated party-line writers.[13] Other authors aim at similar effects. For example, Victor Serge – the anarchist Bolshevik who became one of the most celebrated dissident voices of twentieth-century communism – deploys first- and third-person voices in his memoirs to indicate how completely personal experience becomes enfolded in broader historical movements. 'It has been observed that I show hardly any interest in talking about myself,' Serge explains in his remarkable autobiography, *Memoirs of a Revolutionary*: 'It is hard for me to disentangle my own person from the social processes, the ideas and activities in which it has shared . . . I view personality as a supreme value, only integrated in society and in history.'[14] Serge's novels register the anxiety that revolutionary subjectivity is devalued following the crisis of communism's macro-historical certainties: 'We have offered our lives to History,' notes one character in Serge's final novel, *Unforgiving Years*: '[But] what if the great machine were running off the rails, what if its mental cogs were perverted, its social cogs corrupted?'[15] Similarly, Serge's novels often respond to the

13 The two volumes of Becher's autobiographical novel are *Abschied* (1940) and *Wiederanders* (publ. posthumously in 1970).

14 Victor Serge, *Memoirs of a Revolutionary, 1901–1941* (Oxford: Oxford University Press, 1975), p. 371. Serge's memoirs were published posthumously in 1951.

15 Victor Serge, *Unforgiving Years* (New York: New York Review Books, 2008), p. 18. 'There is nothing left but our defeat,' Serge observes in another novel: 'For the

experience of historical loss by breaking up their central plotline into several separate strands that describe the interweaving, rerouting or abrupt termination of individual bildung narratives: 'We're starting a different life,' observes one of Serge's characters, while the narrator adds parenthetically that 'more accurately he might have said: We are ending one whole life.'[16] In Serge's writings, this fragmentation of biographical coherence effects a splintering of narrative voices and triggers the emergence of an experimental, quasi-modernist polyvocality. The novels by Lessing, Condé and Weiss, to which I will now turn, convey a related sense of fragmentation. However, instead of presenting this dispersal of narrative unity as the aesthetic sign of a profound political disillusionment, they show that the socialist struggle continues to create spaces from which new radical projects can emerge.

'A Bit of Rescue-Work': Subjectivity and the Party Form in Lessing's *The Golden Notebook*

Born to British parents in Persia, Lessing spent much of her childhood in Southern Rhodesia (present-day Zimbabwe). Her experiences in colonial Africa profoundly shaped her writing, as did the time she spent in the Communist Party in Southern Rhodesia and (from the late 1940s) in Great Britain. *The Golden Notebook* fictionalizes Lessing's own biography in the figure of the writer Anna Wulf, and its plotlines skilfully interweave Anna's interest in communism with her personal relationships, as well as with her views on gender, race and identity. The bulk of the novel consists of the four notebooks penned by Anna: a black notebook that provides a record of Anna's life in Southern Rhodesia before and during the Second World War; a yellow notebook containing a novel-in-progress about the painful ending of Anna's love affair; a blue notebook that offers a more intimate chronicle of Anna's dreams and memories; and a red notebook that records Anna's experience as a member of the Communist Party from the 1930s onwards. The novel concludes with Anna's fifth (golden) notebook, in which she tries to tie together the different strands of her life. *The Golden Notebook* is often considered an

moment the dialectic of history has placed us under the wheel.' See Victor Serge, *Midnight in the Century* (New York: New York Review Books, 2008), p. 121.

16 Serge, *Unforgiving Years*, p. 47.

expression of Lessing's comprehensive disillusionment with Soviet-style state communism.[17] Or, more precisely, it is often regarded as a transitional text in Lessing's fictional oeuvre because it combines a searching (but essentially backward-looking) account of communism from the 1930s to the 1950s with a (forward-looking) engagement with the nascent women's liberation movements of the 1960s, to which Lessing would soon commit herself. But, I suggest, we can also read *The Golden Notebook* as a radical bildungsroman that dials up the genre's tone of ideological self-questioning without reneging on the importance of socialism's historical mission. When it is understood in this way, Lessing's novel demonstrates the left bildungsroman's capacity to incorporate even the most extreme forms of ideological (self-)doubt. In doing so, the novel also offers a particularly insightful and artistically sophisticated engagement with the problem of formlessness.

The year 1956 figures as a political watershed year in Lessing's novel, as it comes to symbolize the Soviet CP's totalitarian betrayal of socialism's revolutionary promise. In Anna's account, this betrayal entails a receding – if not quite a total closing down – of socialism's internationalist horizons. As Anna comments in the red notebook that keeps track of her political life, the 'C.P. should be completely changed': what is required after 1956 is 'a genuinely British Party, without the deadly loyalty to Moscow . . . a genuinely democratic Party'; moreover, it will be necessary 'to break all ties with foreign communist parties, in the expectation that other communist parties will also be rejuvenating themselves'.[18] Another entry, dated '20th September, 1956' and ostensibly written after Khrushchev's revelations about Stalin's Purges, notes that '[t]he idea in the air' is 'to start a new "really British C.P."' (428). This gradual nationalization of the International responds to communism's defeats in Western Europe, as well as to the aggressively expansionist policies of the Soviet Union in the newly constituted Eastern Bloc and to its brutal imposition of the Soviet model of cultural life in Central and Eastern Europe.[19] Like other left bildungsromane of the

17 Marion Vlastos, 'Doris Lessing and R. D. Laing: Psychopolitics and Prophecy', *PMLA* 91.2 (1976): 245–58 (247).

18 Doris Lessing, *The Golden Notebook* (New York: Vintage, 1999), p. 427. Subsequent references are given parenthetically.

19 Lessing's analysis of the pressures of national retrenchment is shared by many other radical bildungsromane of the period, including Sartre's *The Last Chance*, Edward Upward's *The Rotten Elements* (the second volume of *The Spiral Ascent*) and *Betrayed*

postwar years, *The Golden Notebook* takes account of what is lost in this process, but the novel also evokes historical moments of positive commitment and political action that lend legitimacy to the socialist struggle in the present. These moments provide a model for the 'new honest' party (428) Anna envisages. Similar to Sartre's *Roads to Freedom* and Weiss's *Aesthetics of Resistance*, the main problem that animates Anna's red notebook is the difficulty of not letting her later disillusionment with communism seep into her recollection of these foundational moments.[20] As a radical bildungsroman, *The Golden Notebook* works – however haltingly and inconclusively – to transform Anna's acute experiences of loss into a redemptive narrative through which (self-)doubt can be understood as contributing to personal and political growth.

Recent work in political theory has identified the party as an institutional structure that can lend a shared direction and durable form to otherwise dispersed revolutionary impulses and desires. In her book *Crowds and Party*, which aims to remobilize the party form for twenty-first-century socialist movements, Jodi Dean offers a key statement of this position:

> The stronger the political organization we build, the greater will be its – and our – expectations. Organizing us, the party compels us, or, differently put, it is the apparatus through which we compel ourselves to do what we must, to do what has to be done because we cannot, will not, acquiesce to inequality, exploitation, and oppression.[21]

When it is viewed in this way, the party bears a family resemblance to the 'earthly home' that Lukács had described as the gravitational endpoint of the left bildungsroman. In *The Golden Notebook*, by contrast, the party figures no longer as the quasi-natural organizational form of

---

Spring (1953) by Lessing's communist friend Jack Lindsay. In the second volume of her autobiography, Lessing records that her disillusionment with the CP was partly grounded in her recognition of the vast national differences existing between party branches. For her recollection of a meeting with then communist Tristan Tzara ('He made it clear that the French CP despised the British CP'), see *Walking in the Shade: Volume Two of My Autobiography, 1949–1962* (London: Harper Collins, 1997), p. 93. Louise Yelin has offered a helpful discussion of national belonging in *The Golden Notebook* in her *From the Margins of Empire: Christina Stead, Doris Lessing, Nadine Gordimer* (Ithaca, NY: Cornell University Press, 1998), pp. 71–90.

20 Sartre's influence on Lessing's novel is discussed in Betsy Draine, *Substance Under Pressure: Artistic Coherence and Evolving Form in the Novels of Doris Lessing* (Madison, WI: University of Wisconsin Press, 1983), pp. 72–3, 82.

21 Dean, *Crowds and Party*, p. 210.

the socialist movement – as the transhistorical object of political identifications – but merely as a transitional moment in an ongoing and open-ended struggle. In the words of Rodrigo Nunes, this shift in emphasis entails a 'move from *organisation as form* to *organising as mediation*': whereas the party as organizational 'form' had promised to endow the socialist struggle with a single historical goal and gestalt, the party understood as mediation 'can in no way be reduced to a form; it exists as activity [and] constant exercise'.[22] This reconfiguration of the party – as transient mediator rather than as fixed form – helps to render *The Golden Notebook* legible as a revisionary post-1956 left bildungsroman.

Lessing's novel considers how – given the crisis of the party form and of the macro-historical teleologies that subtended it – experiences of loss and meaninglessness might be rescued into some new kind of significance. As Anna notes at one point, it is through the act of writing – that is, by recasting her life in the shape of a bildungsroman – that her suffering will acquire meaning: 'The pleasure of recognition, of a bit of rescue-work, so to speak, rescuing the formless into form. Another bit of chaos rescued and "named" . . . And I know why – it's because all the pain, and the killing and the violence is safely held in the story and it can't hurt me' (450). *The Golden Notebook* itself revolts against the optimism of such pronouncements. The novel's resistance to unified biographical narrativization casts doubt on the ability of any artistic 'form' to ensure cohesion or to shore up a stable selfhood in the face of raw experiences of crisis and loss. In this context, Anna's decision to keep four distinct notebooks appears to suggest a tidy compartmentalization of the self, and it raises the question of how her political life is linked to other parts of her identity. Anna's attempt to figure out the connection between her private and activist selves mirrors the key question that Nikolay Chernyshevsky's activist heroine Vera Pavlovna poses to herself after setting up the first of her cooperative workshops: 'Is the workshop really part of my personal life?'[23] Anna's notebooks are not simply the retreat of a private self or the passive receptacle of personal convictions and experiences. Instead, much like the Soviet diaries of the 1930s analysed by the historian Jochen Hellbeck, Anna's notebooks become the medium where the truth of the political struggle is given fresh urgency by being articulated from the inside or

22 Nunes, *Neither Vertical nor Horizontal*, p. 78.

23 Nikolay Chernyshevsky, *What Is to Be Done?* (Ithaca, NY: Cornell University Press, 1989), p. 343.

phenomenologically.[24] While the diaristic fragmentation of *The Golden Notebook* appears to upend Anna's attempt to 'rescu[e] the formless' into the unified narrative 'form' of a bildung narrative, the notebooks also become the place where experiences of homelessness can be contested: the rupture between Anna's different selves is presented as a historical dilemma that will need to be resolved through a new and radical praxis of living, albeit one that is no longer articulated solely through the party form.

As the fifth and final notebook – the golden notebook – makes clear, the possibility of such a new praxis is signalled by Anna's psychological breakdown towards the end of the novel. At a formal level, this mental breakdown corresponds to the disintegration of the novel's linear narrative of formation as well as of the political logic of 'transitivity' that sutures individual biographies to larger macro-historical trajectories. Similar to Anna's collapse, which Lessing held to signal Anna's ultimate liberation from social constraints (including the constraint of the patriarchally organized party form), the dispersal of narrative coherence in the golden notebook marks the point at which Anna's life story begins to escape the artificial constraints of plot that render life as a steady development from youth to mature adulthood. Anna's hysteric collapse, Lessing suggests, can be a conduit to freedom: it indicates the precise moment at which Anna's story begins to follow the open-ended and non-directional movement of her life, rather than pressing her biography into the coercive logic of a tightly coordinated developmental narrative.[25]

When *The Golden Notebook* begins, Anna already appears to have completed her second (political) bildung, having been a member of the CP for four years. However, as the novel unfolds, Anna recognizes that her younger self misconstrued the meaning of the socialist struggle. As

---

24 Hellbeck shows that diary writing in post-revolutionary Russia was integral to the 'goal of remaking the life of society as well as of each individual'. As Hellbeck points out, this also applied to cases where diaristic authorship did not hew closely to the party line. See Jochen Hellbeck, *Revolution on My Mind: Writing a Diary under Stalin* (Cambridge, MA: Harvard University Press, 2009), p. 5.

25 Jodi Dean, whose work on the party form I engaged with earlier, closes her book *Comrade* with a reading of this moment in *The Golden Notebook*. According to Dean, Anna's breakdown is a symptom of 'nonmeaning, incoherence, madness'. This argument makes sense in the light of Dean's own conviction that, without the party form to hold us and give a direction and shape to our lives, we would (politically speaking) be nothing. By contrast, I argue that Lessing's novel gives us a more hopeful understanding of the political possibilities that are created by Anna's experience of crisis. See Jodi Dean, *Comrade: An Essay on Political Belonging* (London: Verso, 2019), p. 135.

her partner, the writer Saul Green, comments in the golden notebook, the overpowering experience of those who witness the political struggle from the inside is not one of imminent plenitude but of ceaseless, work-like dedication to the political task at hand:

> As I crack up out of that 100 per cent revolutionary, I notice I crack up into aspects of everything I hate. That's because I've never lived with my eye on becoming what is known as mature. I've spent all my life, until recently, preparing myself for the moment when someone says: 'Pick up that rifle'; or, 'run that collective farm'; or 'organise that picket line'. I always believed I'd be dead by the time I was thirty. (595)

One of the questions raised by Lessing is what form the socialist struggle will take after the totalitarian excesses of Stalinism seem to have made a revitalization of the movement impossible. In a striking move, Lessing responds to this dilemma by showing that even those mythical foundational moments – the October Revolution, the Popular Front of the 1930s, the Spanish Civil War – were already overdetermined by social and economic contradictions. It turns out that the safety and wholeness that Anna's younger self hoped to enjoy in the party was never to be found there in the first place. Anna increasingly comes to identify her earlier desire to find a home in the CP with the reactionary values of her psychotherapist, the ironically named Mrs Marks. The opening pages of *The Golden Notebook* in which she does so are supposedly quoted from Anna's own novel-in-progress, *Free Women*, a book that fictionalizes the process of bildung described in Anna's subsequent four notebooks. *Free Women* thus marks the endpoint of Anna's bildung, as *The Golden Notebook* proceeds to retrospectively unfold the story of her personal maturation. Lessing scrambles the conventional linearity of the novel of formation to make visible the fraught and involuted itinerary of Anna's political bildung – its errant and tortuous movements as well as its multiple stops and starts.

The inverted chronology of Lessing's novel serves a double purpose: on the one hand, Anna's mingled feelings of personal freedom and ideological disappointment at the beginning of the book are revealed to be the outcome of a set of complex adjustments to historical pressures; on the other, the blurring of the boundary between Anna's novel and her diaristic notebooks unsettles the idea that the shift from autobiography into fiction – from first-person into third-person narration – makes it possible to attain a commandingly detached view of one's life. While *The*

Golden Notebook's shuttling back and forth between narrative levels and points of view has often been identified with the postmodern interest in destabilizing diegetic levels, it in fact encodes the impossibility of attaining an Archimedean point outside historical struggles. As Anna fails to create a continuous story out of the life fragments recorded in the notebooks, Lessing's novel articulates – at the level of its formal construction – the insight that there is 'no home but the struggle'.[26]

Lessing recalled in 1957 that, as a member of the CP in the 1940s, 'my picture of socialism as developed in the Soviet Union was, to say the least, inaccurate'. And yet, Lessing observes, 'after fifteen years of uncomfortable adjustment to reality I still find myself in the possession of an optimism about the future'.[27] Like other authors of radical bildungsromane, Lessing suggests that her second (socialist) bildung was not completed by joining the CP – on the contrary, her time in the CP acted as a catalyst (what Nunes calls a 'mediator') for the development of her later (feminist, anti-colonial, socialist) commitments. Socialism, Lessing explained in 1971, 'has fermented ideas everywhere, [it] has become part of ordinary thinking'; and she also expressed hope that socialist energies, having found their way into 'ordinary thinking', would invigorate the political activities of the New Left.[28] This process of transformation and 'revitaliz[ation]', Anna concludes in her red notebook, will entail an attention to the specific problems that arise in the national contexts of Britain and Rhodesia: commenting on the mid-century 'Old Left', she finds that the CP's 'inner logic of "centralism" made the process of disintegration inevitable because we had no links at all with what African movements there were' (65). The left struggle, if it is to continue, will need to be articulated with anti-colonial liberation movements that break with the vertical structures of the party – even when these new and emerging movements renounce socialist internationalism in favour of a new sense of national (or pan-African) belonging.

26 Upward was another communist writer whose commitment to socialism outlasted the time he spent in the CP. *No Home but the Struggle* is the title of the last volume of Upward's trilogy *The Spiral Ascent.*

27 Doris Lessing, 'The Small Personal Voice', in *Declaration*, ed. Tom Maschler (London: MacGibbon and Kee, 1957), pp. 13–27 (26).

28 Lessing, 'Introduction', in *The Golden Notebook*, pp. xi–xxvi (xvi).

Radicalism, Idealism and Counter-Revolution in Condé's *Hérémakhonon*

Published in 1976, *Hérémakhonon* was the debut novel of the Guadeloupean writer Maryse Condé. Condé would later note that she 'began to be politically conscious' around 1960, in her mid-twenties, thanks to her friendship with a group of African Marxists: 'I became a Marxist because my friends were Marxists.'[29] This political radicalization led her to relocate to Ghana, where she engaged in Marxist activism and imbibed ideas of the Black radical movement by reading works by Julius Nyerere, Malcom X and others. As a semi-autobiographical text, *Hérémakhonon* shares some features with Condé's own life, but it also conveys her keen anxiety about the ways in which the socialist project had become compromised. Most importantly, the novel captures the rapid unravelling of the belief that the concept of *négritude* – the intensely politicized vision of a unified Black culture and consciousness – might serve as an emancipatory rallying call against forms of neocolonialism.

Hérémakhonon recounts the journey to West Africa undertaken by Veronica Mercier, a highly educated Caribbean woman who lives and teaches in Paris. Veronica hopes that her sojourn in Africa will help her attain clarity about her cultural identity and family roots: 'well, perhaps, [I am] a tourist,' she notes of her decision to travel to Africa, 'but one of a new breed, searching out herself, not landscapes.'[30] *Hérémakhonon* offers a formally experimental mosaic of Veronica's recollections, present impressions and future-directed aspirations that troubles the idea of a straightforward search for, and recuperation of, biographical origins. Like Ngũgĩ's *A Grain of Wheat* (which I discussed in the previous chapter), Condé's novel resists the 'romance of decolonization' by showing that the return to a shared homeland is riddled with contradictions.[31] Like other postcolonial novels of formation, *Hérémakhonon* responds to this situation by scrambling the idea of a progressive developmental plot that relies on the concept of a unified

29 Condé, '"I have made peace with my island": An Interview with Maryse Condé', *Callaloo* 38 (1989): 87–133 (101).

30 Maryse Condé, *Hérémakhonon* (London: Lynne Rienner, 2000), p. 3. Subsequent references are given parenthetically.

31 Simon Gikandi, *Ngũgĩ wa Thiong'o* (Cambridge: Cambridge University Press, 2000), p. 72.

bildung.[32] Already on the first page of the novel, we are given glimpses of a parodically accelerated (or merely atavistic) bildung, as Veronica feels transported back in the blink of an eye to her ancestors' African past: 'Consider yourself home,' Veronica is told by the man who picks her up from the airport. In Veronica's imagination, past and present suddenly fuse into a single epiphanic moment of belonging. She feels that the man's greeting 'wipes out three centuries and a half' (4), thereby effecting an instantaneous realization of her journey's goal. As Veronica soon learns, however, the process of her second (African) bildung will be significantly more labyrinthine than this initial experience suggests: upon arriving in Africa, she discovers that the country is run by a corrupt president called Mwalimwana – a realization that sets Veronica on an increasingly tortuous and inconclusive course. As we will see, Veronica's search for her African roots proceeds by way of a series of negations, as she comes to reject one potential (political, historical) telos after another.

Mwalimwana uses his party to rule the country with an iron fist, notwithstanding his propagandistic efforts to cast himself in the role of the nation's benign father (Mwalimwana, we are told, is a Mandé term meaning 'our Father,' 10). In a particularly grim irony, we discover that Hérémakhonon ('Welcome House') refers to the walled-in headquarters of Mwalimwana's regime, where political prisoners are tortured. Far from providing the lost home that Veronica has longed for, Mwalimwana's brand of socialism has thrown the country into turmoil. Veronica is told by a friend:

> Mwalimwana planted this idea of socialism in the country, of equality between master and slave, and that's what you get. Students who no longer obey their teachers . . . Thieves. Criminals who are not afraid of the courts. Mwalimwana now has regrets. He wants to start all over again. He has realized that socialism will kill Africa. Will kill it far more radically than years of colonialism. Yet it will kill it. (71–2)

Mwalimwana's brutal imposition of socialism is intended to supply the momentum that will enable this African society to 'enter history [and] grasp the future,' but it instead comes 'at the price of [society's]

32 On this feature of postcolonial bildungsromane, see Jed Esty, *Unseasonable Youth: Modernism, Colonialism, and the Fiction of Development* (New York: Oxford University Press, 2013).

destruction'.[33] Condé reminds us that the attempt to subject non-European nations to an accelerated process of economic modernization (from rural economy to capitalism to socialism) has produced disastrous consequences. In Mwalimwana's case, the attempt to modernize the country is linked to his own brand of primitivist Afro-essentialism. The country's current ruling caste, we are told,

> were brought up with a certain idea of Africa . . . Oh, they encourage the arts! Have you heard the army's traditional music ensemble? Have you seen the national ballet? They took Paris and New York by storm. The African soul has never been expressed so well. The soul, the soul, they'll kill us to the last man to safeguard it. (90)

The attempt to posit a uniquely African 'soul' is inspired by mid-century celebrations of pan-African *négritude*, but these ideas are here articulated with distinctly Western cultural forms ('ballet'). In tying his political project to the *négritude* movement, Mwalimwana intends to reinforce his own nationalist rhetoric of rooted belonging – and Condé clearly wants her readers to grasp the historical irony of this opportunistic celebration of *négritude*. Yet, as the novel makes clear, this same language also paradoxically works to satisfy the Western desire for an exoticized African otherness: Western intellectuals, Condé's narrator informs us, 'consider Africa the rejuvenation of [their] Western soul, exhausted and dried up by the technological age' (98).

In *Hérémakhonon*, the various teleological political narratives that are held up for examination – from recuperative pan-Africanism to the future-oriented idiom of socialism, with its deep commitment to the possibility of an anti-capitalistic modernity – are rejected in turn. This process of critical appraisal and rejection makes up the substance of Veronica's struggle to find a new home, and it is rendered with compelling psychological depth through Veronica's budding love affair with Ibrahima Sory, a character who is described as 'the most reactionary and retrograde element among Mwalimwana's associates' (63). Initially unaware of Ibrahima's role in the regime (he has been guilty of censorship, murder and the detention and torture of political opponents), Veronica increasingly comes to recognize the inescapably political

33 The quotations here are taken from Simon During's 'Waiting for the Post: Modernity, Colonization, and Writing' (1989), cited in Simon Gikandi, *Writing in Limbo: Modernism and Caribbean Literature* (Ithaca, NY: Cornell University Press, 1992), p. 2.

dimension of her most intimate personal relations: 'If I understand correctly, making love in this country comes down to making a political choice' (64).

Veronica's bildung, then, is essentially negative – it involves rejecting a number of political projects that she comes to deem inadequate. This negative bildung proceeds along several interlinked vectors, from the explicitly political to the intimately personal, and it also includes a critique of Sory's masculinist advocacy of anti-colonial violence. Instead of affirming the political aim of national independence at any cost, *Hérémakhonon* presents us with a contradictory tangle of desires that results from the (sexual) attraction and (moral) disgust that Veronica feels towards Ibrahima.[34] As the novel progresses, Veronica is confounded by her inability to end her romance with Ibrahima. Is it possible, she wonders, that her attraction to Ibrahima is motivated by her own half-conscious rejection of the high-flying revolutionary ideals ('people, revolution, and justice', 94) advocated by her other male friends, most of whom are opposed to Mwalimwana? While Veronica shares her friends' outrage at the brutality of Mwalimwana's regime, she also feels alienated by the self-aggrandizing 'arrogan[ce] and contempt' of their proclamations:

> My revolt is a lure. This piece of truth hits me and goes to my head. I have never realized it so clearly. In fact I'm not escaping from anything. Through Ibrahima Sory I'm trying to get back to them on an idealized level. Rid of their absurdities. Entitled to be what they were – arrogant and contemptuous. Oh Lord, we thank you for having made us different – may the famous prayer no longer have an absurd taste for me. To sum up, I'm not trying to escape them. But to justify myself. (94–5)

Veronica narrowly avoids the type of mental breakdown that is experienced by Lessing's Anna Wulf when she is forced to face the contradictions that exist between her political and private life. And yet, at several points in Condé's narrative, including the passage I have just cited, Veronica reaches a similar recognition of the conflicted and self-defeating duality of her (intimate and political) desires. Like Anna, Veronica

34 At one point in the novel, Condé comments on her protagonist's instinctive opposition to Fanon's masculinist calls for anti-colonial violence (*Hérémakhonon*, p. 30). The literary scholar Julietta Singh offers an insightful critique of Fanon's theoretical investment in 'homogenized male subjectivity': see Julietta Singh, *Unthinking Mastery: Dehumanism and Decolonial Entanglements* (Durham, NC: Duke University Press, 2018), pp. 32–7.

comes to associate single-mindedness of purpose – including her own initial fetishization of the lost object of African ethno-cultural identity – with a quintessentially male practice of politics. Navigating a world in which political opinions are propagated almost exclusively by men, Veronica's bildung takes the form of a process of negations, or of bildung as struggle. Shuttling restlessly between intimations of the past, present and future, the open narrative structure of Condé's novel corresponds to Veronica's inconclusive attempts to find an appropriate object on which to focus her desire to belong – an earthly home that will anchor her sense of self.

In *Hérémakhonon*, the character who provides the closest analogue to Veronica's frustrated search is the young socialist Birame. Birame and Veronica are both introduced at the beginning of the book (Birame is presented to Veronica as 'one of your future students', 8), and Condé stresses the close, almost filial connection that forms between them. Like Veronica, Birame realizes that the historical failure of African socialism – its degeneration into autocratic despotism – leaves him without a political and ideological home. A committed activist, Birame recognizes the signs of socialism's crisis quickly enough: from the party loyalists in 'Mao suits' (37, 43) to Mwalimwana's oratorical impersonation of Fidel Castro (129), Birame everywhere encounters the material markers of a corrupted, party-centric socialism. No other character suffers as much as Birame at the hands of Mwalimwana's dictatorial regime. Arrested for his participation in anti-government protests, he and his fellow protestors are shunted onto a public stage where they are expected to deliver a public apology in front of a jeering crowd. When it is Birame's turn to undergo this public shaming and swear allegiance to the regime, he shouts: 'Never, never. They have betrayed the revolution. Never, never!' (44). Birame is detained and subjected to further torture. Veronica never manages to determine Birame's subsequent fate, but the novel hints that he has been murdered by Mwalimwana's henchmen.

Even though Veronica is concerned for Birame, her feelings towards him remain ambivalent. On the one hand, she admits, 'I never took him seriously. I half listened to his lucubrations' (45); on the other hand, almost in the same sentence, Condé's narrative solicits our admiration for Birame's 'convictions, beliefs, and ideals for which he had the courage to defy Mwalimwana and the soldiers' (45). The figure of Birame continues to haunt *Hérémakhonon*, as Veronica finds herself at every turn reminded of his sacrifice. The brutality with which Birame is treated by the regime continues to define the rest of the novel, and his spectral presence in the narrative gives Veronica's process of bildung added existential urgency. Veronica is initially unsympathetic to Birame's demand that '[w]e need a revolution' (31), but the novel clearly shows up the political limitations of Veronica's own (bourgeois, European) education and invites sympathy with Birame's youthful socialist idealism. Like the 'new people' that Lessing had identified as 'those who keep the dream alive', it is the young Birame who remains convinced that the socialist struggle must continue even in the face of its manifest historical 'betrayal'.[35]

It is important to recall the central place that Birame occupies in *Hérémakhonon*, partly because so much scholarship on the novel has given pride of place to Veronica's own female bildung narrative. Even the novel's most perceptive readers – such as Catherine Ward and Gayatri Chakravorty Spivak – have tended to emphasize the text's critique of negritudinal 'primitive history', as well as the various false starts and ellipses that mark Veronica's personal history (what Spivak calls 'the absent time that haunts the time of *Hérémakhonon*').[36] As these critics point out, the formlessness of Veronica's narrative – with its meandering plotlines and multiple inconclusive stops and starts – appears to suspend the very idea of future-directed bildung. Of course, this reading is not simply wrong: after all, *Hérémakhonon* charts Veronica's slow emancipation from the domineering male figures around her. But Birame's spectral presence in the book acts as an important political supplement to the itinerary of Veronica's own bildung, which ends with her disillusioned return to France: his radical idealism keeps open the temporal horizon of a future socialist politics that is not reducible to the perverted socialism of Mwalimwana's Soviet-style ruling party. Similar to Lessing's *The Golden Notebook*, it remains unclear just how these new struggles outside the party form will unfold. And yet, as the case of Birame's unyielding commitment to the socialist cause powerfully reminds us, future political struggles need to find ways to reinvigorate their allegiance to a broader socialist project – they must resist the defeatist

35 Lessing, *Golden Notebook*, p. 263.

36 Gayatri Chakravorty Spivak, 'The Staging of Time in *Hérémakhonon*', *Cultural Studies* 17.1 (2003): 85–97 (87); Catherine Ward, '"A false sister. A false foreigner": Space, Sexuality, and Identity in Condé's *Hérémakhonon*', *Journal of the African Literature Association* 13.1 (2019): 96–111.

'commitment to "inconsequence"' that would condemn socialism to a truly directionless politics of 'anti-futurity'.[37]

Creating Traditions in Weiss's *The Aesthetics of Resistance*

As I noted earlier, the formal structure of the left bildungsroman is shaped by an unresolved tension between the inside (phenomenological) view of the political struggle and the attempt to make sense of the struggle from an authoritative outside position. Instead of positing a tidy division between these conflicting perspectives, radical bildungsromane often project an intricate dialectic of experiential (first-person) involvement and authorial (third-person) detachment. Weiss's *The Aesthetics of Resistance* offers an important variation on this dynamic by locating the narrator function in a collective 'we' and only occasionally adopting the personal pronoun 'I'. To recall Nunes's phrase, this formal innovation can be understood as an artistic response to the crisis in the macro-historical 'transitivity' of subjective experience: Weiss's first-person plural voice gives us an inside view of the socialist struggle, but it also intimates that the work's narrating self (who looks back on the internationalist socialist movement of the 1930s and 1940s) continues to aspire to a fully collective 'extrapersonal identity'.[38] Weiss's narrator himself notes that he has reached a level of historical 'consciousness' (*Erziehung und Bildung*) that was not available to his youthful self of the 1930s:

> Back then, in the thick of it all, we only saw that everything was full of antagonisms, we couldn't get a sense of the bigger picture. To create an image of our history, we first had to draw lines between makeshift reference points, establish connections above deep craters. We had nothing

37 Daniel J. Elam has argued that certain works of anti-colonial literature are defined by such a 'commitment to "inconsequence"'. See his *World Literature for the Wretched of the Earth: Anticolonial Aesthetics, Postcolonial Politics* (New York: Fordham University Press, 2021), p. 5.

38 I take the phrase 'extrapersonal identity' from Katerina Clark, who uses it in her discussion of post-1917 Soviet novels. These novels, Clark writes, unfold 'the great historical drama of struggle between the forces of spontaneity and the forces of consciousness' by focusing on 'the way one individual mastered his wilful self, became disciplined, and attained to an extrapersonal identity.' See Katerina Clark, *The Soviet Novel: History as Ritual* (Bloomington: Indiana University Press, 2000), pp. 16–17.

> but these mostly divined points, the rest of our landscape was made up of those craters.[39]

Despite this emphasis on the growth of revolutionary consciousness, *The Aesthetics of Resistance* does not fit easily into Lukács's idea of a second (socialist) bildung. In contrast to many other novels I have explored in this book, the first volume of *The Aesthetics of Resistance* adheres quite faithfully to the conventions of the bourgeois novel of formation: Weiss's protagonist appears as a schoolboy and not as a young man on the cusp of his second bildung. Weiss's recourse to the conventions of the nineteenth-century bildungsroman is programmatic as it signals the novel's predominant concern with the question of whether (and how) aspiring proletarian writers can appropriate bourgeois artistic traditions.[40] One of the narrator's closest friends, Max Hodann, confidently proclaims that proletarian literature needs to make a complete break with earlier traditions: 'the workers' literature that we are demanding must from the very outset transcend any limitation, it must not wait for [the right] level of education [*Bildungsstand*]' (1:271; 1:238). By contrast, Weiss's narrator tries to imagine a form of radical bildung that won't require a total break with his old identity. Invoking Goethe's *Wilhelm Meister* as a model for his own enterprise (1:134; 1:115–16), Weiss insists that 'we, on the other hand, had no interest in breaking with the works of the past, we saw a historical continuity between them and the evidentiary signs of new social relations' (2:58; 2:52). Nodding to Trotsky's argument in *Literature and Revolution* (1924) that there exists a continuity between bourgeois literature and proletarian literature, Weiss's narrator is convinced that socialist writers will find ways of moulding bourgeois literary models to their own needs.

Like the radical bildungsromane I discussed in previous chapters, Weiss's novel imagines the socialist struggle as a complex interplay of spontaneous and conscious revolutionary action: 'There were always . . . two apparently contradictory forces working within us,' the narrator observes, 'one demanding patience, discipline, the other spurring on

39 In what follows, I parenthetically provide page numbers for the German text, followed by page numbers for the English translation. See Peter Weiss, *Die Ästhetik des Widerstands*, 3 vols (Frankfurt: Suhrkamp, 1983), 3:239–40; *The Aesthetics of Resistance*, 3 vols (Durham, NC: Duke University Press, 2005–25), 3:238.

40 For a brief discussion of Weiss's novel as a bildungsroman, see Fredric Jameson, 'Foreword: A Monument to Radical Instants', in Weiss, *The Aesthetics of Resistance* (vol. 1), pp. vii–xlix (x).

our radicalism; one constructive, the other raging against rigid relations; and then it turned out that these were just two sides of the same coin, and that both had to be accommodated if we wanted to realize our full potential' (2:54–5; 2:49). Weiss later remarked that the fraught coexistence of instinctive revolt and conscious political action owed much to Jean-Paul Sartre's postwar philosophical and novelistic oeuvre: 'Right after the war we began to read Sartre, whose works reconciled raw revolt – hatred and rage, personal liberation – to a worldview that claimed to be scientific.'[41] The laborious and lengthy discussions about the nature of the socialist revolution that we encounter in *The Aesthetics of Resistance* recall the conversations between Mathieu and Brunet in *The Roads to Freedom*. Much like Sartre's characters, Weiss's protagonist is caught between a hopeful vision of the socialist International and the existing confines of the nation-state. While *The Aesthetics of Resistance* sometimes sounds the high note of a future left internationalism, it is also alive to the elusiveness of a genuinely post-national socialist aesthetic: 'but for my purposes there was no such point of departure, I would have to start with the formless [*dem Formlosen*], the unattached, and seek connections beyond the borders of states and tongues' (1:136; 1:117). Like Lessing, who had attempted to 'rescu[e] the formless into [literary] form', Weiss – in representing his protagonist's incessant crossing of national borders, his decision to fight in Spain, his artistic collaboration with Bertolt Brecht in Sweden, and his support of the Swedish resistance against Nazi occupation – works to create a narrative that is capable of articulating socialism's internationalist horizon.

However, Weiss's protagonist begins to doubt the possibility of realizing these internationalist aspirations in the face of the imminent Second World War. Reconstructing the history of the 1930s, the second volume of *The Aesthetics of Resistance* presents this decade as a period that was shaped by surging nationalism and the unstoppable rise of fascism. With this crisis of left internationalism, Weiss suggests,

41 Peter Weiss, 'Interview mit Heinz Ludwig Arnold', in *Die Ästhetik des Widerstands: Materialien*, ed. Alexander Stephan (Frankfurt/Main: Suhrkamp, 1983), pp. 11–58 (31). Weiss's own hope that the spirit of spontaneous revolt might be carried over into the more intensely self-conscious sphere of post-revolutionary politics also animates his notebooks of the 1970s, written while he was working on *The Aesthetics of Resistance*. Weiss summarizes the narrator's conversations with the German playwright Bertolt Brecht as follows: 'Will there be a future in which the revolution once more becomes "spontaneous" and in which the [socialist] struggle is conducted by people outside the Party's hierarchies? No, impossible, without a strong Party!' See Peter Weiss, *Notizbücher 1971–1980*, vol. 1 (Frankfurt/Main: Suhrkamp, 1981), p. 190.

socialism is in danger of losing its historical direction and becoming a mere utopian dream about the future. As Lukács claimed in *The Theory of the Novel,* this problem can be understood in terms of Hegel's 'bad infinity' – a term that Lukács uses to describe both the post-religious condition of 'transcendental homelessness' and the essentially open-ended and internally decentred form of the novel.[42] Building on Lukács, literary scholars have seized on this Hegelian language to argue that the bourgeois bildungsroman aimed to hem in this 'bad infinity' by providing a positive vision of national closure. As Franco Moretti explains, the nineteenth-century bildungsroman's 'teleological rhetoric – [the idea that] the meaning of events lies in their *finality* – is the narrative equivalent of Hegelian thought, with which it shares a strong *normative* vocation'.[43] By contrast, the radical bildungsroman tends to resist the idea of national closure because the protagonist's embrace of the nation would seem to acknowledge the failure of socialist internationalism.

Weiss's novel is likewise interested in the problem of bad infinity. It homes in on experiences of formlessness that result from the attempt to imagine the socialist struggle outside the traditional organizational form of the party as well as outside familiar political teleologies. Aesthetically, such formlessness manifests in a conspicuous and recurring stylistic feature of Weiss's work: the long continuous passages – some of them running to fifty pages without a paragraph break – that make up the three volumes of his novel. These long passages support Weiss's attempt to offer detailed accounts of particular historical conjunctures, but the absence of any division into paragraphs also expresses the frustration met by the narrator as he faces the sheer 'formlessness' (*das Formlose*) of history.[44] Struggling to grasp the deeper patterns of historical development and suffering from the severed 'transitivity' between subject and party, Weiss's narrator fails to find evidence for a collective proletarian subject of history in the making.

The Aesthetics of Resistance focuses obsessively on traumatic moments 'when the revolutions failed to materialize in the West, when all energy had to focus on preserving the isolated Socialist state' (1:70; 1:59). However, like *The Golden Notebook*, Weiss's novel does not give up on

42 Lukács, *The Theory of the Novel*, pp. 81, 41.

43 Franco Moretti, *The Way of the World: The Bildungsroman in European Culture* (London: Verso, 1987), p. 7 (emphasis in original).

44 Nanni Balestrini aims at a similar effect in *The Unseen* (1987), where he repeatedly allows his prose to break free of the ordering functions of chapters and paragraphs.

the hope that this sense of loss might finally be redeemed by reworking it into a narrative of individual transformation and bildung. Instead of reneging on socialism's internationalist aspirations, Weiss reframes the movement's failure to realize these aspirations as a process of historical deferral or tactical postponement. When the socialist struggle is viewed from up close ('*from the inside*'), it becomes clear that complete political unity – of the proletariat, of socialists, of the Popular Front – is an ideological illusion that does not withstand historical scrutiny: 'No social upheaval,' the narrator concludes, 'has two classes facing one another with precisely defined interests, on the contrary, the fighting camps themselves are assaulted by internal hostility, which constitutes the driving force of the whole violent clash' (1:252; 1:221–2). This logic of internal conflict, in turn, gives rise to a distinctive revolutionary temporality. Revolutions, Weiss's narrator learns, cannot lay claim to a quasi-mythical place outside time – they do not signal the irruption into time of a radically new post-dialectical order. Nor do they ever occur at the right time: 'I saw clearly how impossible it was to establish the Popular Front. This united front had arrived too late [*zu spät*], or perhaps its time had not yet [*noch nicht*] arrived' (3:43–4; 3:40). Instead of inhabiting the optimistic, future-directed Blochian 'Not-Yet' of the utopian imagination, the radical bildungsroman articulates what could be called the 'Not-Now', the series of missed historical opportunities and uncertain futures that characterizes the experience of the socialist struggle.[45] The genre's particular attention to moments of deferral and defeat lends support to Hannah Proctor's critique of overly optimistic or euphoric views of past and present struggles. Such accounts, Proctor notes, typically call on left-wing writers and historians to 'excavate hopeful moments from revolutionary history to stir politically sympathetic readers in the quiescent present.'[46] But, Proctor admits, 'when writing about political disillusionment and exhaustion', this 'rhetorical gesture [is] insufficient': 'However seductive I find this mode of argumentation, experiences of political burnout necessitate contending with hopeful moments in the past that cannot be severed from individuals' subsequent experiences of despair.'[47] The radical bildungsroman does not avoid experiences of political disappointment and left-wing melancholy but rather treats these experiences as a mode of political attachment in

45 Ernst Bloch, *The Principle of Hope* (Cambridge, MA: MIT Press, 1995), pp. 127–46.

46 Proctor, *Burnout*, p. 7.

47 Ibid.

their own right, as 'the very mechanism through which one may be interested in the world'.[48] As a radical bildungsroman, Weiss's novel reckons with experiences of defeat in ways that are not themselves defeatist.[49]

The feeling of being adrift in a present that lacks a clear revolutionary horizon predominates in many radical bildungsromane from the second half of the twentieth century. In the case of Weiss, this feeling also correlates in interesting ways with the experience of exile that had formed the centre of his earlier semi-autobiographical novels *Leavetaking* and *Vanishing Point*.[50] Following his family's narrow escape to Stockholm in 1938, Weiss himself spent the remainder of his life – some four decades – in exile from his native Germany. There is a real sense that Weiss's experience of being adrift in *geographic* terms came to serve as a model for his subsequent reflections (in *The Aesthetics of Resistance*) on the more specifically *temporal* deferral, or indefinite historical postponement, of revolution. As Weiss came to see it, both types of dislocation – the spatial as much as the temporal – could be at once disorientating and liberating. For example, *Leavetaking* gives expression to feelings of 'non-belonging' (*Unzugehörigkeit*) that are shown to result from the absence of a 'firm ground that can be called home' (*heimischen Boden*). This precarious and shifting 'ground' of exile produces as its political corollary an inability 'to take a firm stance vis-à-vis the world's revolutionizing struggles' (*umwälzenden Konflikten*).[51] At the same time, however, Weiss also avers that the non-fixity of the writer's self under conditions of exile liberates it from the 'falsifying' (*verfälschend*) ideological constraints that result from nationally rooted identities.[52] In a related vein, *Vanishing Point* observes that mid-century socialist artists

48 I borrow this description of (political) melancholy from Jonathan Flatley's *Affective Mapping: Melancholia and the Politics of Modernism* (Cambridge, MA: Harvard University Press, 2008), p. 1.

49 In his book-length account of 'left-wing melancholy', the Italian historian Enzo Traverso has pointed out that the analytic effort to account for political resignation is separated from defeatism only by a thin line. Engaging with Perry Anderson's writings on the post-1989 conjuncture, Traverso writes: 'Communism had failed as both a political and an ethical project. It had proclaimed the emancipation of humankind but had created a new form of despotism: why should it survive such a gigantic heterogenesis of ends?' See Enzo Traverso, *Left-Wing Melancholia: Marxism, History, and Memory* (New York: Columbia University Press, 2016), p. 32.

50 See Chapter 2 for a more extended discussion of these two novels.

51 See Peter Weiss, *Abschied von den Eltern* (Frankfurt: Suhrkamp, 2007), pp. 118–19.

52 Ibid., pp. 30, 54, *passim*.

do not belong 'to any particular nation' (*Zugehörigkeit zu einer Nation*) – instead their art emerges from the unsettled 'world of a person on the move' (*Welt eines Fliehenden*).[53] In *Vanishing Point* and *Leavetaking*, this acute and existential sense of homelessness is reimagined as an enabling condition that supports the artistic work of creating a fully internationalist art: 'the language that was my tool (*Werkzeug*) . . . no longer had any connection to my place of birth . . . it became possible to participate in an exchange of ideas that took place all around me and that was no longer tied to any particular country' (*an kein Land gebunden*).[54]

In *The Aesthetics of Resistance*, the deracinated artistic voice of Weiss's early novels is mobilized once more to describe the ambiguous affective states that characterize the revolutionary subject. Many twentieth-century radical bildungsromane oscillate between a mourning of lost opportunities – what Walter Benjamin called 'left-wing melancholy' – and the future-directed revolutionary 'optimism' invoked in Lukács's landmark essay on the left bildungsroman from 1956.[55] *The Aesthetics of Resistance* self-consciously addresses this interplay between melancholic resignation and revolutionary optimism: 'The October Revolution was not a past event, it was something immediately present . . . driving out the weariness, the recent paralyses' (1:256; 1:225). Just as Weiss encourages proletarians to make use of available novelistic forms to express their radical politics, so he enjoins revolutionaries to look back to previous moments of resistance. This view of the struggle is key to the mature socialist vision attained by Weiss's protagonist, but his blend of hope and pessimism also constitutes a distinctive pattern that defines the twentieth-century radical bildungsroman more generally. It's worth emphasizing this point: if we wish to reclaim the political force of the radical bildungsroman tradition, we must not mistake the genre's retrospective stance for contemplative nostalgia or mere quietism.

The Aesthetics of Resistance depicts historical situations in painstaking detail, as though Weiss had placed a huge magnifying glass over each scene. Like Sartre's *The Roads to Freedom*, Weiss's novel blurs the boundary between the bildungsroman and the genre of the historical

53 Peter Weiss, *Fluchtpunkt* (Frankfurt: Suhrkamp, 1965), p. 32, 34.

54 Ibid., pp. 196–7.

55 Lukács, 'Critical Realism and Socialist Realism'. Left-wing melancholy, writes Benjamin, 'takes as much pride in the traces of former spiritual goods as the bourgeois does in his material goods': 'from the beginning all it has in mind is to enjoy itself in a negativistic quiet'. See Walter Benjamin, 'Left-Wing Melancholy: On Erich Kästner's New Book of Poems', *Screen* 15.2 (1974): 28–32 (29–30).

novel – it provides us with a vast historical canvas by weaving the protagonist's individualized narrative into a broader story of tectonic social change.[56] As readers, we are invited to share Weiss's astonishment that this multitude of inert historical facts was once energized by a revolutionary event, like so many iron filings attracted by an invisible yet powerful magnetic force.

We can give additional depth to the two key concepts I introduced in the preceding paragraph – *situation* and *event* – by recalling their place in the work of Alain Badiou. Badiou's thinking addresses many of the same problems that have concerned me in this chapter. This includes the question of how a historical situation, in its sheer material givenness and unordered ('formless') facticity, can become the site of a revolutionary event. In a passage that recalls the intense analytic optic of Weiss's narrator as well as his inconclusive search for shards of messianic time amidst the formlessness of history, Badiou observes that revolutionary 'truth-events' are not 'naturally' or self-evidently part of a historical situation – indeed, Badiou refers to the latter as a sheer 'multiple of [empirical] facts'.[57] The event's '*belonging to the situation of its site*,' Badiou notes, is '*undecidable from the standpoint of the situation itself*' (181, emphasis in original): 'The Revolution [is] supernumerary to the sole numbering of the terms of its site' (180). Using the October Revolution as his principal example, Badiou states that a sequence of historical occurrences becomes 'eventful' by being 'retroactively . . . nominated' as an event. Revolutionary events are sustained through an active process of remembering – for example, by virtue of acts of political resistance that invoke these events as models. This also explains why the backward glance at socialism's twentieth-century triumphs in *The Aesthetics of Resistance* does not lead the narrator and his comrades to give in to left-wing melancholy or political despair. This type of retrospective vision can be rearticulated in a more active register as the radical subject's 'fidelity to the event' (xiii).

Pertinent to the history of the radical bildungsroman and its long line of revolutionary protagonists, Badiou also advances the stronger

56 Conversely, theorists of the left historical novel agreed that 'not every historical novel must necessarily deal with the masses of the people': even socialist historical novels could legitimately focus on individual lives, provided these were representative of larger political struggles. See Mark Serebryansky, 'The Soviet Historical Novel', *International Literature* 4 (1938): 78–86 (80).

57 Alain Badiou, *Being and Event* (London: Continuum, 2011), p. 180. Subsequent references are given in the text.

claim that the socialist subject and the revolutionary truth-event exist in a dialectical relationship. They are, in an important sense, mutually constitutive: on the one hand, 'a subjective intervention names the event, [and] it faithfully connects as many elements of the situation as possible to this name';[58] on the other, 'a subject' is itself 'nothing other than an active fidelity to the event of truth' (xiii). Fidelity to the socialist struggle and revolutionary practice is here imagined as an unconcluded identificatory and participatory process. It does not signal, as established understandings of the bildungsroman would suggest, the attainment of a fixed telos or a redemptive moment of plenitude. The protagonists of the radical bildungsromane that I have discussed in this book are faithful revolutionary subjects in exactly this sense. They try to draw strength from the hopes of earlier generations, even as they recognize the vagaries and the sheer ongoingness of the socialist struggle. As Weiss's narrator notes:

> Back then, we were still clinging to our hopes, for without them, we wouldn't have been able to go on; and I would see how we would reach for those hopes time and again; how we never dismissed them as delusions, even if all signs suggested they were futile; and how our hope had always been stronger than our failures, because in the end, this hope was the very thing that kept us alive. (3:261; 3:261)

The socialist struggle does not depend on a pre-established or automatically self-rejuvenating collective – or, for that matter, on an organizationally fixed party form. Instead, as the novels of Lessing, Condé and Weiss illustrate, the historical continuity of the struggle is made possible through the solidarity of individuals who decide to join the fight for their vision of a better world. Following Badiou it is possible to say that the radical bildungsroman negotiates two kinds of truth: first, a belief in the fundamental rightness of socialism – that is, a belief in the idea that socialism is valid transhistorically and transnationally; and second, the materialist insight that all truths are historically contingent and structurally complex. The novels I have analysed in this book resist the facile reified truths that are held out by a melancholic contemplation of the past or by a naively utopian anticipation of the socialist future. Instead, the protagonists of these novels arrive at the knowledge that the truth of socialism resides in the continuation of the struggle itself. 'The world

58 Bosteels, *Badiou and Politics*, p. 165.

revolution had become very remote,' Weiss's narrator observes: 'It would no longer be a unique act, it would now be a long-lasting process of class struggles, crowded with victories and defeats' (1:118; 1:101). In the wake of the demise of European workers' parties in the 1930s, Weiss continues, some 'scattered names survived with which we, in our isolation, long associated a tradition' (1:33; 1:27). As I have been suggesting, one of the transnational 'traditions' that lent support to the socialist struggle and became a cornerstone of red *Weltliteratur* was the genre of the radical bildungsroman itself.

Coda

The fracturing of the Communist International and the violent excesses of party-centric socialism – both captured so poignantly in the novels by Guido Morselli, Doris Lessing and Peter Weiss, as well as in Uwe Tellkamp's *The Tower* (with which this book began) – did not put an end to desires for radical social transformation. Neither did socialism's profound historical crises mark the end of the literary history of the left bildungsroman. Instead, these crises helped to produce a remarkable further expansion of the experiences, subject positions and types of social discontent that could be represented in the genre. As I have been arguing in this book, the radical bildungsroman had long resisted fetishizing a single (proletarian, male, white) identity that could be treated as normative across a wide range of different conjunctures and national contexts. Karl August Varnhagen von Ense had first drawn attention to this feature of the left bildungsroman in his programmatic description of Goethe's *Wanderjahre*. The socialist novel of formation, Varnhagen observed in 1832, was hospitable to a plurality of different protagonists: these were by no means limited to 'proletarians' (*Proletarier*) but also included the more demographically diverse categories of 'slum-dwellers and oppressed' (*Verwahrloste und Bedrückte*).[1] By the same token, Varnhagen argued, the radical bildungsroman does not limit its attention to a one-size-fits-all experience of alienation. Instead, it homes

1 Karl August Varnhagen von Ense, 'Im Sinne der Wanderer' ['In the Spirit of the Wanderers'], *Über Kunst und Alterthum* 6 (1832): 533–51 (535).

in on a variegated phenomenology of proliferating 'alienations'[2] that extends from the economic sphere to the social and political realm and that affects individuals and groups in uneven ways.

As my account of the radical bildungsroman's history has indicated, the genre can be understood as a type of aesthetico-political sensorium or as a medium of political thought in its own right. To chart the literary history of the genre is to engage in a type of pattern recognition that detects unexpected affinities between writers who seem at first glance to have little in common with each other: Goethe and Godard; Chernyshevsky and Ngũgĩ; Lessing, Condé and Weiss; Gorky and Hikmet. By creating these literary-artistic constellations, the radical bildungsroman poses a challenge to Marxist literary historiography as it is sometimes practised: the genre forces us to consider forms of artistic development that are non-continuous and that operate according to patterns of loss and retrieval rather than according to the relative homogeneity that is often (falsely) assumed to be constitutive of artistic traditions. *Revolutionary Subjects* has unearthed the genre ontology of the radical bildungsroman by tracing some of the continuities and disjunctions that mark its history across a 200-year span. The genre's formal richness, I have suggested, served a broadly universalist political project. It is these universalist aspirations that my Introduction aimed to make visible by calling on the traditions of Marxist humanism. When the genre is understood in this way, even the proletarian protagonists of Soviet novels such as Gladkov's *Cement* or Andrei Platonov's *Chevengur* (1928) can be grasped as figures whose precariously advancing bildung renders them capable of acting as models for a much broader (social, ethnic, racial, gendered) range of revolutionary subjectivities. By offering up a wealth of novelistic characters for readerly identification, the radical bildungsroman lends support to Lukács's remark (in his 1924 book on Lenin) that the 'universality' of the proletarian revolution was not limited to this or that country or social group but rather constituted an all-encompassing 'world-historical horizon'.[3]

Literary form does important political work by abstracting from those elements of a text that would otherwise remain merely contingent. Because the history of literary forms makes it possible to discern

2 Ferenc Fehér et al., 'Notes and Commentary', *Telos* 29 (1976): 160–81 (180). I touch on this essay in the Introduction, alongside a few other responses to Lukács's mid-century *Ontology of Social Being*.

3 Georg Lukács, *Lenin: A Study of the Unity of His Thought* (London: Verso, 2009), p. 12.

commonalities amidst the whirl of historical particularity, my book has tended to privilege questions of literary form at the expense of social context or biographical specificity. I hope it has become clear that, in doing so, I have tried to be faithful to the political aspirations of the radical bildungsroman itself. It is worth recalling that Lukács's theorization of the proletariat's 'universality' as the 'subject-object of history' builds on many of the same early nineteenth-century debates that also helped to fuel German idealist theorizations of bildung.[4] And it should also come as no surprise that the radical bildungsroman's early universalist commitments – its attention to *Proletarier* as well as to the more capacious categories of *Verwahrloste* and *Bedrückte* – remained central to the genre's 200-year history and to Marxist thought more broadly. For example, it is possible to detect echoes of these universalist commitments in the writings of Third World activists and novelists from the 1950s onwards.[5] 'Assuming that Marxism has a relevance, has a meaning, has an applicability to Western Europe,' the Guyanese activist and theorist Walter Rodney wrote in 'Marxism and African Liberation' (1975), 'to what extent does this validity extend geographically? To what extent does its validity extend across time?'[6] 'Black people,' Rodney continues, 'ask the question whether an ideology which was historically generated within the culture of Western Europe in the nineteenth century is, today, in the third quarter of the twentieth century, still valid for another part of the world . . . whether it is valid to other societies at other times.'[7] Rodney firmly believed that anti-colonialist thinking could be energized by ideas that resonate with the body of humanist thought I have traced in this book and that find exemplary expression in the narratives of the radical bildungsroman. Regrettably, this Marxist-humanist genealogy includes the problematic demotion of nonhuman nature to an enabling factor in human self-actualization – a view we encountered as early as Chernyshevsky's *What Is to Be Done?* from 1863. Echoes of these ideas can be heard in Rodney's emphasis on work as an anthropological category and as a central modality of political

4 Georg Lukács, *History and Class Consciousness* (London: Verso, 2009), esp. p. 199. For the German-idealist sources of Lukács's arguments, see his 'Preface to the New Edition' (1967), in *History and Class Consciousness*, pp. ix–xl (xxii–xxiii).

5 On the universalist aspirations of 'third-worldism', see Bruce Robbins, *Criticism and Politics: A Polemical Introduction* (Stanford, CA: Stanford University Press, 2022), pp. 22–3.

6 Walter Rodney, 'Marxism and African Liberation', in *Decolonial Marxism* (London: Verso, 2022), pp. 33–51 (36).

7 Ibid., pp. 36–7.

becoming: 'Man's consciousness is formed in the intervention in nature,' Rodney writes, and 'nature itself is humanized through its interaction with labour.'[8]

Rodney's African liberationist perspective reflects the universalist reframing of the political struggle, of work and of political emancipation that also characterizes the literary history of the radical bildungsroman. For another such perspective, we can turn to the Combahee River Collective (CRC), the Black feminist socialist collective whose exploration of intertwined forms of (racial, gendered, economic) oppression came to have a profound influence on more recent theorizations of intersectionality. The CRC is often credited with developing the concept of identity politics. As such, it might seem to signal a complete break with the universalist aspirations of Marxist humanism or a rebuttal of the implicit identitarian (proletarian, male, white) bias that was integral to so much nineteenth- and early twentieth-century socialist thought. However, as the literary critic Colleen Lye has pointed out, this account of the CRC's politics is almost absurdly reductive. Drawing attention to the Maoist dimension of the CRC's theoretical practice, Lye warns that the Collective's 'identity politics' must not be equated with an irredeemable particularism that would cause 'the ruination of all universal political projects.'[9] In her attempt to salvage the universalist dimension of the CRC's political project, Lye traces echoes of Maoist thought in the group's manifesto ('Collective Statement') from 1977, notably in the text's emphasis on the importance of 'self-criticism.' Invoking Mao's essay 'On Contradiction' (1937), Lye observes that for the CRC, as for Mao, subjectivity – the self – is a key site in the work of collective social transformation: 'identity [has] the dual aspects of particularity and totality, and indeed is the very name for the contradictory relationship that unites them.'[10] Similar to Ding Ling's *The Sun Shines Over the Sanggan River*, Godard's *La Chinoise* and other works discussed in this book, Lye's account suggests that the CRC envisioned a mode of anti-capitalist subjectivity that would be expansive enough to accommodate a large and growing range of non- and counter-hegemonic subject positions.

8 Ibid., p. 38. 'Production,' Rodney continues, 'is not merely the basis of man's existence, but the basis for defining man as a special kind of being with a certain consciousness' (p. 38).

9 Colleen Lye, 'Identity Politics, Criticism, and Self-Criticism,' *The South Atlantic Quarterly* 119.4 (2020): 701–14 (701).

10 Ibid., 701.

Individuality – for Rodney, for the CRC and for the writers and filmmakers I have explored in this book – does not come to rest in a narrowly particularist understanding of the self and its contexts but rather doubles as an imaginative relay for a more expansive set of identifications. As I pointed out in the Introduction, radical bildungsromane serve the purpose of retrospective exploration and historical understanding; in this sense, they do not fit easily into the category of overtly didactic or activist art. The radical novel of formation inherits from the nineteenth-century bildungsroman an interest in producing a reflective knowledge of the relationship between self and world. Its strong reliance on 'autobiographical' experience accordingly serves as a starting point for a broader inquiry into the conditions of possibility for radical change.[11]

The left novel of formation was able to maintain its intellectual and artistic vitality as long as it could draw on the energies of a larger political project: radical *Weltliteratur* was energized by the proximity to socialist *Weltrevolution*. If (as I noted in the preceding chapter) 1956 was a momentous crisis year for the left in this regard, 1989 marked another. Indeed, the case of Tellkamp's *The Tower* – and of many other recent fictions, such as Jenny Erpenbeck's *Kairos* (2021), about the catastrophic personal and collective aftermath of the GDR's demise – indicates that many contemporary novelists find it difficult to reclaim the socialist bildungsroman's universalist aspirations. For more successful recent attempts to make individual development stand in for collective radical hopes, we can look to forms of non-fiction, where the political work of coalition-building is described at an elementary and experiential level. I turn to non-fiction, then, to suggest what happens when revolutionary hope is no longer sufficient to sustain the capacious teleological organization of the long-form novel.

For a recent example of this trend, we can turn to the Catalan trans theorist Paul B. Preciado, whose writings offer rich explorations of transness as a form of political becoming. Preciado's publications include *An Apartment on Uranus* (2020), originally published as a series of columns written for the French periodical *Libération* between 2013 and 2018.[12] Preciado began a process of medical transition in

11 On 'the preference for the autobiographical bildungsroman' among socialist writers, see Georg Lukács, 'Critical Realism and Socialist Realism,' in *The Meaning of Contemporary Realism* (London: Mellon, 1963), pp. 93–135 (111).

12 Paul B. Preciado, *An Apartment on Uranus: Chronicles of the Crossing* (South Pasadena, CA: Semiotext(e), 2020). Subsequent references are given in the text.

2010, and while his book treats a considerable range of topics (extending from questions of gender identity to the 'refugee crisis' in the Mediterranean and the Israel–Palestine conflict), *An Apartment on Uranus* retains an obliquely biographical shape: 'I have preserved the strict chronological order in which these columns were written, since it is also the sequence of this sexual and gender transition, the story of the crossing' (32). At the same time, Preciado insists that the experience of 'the crossing' undercuts any sense of the self as stable or otherwise ontologically grounded, and he proceeds to pit this fluid concept of selfhood against the 'universal principles of European humanism' (91).

And yet, notwithstanding his programmatic disavowal of 'universal[ism]', in Preciado's essays transness itself becomes a kind of meta-signifier for experiences of radical transformation and change. As Virginie Despentes writes in her preface to *An Apartment on Uranus* (a text addressed to Preciado), the book is

> the story of your transition – of your transitions. This central story not of going from one point to another, but of wandering and in-betweenness as the place of life. A constant transformation, without fixed identity, without fixed activity, or address, or country . . . From one language to another, from one theme to another, from one city to another, from one gender to another – transitions are your home. (16–17)

In *An Apartment on Uranus* transitions and crossings are not pictured as the negation of subject formation as such – instead, transformation, change and transition are reframed as the very essence of a new kind of post-foundational radical bildung. Preciado accordingly analogizes transness to other modalities of (social, political, cultural) change:

> I will go so far as to say that it is processes of transition that best allow us to understand the political shift with which we are confronted worldwide. Sex change and migration are two practices that, by calling into question the political and legal architecture of patriarchal colonialism, of sexual difference and racial hierarchy, of family and nation-state, place a living human body inside the limits of citizenship, even of what we understand by 'humanity'. (32)

This account positions *trans* and *crossing* as universals in their own right. Preciado proceeds to align these concepts with a vision of post-national citizenship: 'The intensity of global migratory movements and the violence of neo-nationalist policies urgently demand today a transition . . . that would oppose and transgress the laws of nation-states within which reigns citizenship-capital-earth' (127). Preciado's interest in migration often oscillates uncomfortably between his own privileged position as a Princeton-educated cosmopolitan intellectual and poignant accounts of the 'migratory movements' of immiserated and homeless refugees across the Mediterranean and elsewhere. His attempt to correlate these two types of migration is ethically problematic, but it also recalls the wanderings of exiled revolutionaries and homeless *Bedrückte* that socialist critics of the 1830s and 1840s had foregrounded in their discussions of Goethe's *Wanderjahre*. Like Preciado, these earlier critics and essayists – Varnhagen, Karl Grün, Ludolf Wienbarg and others – had identified wandering and crossing as key tropes for the socialist struggle. As Varnhagen pointed out, Goethe's *Wanderjahre* had instructed its readers to become 'wanderers' and join the collective struggle for a better future.[13] Over the course of the next 200 years, such figures of movement and crossing came to act as motifs that hold together the textual archive of the radical bildungsroman tradition. In Preciado's essays, too, the precarious networks formed by exiles and migrants double as the model for a new kind of grassroots internationalism: 'An unprecedented mode of neoliberal-nationalism is drawing new borders and building new walls . . . Conditions of life without identity papers and without land, with successive moves, migrations, translation, all force us to go beyond the ethnocentric narration of modern Western history and open new forms of democratic actions' (210). Nomadism takes centre stage as the model for a viable future socialist politics.

The residually biographical outline that Preciado gives to many of his books (including his 2023 feature film *Orlando: My Political Biography*) recalls the radical bildungsroman's analogous strategy of 'rescuing the formless into form' by holding together multiple narrative vectors

13 Having discussed Godard's *Lehrjahre*-inspired *La Chinoise* in a previous chapter, I will only note in passing that *Film Socialisme* (2015) is the closest the Goethe-obsessed Godard came to creating a filmic rendition of the concerns of the *Wanderjahre*. The film's diverse and trailing plotlines converge on the drifting cruise ship *Costa Concordia*, as it transpires that the various characters are connected by complex historical webs of colonial guilt and neo-feudal exploitation. Coincidentally, Preciado's keen interest in Godard's work is well documented, for example in his biographical film *Orlando: My Political Biography* (2023) with its visual allusions to the credit sequence and colour scheme of *Pierrot le Fou* (1965) and *La Chinoise*.

through the conceit of a character-centred developmental narrative.[14] However, as Preciado reminds us, transitioning between identities can also involve a momentary suspension of fixed selfhood as such – the kind of immersion in the 'formless' that radical bildungsromane often associate with the tortuous and prolonged process of second bildung.[15] Preciado's prose movingly captures a key aspect of the struggle for radical political change – the formation of a revolutionary subjectivity caught between the old world that is passing and the new world that struggles to be born.

As *Revolutionary Subjects* has documented, the experience of existing in a state of in-betweenness – of being positioned in the midst of historical contradictions – is central to nearly all accounts of radical bildung. 'My identity', writes Stuart Hall in his autobiography *Familiar Stranger* (2017), 'was formed as much by what my circumstances had made me as by the often unrecognized or unconscious struggle against my conditions of formation. This is a contradiction which I have come to believe the identification process always involves: identification always generates this paradox.'[16] The process of making and unmaking that Hall describes here relates partly to his experience as a colonial subject from Jamaica arriving in England in the 1950s. Many members of his generation, Hall observes, found themselves on the move – they experienced a condition of 'natal alienation', that is, 'a situation in which the elemental ties of birth were severed' (71). The building of provisional new homes – ones no longer limited to the confines of a single nation – accordingly becomes the presiding theme of Hall's autobiography. But, as Hall makes clear, this work of construction applies equally to his position as a member of the New Left: 'Really, I was formed as one of the last colonials, and politically I was a child of 1956' (45). For Hall – as for Lessing, Condé, Weiss and the other bildungsroman authors discussed in the previous chapter – being 'a child of 1956' meant that 'history was the carrier of no absolutes

14 I discussed Doris Lessing's succinct formula for the radical bildungsroman's artistic work ('rescuing the formless into form') in Chapter 4. See Doris Lessing, *The Golden Notebook* (New York: Vintage, 1999), p. 427.

15 Like many of the novels and films I have explored in this book, Preciado's texts figure this sense of transition in terms of a proliferation of (narrative) voices: 'In this sense, these [newspaper] columns have at least two authors: this dissonance makes exaggeratedly visible the division of the author into a multiplicity of voices that undergo the crossing – a phenomenon that exists in any written work, but that is usually erased under the unicity of the author's name' (32).

16 Stuart Hall, *Familiar Stranger: A Life Between Two Islands* (London: Penguin, 2018), p. 22.

and conformed to no overarching scriptural commandments' (62). Questions of divided (political, social, cultural) belonging are central to *Familiar Stranger* as 'absolute' macro-historical certainties come to be replaced by an open-ended process of political becoming and precarious acts of political coalition-building.

Like the authors of radical bildungsromane, Hall works to position his personal experiences as allegories for broader political struggles: his life, he concludes, has taken place in a historical 'transition zone' (201). The process of personal-cum-collective transformation that is described in *Familiar Stranger* does not involve a single moment of unmaking, or an event-like turning point, but rather the drawn-out revision of acquired knowledges and modes of thought and feeling, what Hall dubs the 'unlearning [of] the norms in which I had been born and brought up . . . a long, continuing process of disidentification [that] has shaped my life' (3). Like Preciado's essays, Hall's narrative entails a multiplicity of laborious transitions and (dis)identifications – a non-totalizable sequence of projects that the tradition of the radical bildungsroman had associated with the localized teleologies of work. *Familiar Stranger* shares with the radical bildungsroman a profound commitment to making sense of personal experiences of the political struggle. By the same token, Hall's and Preciado's texts echo the radical bildungsroman's central recognition that political change is best imagined in terms of a long series of (social, political, personal) transformations. For those who are immersed in the here and now of the political struggle, they suggest, the urgent and necessary work of producing such transitions matters every bit as much as the more distant vision of some future emancipation.

Index